Life
*Here and
Hereafter*

Life
Here and
Hereafter

by
F. Newton Howden

PROCTOR'S HALL PRESS • *Sewanee*

Unless otherwise indicated, Bible quotations are taken from the Revised Standard Version

*Copyright © 1992 by F. Newton Howden
All rights reserved
Printed in the United States of America*

*Design by Gary Gore—cover photograph by Gary Gore
Composed by Proctor's Hall Press in Adobe Garamond
Printed by Thomson-Shore, Inc.*

*Published by Proctor's Hall Press
Proctor's Hall Road
P.O. Box 856
Sewanee, Tennessee 37375-0856*

*International Standard Book Numbers:
0-9627687-4-X Paperback
0-9627687-3-1 Hardcover*

Library of Congress Catalog Card Number: 92-064193

*To the Memory of
Cornelia Jane Fenton Howden, 1918–1981 (my first wife),
and two of our children,
David Stuart Howden, 1961–1963,
and
Stephanie Ann Mary Howden, 1965–1968*

Contents

	Introduction	ix
	Foreword	xi
	Author's Preface	xv
1	Death as Part of Life	1
2	Sources of Information	8
3	The Universality of Belief in Life after Death	21
4	Old Testament Eschatology	43
5	This Is Life Eternal	75
6	Life Here	88
7	I Am the Good Shepherd	101
8	The Transfiguration	110
9	The Evidence for the Resurrection of Jesus	117
10	Judgment	128
11	Heaven	139
12	Hell	168
13	The Intermediate State	179
14	The End of the World	193
	Appendix	205
	Notes	207
	Index	231

Introduction

A book reviewing human hopes and fears, past and present, regarding questions and wonderings about the future (an ending or a passage, a transition or a new beginning?) is potentially attractive to a wide range of readers. Especially so is a book that translates a scholarly subject known as eschatology into language common to park bench as well as classroom or bar stools as well as Bible classes. To me this is such a book.

Any subject, interesting or otherwise, gains some additional attraction when reflected in writing or conversation by an intelligent friend or impressive acquaintance. My acquaintance with the author of this book, Newton Howden, began in our college days some fifty years ago at the University of the South, Sewanee, Tennessee.

Newton Howden was a college senior in Sewanee when I entered as a freshman. My recollection of Newt is of a solid built, square shouldered, medium-size fellow, pleasant faced with a crooked grin. He appeared comfortable and observant without need to draw attention to himself. If memory serves, he was one of Dr. John McDonald's philosophy majors and rumor had him headed for the ministry. In the critical eye of a freshman considering unannounced a personal vocation to the ministry, Newt Howden appeared a competent prospect. Remembering how often and easily opinions have lacked accuracy, missed the mark, been in error, it is comforting to have one affirmed, especially when of and by an admirable acquaintance and friend.

Likewise, to engage in serious consideration of a life's ending, be it personal or the "end of the age," the termination, exit, transition, conclusion, coming of a "new age," an entrance, eternal experience, no exit, ever—admittedly it is easier and more encouragingly approached and pursued with a perceptive, reasoning, logical, intelligent friend. Be the friendship and consideration shared in series of conversation or in writing of letters or books, both the end results and progress toward same are the

Introduction

more apt to be enlightened and encouraged when shared with one who proves to be both enlightened and friendly.

Here personal experience prompts an invitation to anyone reading thus far to continue. See for yourself if the above observations are correct: see if you don't find enlightenment and encouragement from a friendly reflector.

As noted in the Preface, with "prayers and blessing" this book is an offering to all who wonder "about the subject of eternal life," and an invitation to share "that quest." It's a friendly offer from one who during many years of pastoral ministry as a parish priest has blended the learnings and insights provided by "all sorts and conditions" of those among whom he has lived and served with sufficient scholarly discipline to provide research and writing. He has recognized the need to test assumptions.

Newton Howden, after obtaining a degree from the General Theological Seminary in New York, served congregations in New York, Vermont, and Connecticut. For a time, in addition to his parish duties, he served as a professor of humanities in a Connecticut college. When he became of sufficient age to enter "the realm of unofficialdom," he sought adventure in Tunbridge Wells, England, where he continues to assist with pastoral service.

To be appreciated is a book or conversation of friendly sharing that in the present prompts recall from the past of friends and events, of hopes and fears and wonderings, while offering interesting information and stimulating thought about the future, the ages ending, human destiny, experience beyond ages, the perceived possibility that now is present reality amid the past and the future within the eternal. This is such a book, thought provoking, and pleasant reading.

JOHN M. ALLIN
Twenty-third Presiding Bishop
The Episcopal Church USA

Foreword

To the world of Jesus' and Paul's day, Christianity offered two supreme gifts. To the Jew it presented a Messiah—not just a conquering hero to avenge Israel's wrongs but one who was *demonstrated* to be Judge of the earth, King of kings, Lord of lords, *by resurrection from the dead.*

To the Gentile, however, *that resurrection was itself the supreme gift.* Upon the human mind, all over the Mediterranean world, there lay a pall, heavy and suffocating. It was *the problem of death.* Does our existence here on earth have meaning? Is there life beyond this one? Or is death the end, the final, grisly mockery of all our hopes and endeavors? The young Gentile mind sought answers in many places. Nearly everybody had heard of ghosts, and some people claimed to have seen them; but what really is a ghost? Everybody knew, too, about the gods of Mount Olympus, but they were often as naughty as the naughtiest human and were of no help on this issue.

Plato was far better. He stated the case for immortality, with arguments so cogent as to be nearly impossible to refute. But win an argument, reduce the opponent to silence as one may, that still is not enough. It takes more than the conclusion of an argument to establish faith either in a Supreme Being or in eternal life.

So the young Gentile tried one or another "mystery religion." A mystery religion focused on one of the lesser gods, say Osiris, or Mithra, or some other. The seeker then went through a prescribed ritual which, it was claimed, would merge his life with the life of the chosen deity. The ritual might involve a sacred meal, or a *taurobolium* (baptism in the blood of a bull), or some other rite. Thus united with the selected god, one caught and absorbed that god's immunity to death. One would hereafter be carried beyond the termination of this life into the immortality that one now shared with the god. But not everybody was able to find help in this fashion, and sometimes mystery religions proved to be grossly unpleasant and repugnant to a sensitive mind.

Into this anxious, questing ambience came Judaism. Victorious Greeks and, even more, the conquering Romans had opened Mediterranean waters to travel and its ports to ever-increasing commerce. Many Jews proceeded to emigrate from their homeland to seek fortunes elsewhere. By Jesus' time more Jews dwelt outside Palestine that in it. Wherever they settled, moreover, the Jews established synagogues. The young Gentile, yearning for an answer to his grinding question, often stopped to listen in at the synagogue service. To be sure, Judaism proffered scant help toward solving his big problem, but he did find here a great deal to admire: the firm insistence on only one God, the high moral code, the ability to inspire intense, even fanatical loyalty in its devotees. Many a Gentile was drawn to Judaism and became a proselyte. Others, recoiling from the thought of circumcision, still undertook to keep the Jewish Sabbath, to observe such other ordinances as they were able, and to attend synagogue worship. These last were called "God-fearers" or "men that fear God." (It was a man's world; when the head of a household was converted, he generally brought all his household with him.) Peter ministered to at least one God-fearer and his family (Acts 10:2, 22). Paul addressed them particularly when he spoke in the synagogue at Pisidian Antioch (Acts 13:16).

The synagogue was, in fact, the one instrumentality that was available to Jewish Christians throughout the Mediterranean world when they sought to propagate their new-found faith. Synagogue services were somewhat like Christian church services today. The congregation chanted psalms, recited the *Shema*—"Hear, O Israel, the Lord our God is one Lord . . ."—and listened to a Scripture reading and to its exposition by a speaker. Just here was the greatest difference from our usage today. The speaker then could be chosen quite informally—even, at times, after the service had begun. Thus the Christian Jew, seeking to proclaim Jesus as Israel's Messiah, found ready opportunity, even on his first visit to a town. Some Jews in the congregation, hearing the new speaker, would heartily welcome his "good news," his conviction that the Messiah was Jesus. Others, however, would be repelled, deeply angered, at the report that the Messiah had been scourged, dragged through the streets of Jerusalem, and crucified as a common felon at the hands of the hated Romans. These Jews would stop their ears or else shout to drown out the speaker. Afterward they would try and sometimes would succeed in having the speaker scourged, jailed, or harried out of town. Often, however, these efforts were unsuccessful.

Now look at the young Gentile, be he proselyte or God-fearer or com-

Foreword

plete stranger, as he sits there. Suddenly he is hearing a new, startling, thrilling answer to this terrible problem of death. And this answer comes not from myth or mystery or fantasy or debate. It comes from actual history, in which the speaker has himself shared: At this time, in these places, under these circumstances this man lived this life, died this death, and rose this resurrection!

After the service these Gentile listeners, and not a few Jews also, will gather around the speaker and say, "We would hear more of this matter." So the speaker arranges, perhaps tomorrow, Sunday, to meet with these inquirers and give them more of this gospel. If his angry opponents do not thwart him, he goes on to form these inquirers into a solid group. They meet one or more times a week, perhaps in a public hall, more commonly in someone's home. The speaker, anxious to carry his good news to still other places and climes, appoints leaders who shall keep the group alive and active after he leaves. The group has become a parish.

So Christianity spread and, in time, conquered much of Europe. Its word to a needy world was early summarized in a pastoral letter:

> Our savior Christ Jesus abolished death and brought life and immortality to light through the gospel.
>
> II Tim 1:10

That was and is the winning claim of the Christian faith.

That is why one warmly welcomes the present book by my good friend Frank Newton Howden. The reader will find here a mine of information, much of which would be hard to come by elsewhere. With skill and scholarship the author touches on almost every phase of human thinking about the life beyond. Most of all he deals with Christian belief, its history and its import for us today. There is thorough treatment of Church teaching about eternal life, rewards and punishments, the "intermediate state" between death and Heaven, and the final consummation of God's purpose. Evidence supporting these teachings is garnered and carefully weighed. (If some readers would weigh some items differently, that is only to be expected.) For all its fulness, the book is easy and pleasant to read. It is an honor and a privilege to have a share in presenting it to the public.

PIERSON PARKER
Emeritus Professor of New Testament
The General Theological Seminary

"Mac, you sure this is Hellgate, Washington?"

Preface

The cartoon on the opposite page—an advertisement by the Rand McNally Company—appeared during World War II. At the time maps were scarce, and some of the maps available were not as dependable as they might have been. The point is well taken: If you follow an erroneous map, you may well end up in an unexpected place—one very unlike your intended destination.

The moral for our purpose should be obvious. If it is important to follow accurate maps directing us along asphalt and concrete roads, then how much more important it is to know which way we are traveling through life; for we want to make certain that the way we choose leads to our intended destination on the other side of life.

This book is about life after death—but more than that. It is, as the title implies, about this life here in terms of our life to come.

Why write such a book? Why not concentrate on this life and this world and let the future take care of itself? The answer to this question is the logical sequitur to the cartoon: If we are not concerned about our destination, then we will not be concerned about which road we travel now. It also follows, if we pay no attention to choice of roads or to destinations, we may end up like the gentlemen in our cartoon—quite surprised when we discover ourselves amid strange surroundings.

It is not popular nowadays to consider the possibility of Hell, but who knows what kind of a hell awaits us at the completion of a life in which we haven't taken an interest in where we are going?

As death approaches almost everyone begins to grope toward the idea that there is something beyond this world. But groping at the end is not the Christian way. Rather, a Christian exchanges for this terminal groping a proper orientation throughout the whole of his life.

The purpose of this book is to help people understand that there is a life beyond the grave—a good life hereafter for the faithful Christian—and, despite the many unknown elements, that there are definite things we can

Preface

and should know about the future. Because of that knowledge, our lives can and should be considerably different.

For whom is this book intended? The aim is to meet the needs of both clergy and laymen. It is hoped that the pastoral clergy will find the book useful in clarifying their thinking on the subject of life after death and in communicating this area of the Faith to their spiritual charges. At the same time, it is hoped that the well-informed layman will find the book both enjoyable and edifying. For the benefit of the clergy I have tried not to labor the obvious—though not always successfully; and for the benefit of the laity I have tried to keep the technical vocabulary simple and employ annotations liberally as guides to further reading.

Though my training and background is in the American Episcopal Church, it is hoped that Christians of all denominations will find the book useful. To the best of my knowledge and belief, all that is written here is consistent with the main stream of orthodox Christianity. It is a faith common to many, as J. V. L. Casserley made plain in his book *No Faith of My Own* (Longmans, New York, 1950). On these fundamentals of Christian faith I can make no claims of authorship.

My prayers and blessing go out to all who have wondered about the subject of eternal life and who seek the answer the New Testament and the Christian Church have to give. It is sincerely hoped that this book will help to satisfy that quest and bring all who read it closer to our Lord.

In the writing of this book I am indebted to many people, members of my family, parishioners, and scholars, all of whom helped with valuable suggestions and the reading of all or parts of the manuscript. Principally, I would like to mention Cornelia Jane Fenton Howden (my late wife), Mary Valerie Howden (my second wife), the Rev. Dr. Pierson Parker (retired professor of New Testament at the General Theological Seminary), Bishop John Maury Allin (former presiding bishop of the Episcopal Church), Dr. Arah Danelian (professor of physics at the University of London), Canon Benedict H. Hanson, Miss Doris Hollenstein (my secretary at Trinity Church, Waterbury, Connecticut), Miss Amy Davy (our part-time secretary at Trinity, Lime Rock), Dr. Florence Sandler (Department of English, the University of Puget Sound), the Rev. Dr. Moultrie Guerry (former chaplain at the University of the South), Mrs. Thelma Lebeaux and Mrs. Trudy Nicholson (friends), Raydon Ronshaugen, Miss Josephine McEntee, and Mrs. Faith Campbell (parishioners at Trinity).

Life
Here and Hereafter

1

Death as Part of Life

It is a well-worn cliché: The only things in this life of which we can be absolutely sure are death and taxes.[1] That statement is only half true, for there are a few isolated areas on this globe where a person can go perfectly secure in the knowledge that no tax collector will seek him out. But escaping death—that is another matter. People dodge it, pretend it isn't true, sentimentalize it as "sleep," soften it as just "passing away," or distort it by the use of cosmetics, colorful coffins with inner-spring mattresses, and lush funeral parlors steeped in somber organ music. Despite all our ostrich maneuvers, death remains the one event in this life of which we can be absolutely certain.

We moderns have been able to add a few years to our lives by the rightful use of medical science—and that is all to the good—but all our twentieth-century ingenuity has done little more than postpone death. No matter how medicated or charmed a life may be, eventually medicine can go no further, the charm wears off, and death at the last reaches out to claim its own.

Toward life's termination the human race takes three different attitudes:

1. Ignore the inevitability of death, pretend it isn't there, live life while you can and for yourself as much as you can, without any regard for the possibility that it is limited. Eat, drink, and be merry, and don't give a passing thought to tomorrow.

2. Acknowledge the inevitability of death but, from the realization of

death's imminence and apparent finality, conclude that all life is futile.

3. Be well aware of death, but accept it as part of life—as something God-given and, therefore, good when the time comes.

Only the last two of these three answers are logical, but, oddly enough, many a man or woman of our day clings to the first. The modern human being seems to pretend that this wonderful life will go on for ever. When someone is dying of an incurable disease, the typical relative instructs visitors not to tell the dying person about his situation. He keeps up the cheery line—"Oh, you look fine this morning. You're going to be up and at 'em in a couple of days."

Here were my instructions given by a neighbor not more than a few weeks after I was ordained: "My sister is up at the hospital dying of cancer. The doctor says that at most she can live only three weeks. If you do go to see her, go just as a friend, not as a priest, and in no way give the girl any idea she is dying."

Most of us have had relatives or friends in the process of leaving this world and have received similar instructions—"Pretend there's nothing wrong." Even before death is near, the average American will have been schooled in refusing to think about the possibility of death. As William Hazlitt once wrote in an essay, "No young man believes he will ever die."[2] Quite so. The same can be said of a great many elderly people, too. The average person is living this life convinced, on the surface anyway, that he is going to live it forever.

Perhaps best known of the ancient proponents of this philosophy of living without regard for death is Epicurus (341–270 B.C.). From his name we derive the word *epicure*,[3] for he taught that the true life is the life of pleasure. Moreover, he was an atheist, firmly convinced that there is nothing beyond this world. As he put it, "Where life is, death is not; and where death is, life is not."[4] In other words, don't ever think about death, because when it comes you will not know that you ever had life; and when you have life and know it, you certainly do not have death. Enjoy the present moment, he said; think neither about the past nor the future.

Though the average person you meet today is not an atheist and though he isn't particularly philosophical about things, he still follows in Epicurus's footsteps; he prefers to ignore death and pretend it will never arrive.

That, then, is the first answer to the problem of death. Illogical though it is, it is the answer a great many moderns endorse by the way they live their lives.

Death as Part of Life

The second answer to the question of death, though not a popular one, is as old as the first. It is the answer of the pessimist: You can't win, so why try? Shakespeare put this answer into the mouth of Macbeth when the news of the queen's death is brought to him:

> Life's but a walking shadow, a poor player,
> That struts and frets his hour upon the stage
> And then is heard no more.
> *Macbeth*, act 5, scene 5

Centuries before Christ, even a hundred or so years before Epicurus, there lived in the Greek colony of Ceos (an island in the Aegean Sea) a sophist by the name of Prodicus. His teachings stirred up quite a rumpus for a time, because many of his followers were committing suicide, and since somebody had to bury these people, it presented quite a problem to the community. One might say Prodicus had the original graveyard voice, for, despite his frail body, he had a powerful deep voice, and when he spoke a profound emotional shock ran through the ranks of his audience.

Prodicus, dubbed the earliest of the pessimists, felt keenly the evils of the world to the point where he regarded early death as a blessing. In his teachings he would describe the five stages of human existence, from the cradle to the grave. The newborn child greets his home with wailing. In like manner, Prodicus would describe the sufferings of each stage of life on up to the gray hairs of old age. As he finished with each stage he would reiterate, "If life could end here, that would be good, for then suffering for that person would come to an end."[5]

Pessimism and the disparaging of life have continued in one form or another down through the ages. A classic example in the philosophical circles of the last century is Arthur Schopenhauer (1788–1860). In his book *The World as Will and Idea* he states that pessimism follows from the very nature of will. "For one wish that is satisfied there remain at least ten that are denied. . . . It is like the alms thrown to a beggar, that keeps him alive today that his misery may be prolonged till the morrow."[6] "In [the] evident disproportion between the trouble and the reward, the will to live appears to us . . . if taken objectively, as a fool, or subjectively, as a delusion, seized by which everything living works with the utmost exertion of its strength for something that is of no value."[7]

Or, to bring this down to our own day, we have the English philosopher Lord Bertrand Russell. Lacking any belief in God (as with just about all pessimists), Russell concludes that man's "origin, his growth, his hopes and fears, his loves and his beliefs, are but the outcome of accidental collocation of atoms," and that "all the labours of the ages, all the devotions, all the inspiration, all the noonday brightness of human genius, are destined to extinction" and "must inevitably be buried beneath the debris of a universe in ruins.... Only on the firm foundation of unyielding despair, can the soul's habitation henceforth be safely built."[8]

Another painter of a picture of despair is the French existentialist Jean-Paul Sartre. *Absurd* is his favorite adjective applied to our world. "I knew it was the World, the naked World suddenly revealing itself, and I choked with rage at this gross, absurd being."[9] This absurdity of existence generates in man a feeling of nausea or disgust at the lack of purpose in all existence, at this disordered mass of reality. Sartre's writings have a constant recurrence of such words as *vomit, stench, disgust, sickening*. The lack of purpose, the nonexistence of God mean that there is no law of morality.[10] Sartre would not recommend suicide as a way out, but certainly the implications of his philosophy make it a desirable possibility, for "all human activities ... are doomed to failure."[11]

A modern writer who has gone a step further than Sartre and spelled out the logical implications of a disparagement of life is another Frenchman, Albert Camus, who also has been termed an existentialist. The subject of suicide he discusses with terrifying candor in his *Myth of Sisyphus*. As Camus reminds us, in Greek mythology the gods had condemned Sisyphus ceaselessly to roll a rock to the top of a mountain; he would never succeed in his task, for, as he neared the top, the stone would slide back, and he must begin all over again. Camus points out, "They had thought with some reason that there is no more dreadful punishment than ... hopeless labor." This for Camus is our world. "It is legitimate and necessary to wonder whether life has any meaning. Therefore, it is legitimate to meet the problem of suicide face to face." Camus doesn't recommend suicide as such; but he claims, "Dying voluntarily implies that you have recognized ... the absence of any profound reason for living, the insane character of that daily agitation, and the uselessness of suffering."[12]

That, then, is the second answer to the problem of death—to welcome it as a good thing, for life is bad.

The third answer is the Christian one, to regard both life and death as gifts from God. The Epicurean says, "Only life is real." The Pessimist says, "Only death is real." The Christian says, "Both are real." More than that, the Christian says death is part of life. He neither welcomes it (under normal circumstances) nor fears it. The Christian, accepting birth and life as gifts from God, also accepts death as His gift. Since he was born into this world as a result of God's creative activity, the Christian realizes that this life is a good one. He also realizes that our Lord Jesus, by being born into this world and living in it, sanctified the whole of this life.

This body that the Christian has is entrusted to him for proper keeping, for, as St. Paul reminds us, the body is the "Temple of the Holy Ghost,"[13] and as such is sacred. The unnatural shortening of life or the neglect or abuse of the body is contrary to God's purpose. The Christian must, therefore, take advantage of medical science to stay healthy; he must pray for healing when necessary; it is his duty to keep his body in repair, to keep physically fit.

At the same time the Christian knows that one day his body will wear out and must be discarded. For some individuals this happens suddenly; for most it is a gradual process. As it is sometimes said, no sooner are we born than we begin to die.

Actually our bodies wear out in much the same manner as do the material things that we manufacture and depend on for so much. If we keep our automobiles long enough, we find that first a tire needs replacing, then perhaps the clutch, or maybe the transmission fails. Anyone who has run an old car is well aware that it is one repair job after another. Yet finally a time comes when we just give up repairing the old machine and abandon it as a contribution to America's rubbish heap.

Our bodies are not very different from that in terms of wearing out and the constant need for repair, except that the human machine is far more durable than any of our material creations and often is able to repair itself. Just the same, as with our machines, the element of wear and failure does take place. In one person, the heart begins to fail; with another it is the bone structure, or a troublesome gall bladder, or, as with the automobile, it can all be demolished in one accident (God permits that, too, as we all sadly know); regardless, something will happen sooner or later, for the body is not meant to last forever. And, although we do well to pray for health, we must not think that God is letting us down if, instead of getting better, our bodies continue to wear out; for, as with the automobile, there is a built-in obsolescence factor.

Unless our lives are cut short by some tragedy, we all share in the sorrow of seeing a parent or a loved one die and leave us. Also, if our children live a normal life-span, they will share a like experience of seeing us go on before them. That is the cycle of life—birth, childhood, growing up, adulthood, marriage, family, maturity, old age, often sickness, and finally death. If this cycle of life and death appears to be a horrible tragedy the Almighty has inflicted upon us, consider for a moment the alternative—a world where there is no death. Anyone who has studied the problem of overpopulation realizes this would soon mean no births, for our planet has limited resources. A far greater tragedy than a world without death would be a stagnant world where there were no births—no comings nor goings.

All this daily dying the Epicurean would ignore; the Pessimist would see only the tragedy of it; but the Christian recognizes it as part of God's great plan for the creation and development of human personalities, all designed as preparations for that which follows death, preparations for the sharing in His eternity, where there are no limits in space or time.

When the human wearing-out process is completed and the body ends its usefulness, when the time comes to leave this earth, the Christian takes that journey unafraid, knowing that all will continue safely in God's care.

We need not stick strictly to theology as such for this reconciliation of life and death. Modern psychiatry has shown us that the normal life is lived to the full only with the acceptance of the inevitability of death. The world-famous psychiatrist Dr. Carl Jung gives us some useful thoughts on the subject:

> I have observed that a life directed to an aim is in general better, richer, and healthier than an aimless one, and that it is better to go forward with the stream of time than backwards against it. To the psychotherapist an old man who cannot bid farewell to life appears as feeble and sickly as a young man who is unable to embrace it. And, as a matter of fact, it is in many cases a question of the selfsame childish greediness, the same fear, the same defiance and willfulness, in the one as in the other. As a doctor I am convinced that it is gygienic—if I may use the word—to discover in death a goal toward which one can strive, and that shrinking away from it is something unhealthy and abnormal which robs the second half of life of its purpose.[14]
>
> Natural life is the nourishing soil of the soul. Anyone who fails to go along with life remains suspended, stiff and rigid in mid-air. That is why so many people get wooden in old age; they look back and cling to the past with a secret fear of death in their hearts. They withdraw from the

life-process, at least psychologically, and consequently remain fixed like nostalgic pillars of salt, with vivid recollections of youth but no living relation to the present. From the middle of life onward, only he ... remains vitally alive who is ready to *die with life*.... The negation of life's fulfillment is synonymous with the refusal to accept its ending. Both mean not wanting to live, and not wanting to live is identical with not wanting to die. Waxing and waning make one curve.[15]

How then should a Christian die? Our Lord from the cross supplies the answer—his last words in the physical body—"Father, into thy hands I commend my spirit."[16]

That is how a Christian faces both life and death. Having lived through this life as a faithful servant of his Creator, not shrinking from life, but, like his Lord, participating in it to the full, he goes on cheerfully toward its end and finally leaves it unafraid, confident that all is well in the hands of a loving, merciful, and purposeful God.

2

Sources of Information

One summer my family and I spent August in Rumford, Maine. It was one of those vacation jobs, where I was in charge of St. Barnabas' Church. In the course of our stay there the senior warden (the layman in charge of things) happened by the rectory and found me busy at the typewriter, surrounded by an impressive clutter of books and papers. My wife Jane felt called upon to volunteer an explanation: "He's writing a book on life after death."

There followed an awkward silence. Our visitor stood there aghast, unable to believe that any normal person could be so presumptuous as to pretend knowledge of that which lay beyond bodily contact. Finally he stammered, "How does he know about such things? Has he ever been there?"

A number of years ago, before American laxity with the mother tongue became as widely accepted throughout the world as it is today, the story was told of two geologists—an American and an Englishman—flying over the mouth of an active volcano. Just as they reached the very center and got a good whiff of the fumes, the American looked over the side of the cockpit and exclaimed, "Wow! That sure looks like Hell down there." To which the Englishman properly replied, "My! How you Americans *do* travel! You know about the strangest places!"

Neither the American geologist of this story nor I have ever been there—neither below nor above. Of course there are some hellish aspects of this globe combined with, we trust, many heavenly ones, which we can project into the future; but, for the most part, a church writer on the afterlife depends for his information on quite other than first-hand evidence.

On reflection, though, it occurs to me that our Rumford senior warden really should not have appeared so amazed at hearing that someone was writing about Hell, because Rumford is dominated by a huge paper plant which for years has created tremendous quantities of sulphurous acid fumes. If any place ever smelled like the traditional description of Hell, it was that community. More than that, as our guide through the paper plant informed us, the pollution helped shorten the waiting period for entrance into the next world for many, because, as he candidly admitted, "It is a well-substantiated fact that the life-expectancy of those living in this valley is ten years below the national average." Despite the free-vacation inducement, my family refused to return to Rumford for a second summer. To Jane nothing the medievalists had ever written about the place of eternal punishment could be worse!

But to get on with the answer to how one can know anything about life after death, most churchmen would contend that there are four valid, objective sources of information:

1. *The Bible as a whole.* The Old Testament doesn't give us much information, but it does give us some. The Old Testament is the particular concern of chapter 4. All that need be mentioned at this point is that we do have in the Old Testament such items as King Saul's visit to a medium (I Samuel 28:3–25), which, though roundly condemned by the narrator, does reveal a widespread practice of the day. We also have visions from the writer of the Book of Daniel. We have revelations from Isaiah and the other prophets. There are snatches of insight in the Psalms and in Job. Scholars have been able to interpret some of the strange passages in the early books of the Bible (Genesis, Exodus, etc.) in terms of what they know about the beliefs of life after death held by Semitic peoples other than the Hebrews. Then, too, there is the Apocrypha section of the Old Testament—where you find such valuable books as Ecclesiasticus and the Wisdom of Solomon, books which express a sure and certain belief in life after death.*

---

*The Apocrypha consists of fourteen books placed between the Old and the New Testaments in some editions of the King James version of the Bible. (You can usually purchase the King James Bible with or without the Apocrypha.) In the Revised Standard Version the Apocrypha is found at the end, after the books of the New Testament. In the usual Roman Catholic

Sources of Information

Our main source of biblical information, however, is the New Testament. Our Lord made it clear, throughout the whole of his teaching ministry, that the real life must be orientated toward the eternal background. He tells the story of the Rich Fool to illustrate the folly of amassing fortunes in this world while neglecting one's ultimate destiny, and he concludes that parable with the clear warning: "'Fool! This night your soul is required of you; and the things you have prepared, whose will they be?' So is he who lays up treasure for himself, and is not rich toward God."[1] The theme of the Kingdom of God underscores the whole of Jesus' teaching, and he promises all who believe in him a share in the Heavenly Kingdom. "Everyone who has left houses or brothers or sisters or father or mother or children or lands, for my name's sake, will receive a hundredfold, and inherit eternal life."[2] Jesus also had much to say about the nature of life after death. Further he spoke frequently about judgment and the possibility of Hell.[3] More than that, he *demonstrated* something of the world beyond by two great acts—his Transfiguration[4] and his Resurrection.[5]

The New Testament epistle writers, too, have much to say about life after death, especially the Apostle Paul. The one other New Testament writer who dwells on this subject is John of Patmos, whose visions we have in the last book of the Bible. All of this material I will treat later in this book.

---

editions of the Bible, these books (with some minor exceptions) are found interspersed with the other books of the Old Testament, generally in places in accord with their contents. It was during the time when Greek was the international language that there came into existence the Septuagint, a translation by Alexandrian Jews of the entire Old Testament into Greek, and this Septuagint included these fourteen books, with the exception of II Esdras (the original of which is extant only in the Latin). This Septuagint was the Bible used by many of the Jews of the New Testament period. The Old Testament quotations found in the New Testament are from this translation. Consequently, this Greek version of the Bible, including the Apocrypha, was accepted by all the early Christians. The word *apocrypha* (Greek, meaning "hidden things") first came to be used by St. Jerome (c. 342–420 A.D.), who in his translation of the Bible into the Latin of his day noted that these books were of uncertain origin, since they were not to be found in the Hebrew text. It remained for Martin Luther and the Protestant Reformers, in 1543, to separate these books into a section of their own and to question their inspiration. Despite this questioning, the Apocrypha has remained officially part of the Bible of the Anglican Communion, and many of the lessons appointed for divine services are taken from it. When the bishops at the Savoy Conference (1661) were asked by the Puritans to omit all lessons from the Apocrypha, they answered, "It is heartily to be wished that sermons were as good."

2. *Parapsychological evidence, both ancient and modern.* As far back as man has been able to write, we have recorded experiences by sane and sober people—of all races and stages of culture—who have actually seen spirits or ghosts of the departed. At the same time there are many recorded accounts of out-of-body experiences of those still in this world. These things will be treated in the next chapter. At this point one example of an appearance by one who was departed will suffice, an experience that could have happened to anybody, but which happened in this instance to the famous radio personality of the forties and fifties, Arthur Godfrey:

> After World War II, while on Pacific sea duty in the Navy, Godfrey was strangely awakened one night. Rubbing his eyes in the half-light, he saw a vision at the foot of his bed. It was his father, speaking to him softly in a voice the son knew well. He had come to say "goodbye" but he didn't want Arthur to grieve, as it was only a farewell.
>
> Then the vision disappeared. Godfrey looked at the clock by his bed. It was 2:10 A.M. Eventually he drifted fitfully off to sleep, but when morning came, the "dream" was still vivid in his mind. Later that day there was a wireless communication relayed from his house. Godfrey's father had died during the night.
>
> The time of death? Shortly after 2 A.M.![6]

3. *Mystical experience.* Mystical experience can be biblical (as with, for example, St. Paul or John of Patmos), or it can be found in the life of the Christian Church, or in the lives of people outside the Church. It might include some parapsychological experiences, but it is more than that. Mystical insight is the ability to see and hear beyond the senses, what most of us can't, or only occasionally can, see or hear. Here are two examples from the Venerable Bede's English history:

> Following the death of the Christian King Sabert of the East Saxons, the land returned to idolatry. The Christian bishops concluded that it would be better for them to return to their own country where they could serve God in freedom. Mellitus and Justus left England first and settled in Gaul. Laurentius (the second Archbishop of Canterbury) was to follow shortly, but first he would spend a last night in the Kentish Church of St. Peter and St. Paul. . . . After long and fervent prayers for the sadly afflicted Church, he lay down and fell asleep. In the middle of the night, blessed Peter . . . appeared to him, and demanded to know why he intended to abandon the flock entrusted to his care, and asked to what shepherds he would commit Christ's sheep left among the

wolves when he fled. "Have you forgotten my example?" asked Peter. "For the sake of the little ones whom Christ entrusted to me as proof of His love, I suffered chains, blows, imprisonment, and pain. Finally, I endured the death of crucifixion at the hands of unbelievers and enemies of Christ, so that at last I might be crowned with Him." Deeply moved by the words and scourging of blessed Peter [which apparently went along with the conversation of that night], Christ's servant Laurentius sought audience with the king early next morning, and removing his garment, showed him the marks of the lash. The king was astounded, and enquired who had dared to scourge so eminent a man; and when he learned that it was for his own salvation that the archbishop had suffered so severely at the hands of Christ's own Apostle, he was greatly alarmed. He renounced his idolatry, gave up his unlawful wife, accepted the Christian Faith, and was baptized, henceforward promoting the welfare of the Church with every means at his disposal.[7]

Regardless of what the reader may think of this account and others like it, it should be pointed out that this experience was positive enough to change the course of history, for the Archbishop remained at his post in Kent and the two exiled bishops—Mellitus and Justus—were sent for and given permission to return to Britain and set their churches in order.

Although not as history-shaping as the above, another once-in-a-lifetime mystical experience comes from Bede's biography of St. Chad, Bishop of Mercia. Here we read of a Brother Owini who was busy working in the grounds around the oratory, while Chad was reading and praying inside:

> Suddenly, as he afterwards related, he heard the sound of sweet and joyful singing coming down from heaven to earth. The sound seemed at first to emanate from the south-east, gradually coming closer to him until it centered over the roof of the oratory where the bishop was at prayer. It then entered the oratory, and seemed to fill both it and the surrounding air. He listened closely to what he heard, and after about half an hour, the song of joy rose from the roof of the oratory, and returned to heaven.... Owini stood astonished for a while, turning over in his mind what this might portend, when the bishop threw open the oratory window, and in his customary way clapped his hands to summon him indoors. When he hurried in, the bishop said: "Go at once to the church, and fetch seven of the brethren here, and come back with them yourself." On their arrival, he first urged them to live in love and peace with each other and with all the faithful, and to be constant and tireless in keeping the rules of monastic discipline.... He then an-

nounced that his own death was drawing near, saying: "The welcome guest who has visited many of our brethren has come to me today, and has deigned to summon me out of this world. Therefore return to the church, and ask the brethren to commend my passing to our Lord in their prayers. And let each prepare for his own passing by vigils, prayers, and good deeds, for no man knows the hour of his death." Having said this and much besides, he gave them his blessing, and they left him sadly; but the brother who had heard the heavenly music came back alone and flung himself to the ground, saying: "Father, I beg you to let me ask a question." "Ask what you wish," Chad replied. "Tell me, I pray," he asked, "what was the glad song that I heard coming down from heaven upon this oratory, and that later returned to heaven?" "Since you have heard the singing and were aware of the coming of the heavenly company," Chad answered, "I command you in the name of our Lord not to tell anyone of this before my death. For they were angelic spirits, who came to summon me to the heavenly reward that I have always hoped and longed for, and they have promised to return in seven days and take me with them." All took place as he had been told, for Chad was quickly attacked by a disease which steadily grew worse until the seventh day. Then he prepared for death by receiving the Body and Blood of our Lord, his holy soul was released from the prisonhouse of the body, and, one may rightly believe, was "taken by the angels to the joys of heaven."[8]

The pages of church history are filled with accounts like these. I myself ran into a story of heavenly music during my last summer before retirement, when I got to know a Mrs. Natalie Norwall, who shared a room with one our parishioners at Geer Memorial Hospital, in Canaan, Connecticut. She had been blind for the past three or so years. This is the story she told me:

It was about ten years ago that this strange event happened. A baby boy was born to a Roman Catholic family, who lived near me in Canaan. The child was very beautiful, but, sadly, unable to speak because of a birth injury. He had other problems, too, and died at the age of two.

The evening of the funeral I went to bed early, at ten o'clock. No sooner had I put my head on the pillow, when I heard the sweetest music I had ever experienced in all my life. I sat up at once, because nothing like that had ever happened to me before.

The next night I went over to the home of the boy's family, at the same time a number of other people were there. While our hostess served tea and coffee, conversation naturally followed. A man by the name of George was there, a rough-spoken character, not at all the kind of person who seemed to be religious. In the course of the conversation he told how the strangest thing happened the previous night; he heard, apparently from nowhere, this wonderful music.

"What time did it happen?" I asked him.

"At about ten o'clock," he replied.

That was exactly the time it had happened to me, and in precisely the same way.

I found this a puzzling experience. It was really the most beautiful music I've ever heard in all my life. I used to sing in our choir [at the Methodist Church] and have heard and sung all kinds of music, but *never* music as sweet as I heard that night following this little boy's funeral.

The skeptic who hears accounts like these is inclined to say, "I don't believe in visions; it's just the imaginations of these people working overtime." Sometimes that might be the case; we would not doubt for a moment that there are mentally ill people who have hallucinations of the impossible. But most of the people who report such experiences show no hallucinatory characteristics whatsoever, as judged by the standards of psychiatrists.[9]

Those people we term "mystics" have had many insights into the world beyond. With most people, however, these experiences are rare, most likely of the once-in-a-lifetime variety. Perhaps the Blessed Virgin Mary fits into this category; she, so far as the biblical record shows, had only one out-of-this-world experience, the one when the Archangel Gabriel visited her at the time we call the Annunciation (Luke 1:26–38).

On the other hand it is quite surprising to discover just how many ordinary people have had at least one mystical insight during the course of a lifetime. Most people are loathe to talk about their experiences for fear of ridicule, but I continue to be amazed when the subject opens up to hear ordinary folk relate instances in which they have been given the gift of seeing into the next world.

A few years ago the magazine edition of the Sunday *New York Times* had a well-researched article entitled, "Are we a nation of mystics?"[10] The authors of this article began by giving us a typical mystical experience, one which John Buchan, novelist and Governor General of Canada, had:

I had been ploughing all day in the black dust of the Lichenburg roads, and had come very late to a place called the Eye of Malmani. . . . We watered our horses and went supperless to bed. Next morning I bathed in one of the Malmani pools—and icy cold it was—and then basked in the early sunshine while breakfast was cooking. The water made a pleasant music, and nearby was a covert of willows filled with singing birds. Then and there came on me the hour of revelation, when, though savagely hungry, I forgot about breakfast. Scents, sights, and sounds blended into a harmony so perfect that it transcended human expression, even human thought. It was like a glimpse of the peace of eternity.

After relating another such account the authors make this statement: "Such extraordinary experiences—intense, overwhelming, indescribable—are recorded at every time in history and in every place on the globe and, as we shall argue later, are widespread, almost commonplace, in American society today." That such experiences are commonplace in a materialistic country like America seems beyond belief, but the authors back this up by a survey involving 1,500 adult Americans, in which they discovered that 40 percent had had at least one mystical experience, while many said they had had several. Further the surveyors discovered that certain groups are more likely to have such experiences than others, as for example, the college-educated and those in the above average income bracket. Though Episcopalians seem to have them more frequently than any other religious group (no reason given), Roman Catholics, Protestants, Jews, and nonreligious people have had such experiences. However, the more religious a person is the more likely he is to be possessed of mystical insight. A survey by the Gallup Poll found that a third of all Americans have had a mystical or religious experience.[11]

Though no one has a monopoly on mysticism, there are three cases of the more gifted mystic I would like to present to the reader—one from Medieval Europe and two from modern United States.

My medieval mystic is St. Hildegard of Bingen, a woman who lived at the time of the great Church-State power struggles and became in her day a tremendous influence for good in the life of a Church which sorely needed a new vision of holiness. She was a confidante of kings and popes, and all who knew her felt the presence of sainthood. From her early childhood to her death she had innumerable visions. As she put it,

> Up to my fifteenth year I saw much, and related some of the things seen to others, who would inquire with astonishment, whence such things

might come. I also wondered and during my sickness I asked one of my nurses whether she saw such things. When she answered no, a great fear befell me. Frequently, in my conversation, I would relate future things, which I saw as if present, but noting the amazement of my listeners, I became more reticent.[12]

These visions came to Hildegard in a way fairly typical of mystics. As Evelyn Underhill points out, all mystics have their visions in terms of light, "a kind of radiance, a flooding of the personality with new light.... It is what Whitman termed 'Light rare, untellable' or what St. Theresa would claim to be 'a light which knows no night; but rather, as it is always light, nothing ever disturbs it.'"[13] So, too, when St. Paul describes his seeing the Risen Christ on the Damascus Road, he speaks of a light "brighter than the sun."[14] This St. Hildegard terms "Lux vivens" (a living Light) or "Inner Light, brighter than the sun." The nature of this light is brought out in one of her books written late in life:

> From my infancy until now, when I am in the seventieth year of my age, my soul has always beheld this light, and in it my soul soars to the summit of the firmament and into a different air and spreads itself among different peoples, however remote they may be. Therefore I perceive these things in my soul, as I saw them through dissolving clouds.... I do not hear them with my outer ears, nor perceive them by the ponderings of my heart, nor by any assistance of the five senses, but only in my soul, my eyes being open and not sightless as in a trance.... I write whatever I see or hear in the Light, nor do I put down any other words, but I tell my message in the rude Latin words I read it in, in the Light. For the Light does not teach me to write as the learned write; the words in the Light are not like words from human lips but like a flashing flame and a cloud passing through the clear air....
>
> Within that brightness I sometimes see another Light for which the name "Lux Vivens" has been given me. When and how I see it I cannot tell, but sometimes when I see it, all pain and sadness are lifted from me and I seem a simple girl again and no longer an old woman.[15]

Among the other famous Christian mystics of history are St. Augustine of Hippo, St. Bernard of Clairvaux, Meister Eckhart, St. Theresa of Avila, St. Francis of Assisi, St. John of the Cross, and St. Catherine of Siena.

First among the two modern mystics from which I would quote is Helen Fiske Evans, an Episcopalian and daughter of the Fiske who was once president of the Metropolitan Life Insurance Company. Her book,

The Garden of the Little Flower and Other Mystical Experiences,[16] was written at the request of two bishops of our Church, two bishops of very contrasting churchmanship, by the way—Noble C. Powell of Maryland and Reginald Mallet of Indiana. Bishop Powell, who writes the Foreword, describes the book as "evidence of the influence of the lovely saint [Saint Thérèse of Lisieux] upon a deeply spiritual person." While Bishop Powell admits to no mystical experiences of his own, he is fully appreciative of Mrs. Evans's gifts and says he has come to know her as a very real and practical person, no visionary.[17] Bishop Mallet, on the other hand, did have one supernatural experience, while simply going over the manuscript with Mrs. Evans.[18] It happened quite often that way with people who came in contact with this saintly person; there were wonderful odors of flowers when no flowers or perfumes were anywhere around. It is impossible to do justice to Mrs. Evans's story in just a paragraph or so. But there isn't room in this book for the full treatment the work deserves. Here is just one sample:

> While I was saying my prayers . . . I had a vision of great beauty which has ever since then seemed to suggest an important message for me. Our Lord appeared, standing in front of the priedieu . . . His robes were a brilliant and glistening white. At His left stood St. Thérèse, . . . and she was looking up at Him intently.[19]

While this passage gives no particular information about the world beyond ours, I cite it primarily to underscore the fact that, though most of us are unable to see them, we are surrounded by "a great cloud of witnesses,"[20] and there are those who frequently do see them.

The second modern mystic I would like to introduce to the reader I call "A Mystic from Vermont." The manuscript she wrote remains unpublished (at her request), and though I promised not to use her name, I am permitted to quote excerpts from her manuscript—what she calls "The Story of John"—whenever I feel it would help others believe in the reality of the spiritual world. (I have in my files a complete copy of the manuscript.) I learned about Mrs. P. (as we will call her) purely by accident and arranged through a third party for an interview. I found Mrs. P. to be a very pleasant, intelligent woman, a retired high-school English teacher, then living in Burlington. She is the author of two books of poetry and was a faithful member of the Congregational Church of her city. Her gifts have been revealed to only a very few people. Anyone coming in contact with her would simply report, "She's a charming and most intelligent person."

Early in Mrs. P's life she had some mystical experiences, but her gifts in this direction remained largely dormant until December 1950, about a year before I became the rector of St. Luke's Church, in St. Albans, Vermont. As it happened, her grandson John was driving back from a Navy cruise when he had a fatal accident. Mrs. P., on hearing of the tragedy, naturally left her home in Burlington and went down to Reading, Massachusetts, to stay at the home of her daughter (John's mother). A few days after the funeral, while sitting in her room at this house, she heard a voice: "May I ask a favor?" Mrs. P. was completely taken off guard, and without looking up she answered, "What is it?" The voice continued, "This is John. Will you please stop calling my name?" Without realizing how strange this conversation was, she answered, "Why, I haven't called your name, John." But John insisted, "Oh, yes you have. I've heard you again and again, saying, 'O John, John, John,' with such pain in your voice; I just can't take it, and you know I'm a pretty husky fellow." He then laughed lightly. At this point Mrs. P. looked up and saw John standing beside her. The mystical relationship went on from that day and continued for about three years, during which time John developed from what appeared to be an "earth bound" person to one "in glory."

In the preface to the manuscript which describes it all, Mrs. P. writes of her philosophy and theology:

> This is to certify that the experiences recorded here actually happened, that they were nothing I ever dreamed could possibly happen; and that they were a continual surprise to me in their almost incredible and wonderful development.
>
> The messages that came to me were taken down verbatim. Their revelation and corroboration of Bible truths have been a constant inspiration and help to me. *I do wish to state that I am not a spiritualist* [italics mine]. But because I am deeply and inexpressibly grateful to my Heavenly Father for so blessing John and me as to permit him to return to earth to witness for the Saviour and to help lead his family to Him; I am making this Witnessing known to a few to whom I feel led by the Holy Spirit to go.

Later on in this book there will be a few other references to the mystical insights of Mrs. P. The material used corroborates that of other Christians similarly gifted.

Mystics have contributed far more than most people realize to religious development. Without the mystics we would have very little insight into the world beyond this one. Without the mystics the Bible could never have been written. Without the mystics the life of the Church would lack an essential nourishment. As Evelyn Underhill words it, "In the great mystics we see the highest and widest development of that consciousness to which the human race has yet attained."[21]

Mystics in the Christian-Hebrew tradition, we should also point out, have never been aloof from the world and its needs. The Prophet Isaiah was able to see his vision of the Holy God and the seraphim at the same time he heard the command to speak out for God against the social injustices of his age.[22] In like manner St. Hildegard saw the God of Light coming to her and demanding that she no longer be silent but speak out against the self-indulgences of her day. St. Catherine of Siena, born into a situation where there was constant war between her city and neighboring Perugia, dedicated her life to peace and worked to care for the wounded and bury the dead. So it is with all true mystics; they never separate themselves from the world and concern for God's people.

Also let us underscore the fact that, as our Mystic from Vermont implied, mysticism is not spiritualism. Mysticism comes unsolicited and it comes for the most part to the holy, to those who have cultivated a devout prayer life and are grounded in the Faith. Spiritualism and the world of Ouija boards and hallucinogens have, on the other hand, been a self-seeking search for personal gratification. As one ex-spiritualist (now a Christian) told me, once you open the sluice gate to the spiritualist world, all kinds of forces come through, both good and demonic, and few dabblers in the occult can tell the difference.

Finally, mysticism always produces fruit; it always brings about a furthering of God's purposes in the world.

4. *The evidence of the Church's teaching.* This includes the evidence from deduction—Christian man's logical thinking, worked out under the guidance of the Holy Spirit. All the evidence we have cited above—the evidence of the scriptures, the evidence of parapsychology, the evidence of mystical experiences—comes into the life of the Church to be judged, some to be rejected, some to be assimilated.

The Church, as the body of all faithful believers under the headship of Christ and under the guidance of the Holy Spirit, can formulate doctrine, deducing logical conclusions from what it already knows to be true.

An example of this deductive process might go like this: God is a God of mercy and justice; that we know to be true from the teachings of both the Old and New Testaments. Consequently any doctrine of life after death that is inconsistent with either one of these characteristics of God is untrue.

One of the patristic writers, Origen (c. 185–254 A.D.), makes this continuing development of theology clear. He calls attention to St. John 16:12-13: "I have yet many things to say to you, but you cannot bear them now. When the spirit of Truth comes, he will guide you into all truth; for he will not speak on his own authority, but whatever he hears he will speak." Commenting on this, Origen says of our Lord and his disciples:

> There were many of the subjects which He had to explain to them; but as He saw that it was a work of exceeding difficulty to root out of the mind opinions that have been almost born with man ... He postponed such a task to a future season—that is, namely, which followed His passion and resurrection.[23]

In other words the Church, indwelt by the Holy Spirit, is led into logical deductions from Holy Scripture and other human experience. Nothing the Church teaches can be contrary to Holy Scripture. And note well, too, any item of mystical experience or any teaching by an individual must be in harmony with the Scriptures and with the whole Church before we can regard it as valid.

What we say, then, about these matters of life and death is not irresponsible speculation. Rather, we trust it emerges from the guidance of the Holy Spirit and stands the test of logic, the test of the ages, the test of human experience, the test of Scripture, and is in keeping with what the Universal Church teaches.

3

The Universality of Belief in Life After Death

An agnostic of my Vermont parish once said, "All peoples believe in life after death; there is nothing exclusively Christian about that." The man was quite right. In fact we can go a step further and candidly admit there is nothing exclusively religious about such a belief either. Primitive man came to the conviction that there is a future life quite outside of anything to do with a belief in any god or gods. As we shall see later on in this book, Christianity's concept of eternal life is quite different from primitive man's belief in the survival after death as such. However it is with primitive man's beliefs and his experiences that we find a good starting point to appeal to the agnostic of our day.

First, although you may find many contemporaries of the civilized world who reject belief in an afterlife, when it comes to modern man living on the primitive level, you cannot find a race or a tribe anywhere over the whole earth that *does not* believe in life beyond the grave. This fact has been well established by innumerable anthropologists.[1]

This universality of belief in life after death is not only a fact of our age but a fact of every age, as far back as archeology can trace man. Visiting the Orkney Islands to the north of Scotland in the spring of 1987, I entered and photographed the chambered tomb of Maes Howe, one of the greatest architectural structures of primitive man. I was amazed to see the craftsmanship involved. By the use of large flagstones (megaliths), and a drystone technique, each stone had been laid flat to overhang the one beneath it so that, at the proper height, it had been possible to roof over the walls with one large slab. The date of the tomb of Maes Howe is 2700 B.C., but similar structures in the western part of the continent of Europe go back as far as 5000 B.C., centuries before the construction of the Egyptian pyramids.[2]

Nearby the burial chamber of Maes Howe are the Standing Stones of Stenness and the Ring of Brodgar, burial sites dating to the early third millennium B.C. Impressive as these monuments are, they are but a few among many similar burial sites of the British Isles. Of course the most impressive stone ring is Stonehenge on Salisbury Plain. It has been estimated that there are 1,000 megalithic tombs, about 35,000 round barrows, more than 900 stone circles and about 3,000 hill forts in Great Britain.[3] All of this underscores the generally accepted belief that long before man built stone houses for the living, he built stone tombs for the well-being of the dead.[4]

Archaeologists have discovered in digging up the graves of early man that often, buried with the body, is a hunting weapon and an earthenware vessel filled with rice or wheat, or perhaps some dried beans or kernels of corn. Surely these primitive people must have discovered that the food buried with the body remained untouched by the departed, but that fact did not deter them. They persisted in leaving offerings needful for the dead so that they would be well prepared for their journey into the great beyond.[5] The idea behind these practices is that the *spirits* of both the food and the weapons would journey on with the *spirits* of the departed and sustain them in their new life. Often the spear or other hunting weapon would be broken before it was placed in the grave so that its spirit would be released from the material and accompany the user.

This line of reasoning appears in the story of an old countrywoman in Lincolnshire, England, an incident which occurred in the late nineteenth century. Having forgotten to put her dead husband's mug and jug into his coffin, she rushed up and broke them over the grave, explaining to her bewildered rector, "I deads 'em over his grave, and when their ghoastes get over on yon side he'll holler out, 'Yon's mine; hand 'em over to me,' and I'd like to see them as would stop him a-having of them an' all."[6]

British archaeologist Sir Charles Leonard Woolley, in the 1920s, discovered that the early kings of Ur in Mesopotamia (c. 2700 B.C.) made a practice of having buried with their own bodies members of the royal bodyguard, together with female attendants, still robed in their finery. Frequently, too, were found a sledge-chariot and ox-wagons, with oxen yoked to the royal chariots. There is no evidence of struggle in all these findings, for the bodies lie in orderly rows, the soldiers with their weapons beside them. In one case Woolley found the king's body surrounded by the bodies of six men and sixty-eight women of the court. Each of the women had the decayed remains of a small silver head band, except for one, a lady of the court who was apparently late for the ceremony. Still rolled up in the pocket of her robe was the silver band, which she evidently had not had time to put on, and so it was protected from corrosion and enabled to survive intact to tell the story. Woolley speculates that all these people entered the burial-pit alive, together with the ox-wagons and the sledge-chariot, and then took poison or a sleeping draught.[7] Obviously they accepted the custom of their day: the king must continue to be served in the manner to which he had become accustomed, even in the afterlife.

China's first emperor, Ch'in Shih Huang, also wanted to be waited upon by his retinue in the afterlife just as he had been while on earth. Living some 2,200 years ago, the man responsible for the Great Wall of China, among other spectacular engineering feats, arranged to have a vast tomb built in the ancient Shensi province, in the Yellow River Valley near Sian. This tomb he peopled with a 6,000 strong terra cotta army, arrayed in battle formation, complete with horses and chariots ready for combat. In this way he would be properly prepared to meet his honorable ancestors.

Many of us have had the opportunity to see samples of this army in exhibitions in various major cities, as I myself have in London. The amazing thing about this army is that each soldier is different, life-sized and obviously "molded upon a real person, one of the emperor's own warriors, servants or footmen." Evidently the use of terra cotta figures represented a more humane way of solving the problem of being waited upon in the afterlife, for as one observer of the site notes, "Evidence found in older graves of the area indicates that during the period of slavery, live slaves, wives, horses, and the like were buried with the aristocracy in accordance with the belief that they would continue to serve in the next life." All was not entirely humane with the terra cotta burial, however, for after the emperor's body was put in place, the pallbearers were ordered to be sealed inside.[8]

Along with these burial practices demonstrating belief in the continuity of life, it is also a matter of record that ancestor worship is one of the most universal religious practices of all people. In no primitive society does death separate a person from his social unit, i.e., his family, his clan, tribe, or his village. We find among many peoples that the dead are treated in much the same manner as older living members of the community. Neglect of the dead, or regarding them as of no account after burial, is rare indeed. The almost universal attitude is one of either worship or fear.

The ancient Egyptians, as we well know, developed burial to a fine art. The bodies would be steeped in natron, or soda, and so preserved for thousands of years. The pyramids of Egypt were built as tombs for the kings and queens of the fourth dynasty. The tomb chambers were decorated with religious texts calculated to secure the safety of the dead monarch and to provide him with crib-notes of what to say to the gods when he stood before the judgment. The custom spread to the more important subjects, the idea being that the preservation of the remains and a proper burial insured acceptance of the spirit into the realm of the blest.

The universality of belief in survival after death should be well established at this point. We have examples from various times in history, from different parts of the globe—people who have absolutely no connection with each other. Though widely separated by deserts, by oceans, or by mountain ranges, and by time, they all agree there is life after death. How is it that they have all come to that same conclusion and all independently of one another?

The answer is simple, though perhaps seemingly naïve to the sophisticate: Primitive man, not hampered by our concern for the niceties of civilization, has a sixth sense well developed to observe what now have come to be labeled "parapsychological phenomena." *Man has had experiences and seen sights that he could explain only by belief in survival after death.* Even if you argue, as some have, that this belief is simply passed on from the original humans to succeeding generations, you must also explain why the belief is sustained and nourished.

This conviction, then, that there is an afterlife comes not from intuition or desire, but from first-hand experience.[9] What primitive peoples believe about the nature of the afterlife is another story, one which will be considered in the next two chapters; all we want to establish at this point is that primitive man, through experience and not through his religion, has come to believe in life beyond the grave.

It was in the late winter of 1965 that the Rev. Daudi W. Udali, an Anglican priest from the Diocese of Maseno, Kenya, East Africa, was a guest in our home in Waterbury, Connecticut. One evening, we asked

The Universality of Belief in Life after Death

him about this whole idea of primitive sensibility to spiritual presences. In answer, he spent the next two hours relating one story after another, of which, for the sake of space, I shall retell only two. Here they are in Father Udali's own words:

> In Maragolia, where I now live, a neighbor told me a story about her son. In this part of Africa, when a father of either parent dies, it is the custom to name the son after the deceased grandfather. So it happened that this young mother had a son after her father's death. But the mother, for some unexplained reason, refused to follow the prevailing custom and named her son, not Agade (her father's name), but some other name. The child was not many weeks old before the parents realized that he had been born blind.
>
> One day, some months later, the mother was sitting on the ground outside the grass hut, holding her child, just looking down at him and wondering, "What can I now do with this blind child?"
>
> Then it was that the father appeared, *her* father, all properly dressed, holding a walking stick in his hand. He greeted the daughter in the fashion of the tribe. She looked up and immediately recognized that it was her father who had died. He said, "Why have you not named the child my name?"
>
> As the mother explained to me, she was not afraid and had the courage to talk. She answered, "The child is blind. We don't know what to do with him."
>
> The father answered, "If you name him my name, he will be all right." Thereupon he disappeared.
>
> When the husband of the woman came in from the fields, she related the strange event of the day. They both agreed that they should give the boy her father's name, and that very same day they renamed him Agade. Also that same day his eyes opened and he could see. He is a big boy now, and the home is a happy one.
>
> Things like this happen in many places. Some don't want to talk about it, but some do.
>
> In another part of our land there were two sisters. One of them married and left the community and moved some distance away through the bush country. The sister who remained home shortly thereafter died. The surviving sister had no knowledge of her death until her ghost appeared and said, "Your sister has died at home, but you have not gone home to mourn with the other members of the family."
>
> She answered, "I do not know the way, so how can I go?"
>
> The ghost replied, "I know the way. I can guide you." She appeared

to her sister as a normal, flesh-and-blood person, not like a ghost. So the two of them journeyed along together, talking all the time.

Finally, they arrived in front of their parents' home. The one who was alive turned to the other and asked, "Can you get into this house?" "No," was the answer. "You go in first. I will follow."

But she never did follow. She just disappeared.

The people in the house asked, "How were you able to get here? You didn't know the way." She explained, "There were two of us."

So they looked outside to where the sister was supposed to be waiting, but could see no one. Naturally, they didn't believe her, with the consequence that a heated argument ensued. The girl insisted that if she had not had a guide she couldn't possibly have come.

They all agreed that the best way to verify the story was to go out on the road and ask any who might have seen the two of them walking along together. They found a group of men who were doing some construction work on the road and put the question to them. Their answer: "No, we saw you only, alone, but you were talking to yourself. We thought you had gone out of your mind, talking to yourself that way."

The girl insisted, "There were two of us, even if you didn't see us both."

Her account finally became accepted by the family, because there was no other way to explain her safe arrival at the home. As they put it, "It must have been a ghost and not a real person. It appeared just to her, so that she could see it, but others could not."*

In the bush country the return of ghosts is an accepted fact, but this is not something a family wants. After the death it used to be the custom to watch at the graveyard or at the place of death in the house until someone would say, "I see the ghost go." After he had gone everything would be all right.

These spirits would come only if something were wrong, as, for

---

* Susy Smith, in her book *Prominent American Ghosts*, makes the point that not everyone is able to see an apparition, "even when others in the room with him are observing it. Certain individuals may see and hear it; others may experience it visually but not auditorily; still others may hear it speak but not be able to see it. . . ." This fact is further illustrated in Smith's book in chapter 1, titled "The Late Mrs. Nelly Butler" (World Publishing Company, Cleveland, Ohio, 1967, pp. ix, 26). Over one hundred people in the small community of Machias, Maine, testified to either seeing or hearing the apparition of Mrs. Butler. Many of these are sworn testimonies. But there still remained a few of the community who saw or heard nothing. In the case of poltergeists, however, where the manifestations are purely objective, everyone present witnesses the same phenomena.

example, if you troubled a person in his old age. When a person gets old, if you mistreat him, he will return as a ghost and trouble the family. If the elderly one would be cursing you all the time and complaining, "I'm dying and you don't take care of me," then he will come back and trouble you. A wife who doesn't love her husband's parents can cause the ghost to come. Sometimes such a ghost troubles the wife and sometimes the husband and sometimes the children. So people realize that you should take care of parents in their old age and have them bless you instead of curse you. This is the way the blessing goes: "My son should get all blessings; nothing bad should fall on him." When that happens, all is well, and nothing ever appears like a ghost.

The interesting and very important fact about all these experiences that take place in primitive lands is that they also actually do take place in our present age, in our own civilized world and with civilized people, though of course to a much lesser degree. Many have come to believe in life after death because of a personal encounter with the spiritual world and, unfortunately, *only because* of this personal encounter.

The subject of the life beyond came up for discussion at our Couples' Club in my parish in St. Albans, Vermont. We went around the circle of the fourteen couples present, asking each individual whether or not he or she believed in anything like immortality. The answers were quite definite: Despite the fact that this was largely a church organization, seven of those present did *not* believe in any survival of the soul, declaring such a possibility simply wishful thinking. There were two or three who weren't sure. The others, though, were certain beyond any doubt, and, much to my surprise, that certainty came simply because in each case there was some experience, some contact with a loved one no longer living in this world. A few of our members shared their experiences, the most impressive of which came from a young executive, then in his thirties, a college graduate. He had been an officer in the Navy during World War II.

The event he shared with us took place on shipboard somewhere in the north Atlantic. Fighting had been heavy, and as it continued there seemed small chance of survival. Night fell. As he stood by the rail of the ship and looked over the waters at the blazing enemy guns, he felt a familiar hand resting on his shoulder. It was his father who had returned from the life beyond for that moment to assure his son that there was no need to worry or to fear for the battle would soon be over and all on board would return safely home. And so it was.

An elderly woman parishioner of my Waterbury parish told me of her encounter with a deceased loved one: One night she was sitting up in bed, unable to sleep. Her mother had died a year previously; the woman was very blue and felt that with her mother's death everything worthwhile had gone out of her life. Then, without warning, her mother in spirit form stood at the foot of her bed and smiled.

"Please come back, Mother," the daughter pleaded. "I need you."

Her mother looked benignly at her as she replied, "I can't do that, my child. I have other things to do now. Please don't pine away your life. You have other things to do too."

A moment later she vanished. But the fleeting visit did accomplish its purpose, for, as the parishioner herself put it, "Everything was all right from that time on, and I completely recovered from feeling sorry for myself."

Another story of helpfulness from a deceased parent came to me through a chance conversation with a high school teacher in Burlington, Vermont. This woman had been brought up a Seventh Day Adventist (a denomination which teaches there is no immortality until the "Day of Resurrection"). She volunteered the information: "I can no longer agree with my church on this matter of the soul's sleeping until the last day." She went on to describe how one day she was swimming in Lake Champlain, going out alone and too far. She heard a voice warning her not to go out any farther. The voice, she maintained, was unmistakably that of her father. "I would know it anywhere, and, besides, there was no one else around." On this occasion and on two other occasions he came back to earth when there was a need. She was so certain of his presence that she was compelled to abandon all her former teaching on this subject.

One of my favorite stories from the unseen world of the departed comes by way of my good friend, the Rev. Randall P. Mendelsohn. At the time he told me this story, he was priest-in-charge of St. John's-in-the-Wilderness, Allakaket, Alaska. Here is his account as he told it:

> Miss Amelia Hill was a mission nurse in charge of St. John's-in-the-Wilderness for roughly thirty years. She began her career in 1922, when traveling to Alaska was quite an ordeal. Miss Hill arrived in the Territory by steamer, via the Inland Passage. She then took the U.S.-owned railway to Tanana, and from there she went by way of a river boat down the Tanana River and then down the Yukon River to Koyukuk Station, at the mouth of the Koyukuk River. There she changed to a much smaller

boat, a barge-type craft, to travel up the Koyukuk River. Sleeping accommodations were rather poor on these barges. One just lay down on the open deck, sometimes under a tarpaulin. During the night—which actually wasn't dark, because it was the time of the midnight sun—Miss Hill awoke to find a priest pacing up and down the barge, near her sleeping place. Walking back and forth, back and forth, he finally turned to her and said, "You are Miss Amelia Hill?" She acknowledged that she was. He continued, "You are going to Allakaket as a mission nurse?" "Yes," she replied. He then told her that she would have a very hard time in the village, but to "stick it out," for it would be well worth the effort. With that he turned and walked away, continuing his pacing.

Miss Hill thought nothing of this man's appearance, as people were always getting on and off these barges at various points up and down the river. She simply assumed that he had come aboard during one of the stops, while she was asleep, and when she fell back to sleep and again awakened in the morning and found him gone, she concluded that he had left the barge at another one of those stops.

Further up the river, at Allakaket, she got off the barge herself. At the dock she was met by some of the people of the Mission and taken directly to the Mission House. As she opened the door, there facing her in the hallway was a framed picture of a priest—a portrait of the man she had spoken to on the barge the previous night.

"Who is that?" Miss Hill inquired. "That," responded a bystander, "is Hudson Stuck, the archdeacon of the Yukon. He died just last year, you know."

Much more so than America does England have ghosts. In fact, as *Life* magazine once put it, "To say that the British believe in ghosts is, in fact, an understatement. On closer investigation it might be more accurate to say that the British *have* ghosts, just as the U.S. has termites, and with somewhat the same results."[10] Indeed, since my retirement to England, I have found it to be so. Every week our area newspaper has another story about some haunted public house or old home, and everywhere I have traveled in this country, I have picked up another book with a title like *Ghosts of Sussex* or *Ghosts of Kent*. There are even canal tunnels that are haunted. And churches, too, for I had hardly begun to help out at St. Barnabas' Church in Tunbridge Wells when I was told about the specter of a former curate often seen kneeling before the Blessed Sacrament or clothed in his cassock and wearing a biretta, solemnly walking down the aisle. Any stranger who learns I'm writing on this subject can give me a whole catalog of stories. There are thousands of them, I've been told.

It will be difficult, but for the sake of space, I'll limit myself to just two English hauntings: The first one is told of an old vicarage in Gloucestershire:

> The house had rambling old kitchens beneath it, no longer used by the family, now provided with a modern one above. At times there were sounds below, as though people were walking about. One day the vicar went down to see if he could find the cause, and in the kitchen he was met by a monk. He was much surprised, as there had been no monastery anywhere near since the time of their dissolution, and only a half-ruined building was left to show where once there had been a flourishing order.
>
> The monk did not answer his greeting, but looked sadly at him and walked across the kitchen and was gone.
>
> This happened several times, and the family got used to the sad but friendly monk.
>
> One day it was noticed that the old kitchen floor appeared to be sagging in the middle, and although the old place was no longer used, it was decided that it had better be repaired. So the local carpenter was called in. There was nothing for it, he said, but to take the floor up to find the cause of the trouble.
>
> When this was done, it was found that the floor rested on two huge old wooden beams, almost rotted through from age and damp . . . and beneath it was a large and deep tank of water, perhaps the water supply in olden days.
>
> The floor was safely repaired, and the kindly monk was never seen again.[11]

Another English item which received world-wide publicity concerns a ghost-organist. Here is the account as it appeared in one of our American church papers:

THIS "REAL GONE" GHOST
PLAYS HAUNTING MELODIES

> An organ-playing ghost is being evicted from the chapel in Torquay, England, which has been his "happy haunting ground" for the past seventy-three years. The vicar, the Rev. Anthony Rouse, is having an eighty-year-old "haunted organ" removed from his church in the hopes that the ghost who plays it will go, too.
>
> Mr. Rouse stated that the music-loving ghost has been around since 1883 when the church organist, Henry Ditton-Newman, died. As a result the parish has had a hard time holding on to their organists and

The Universality of Belief in Life after Death

one temporary organist has refused to play because he could "feel" someone sitting in the organ stall with him.

The vicar and several churchgoers say the old church organ often plays at night when there is no one in the church. Mr. Rouse says he also has heard mysterious footsteps in the church.

Mr. Rouse twice held special exorcism services in the church to chase the ghost away. But to make doubly sure, he is going to replace the old organ with a new one.[12]

The sequel to this story was told in a later issue of the same paper.[13] The vicar explained that the much-publicized story was a little misleading. Contrary to the way it was generally reported, the ghost was a welcome guest at the church, and the only reason the organ was removed was that it was worn out. The vicar also explained that the late organist (who died while still a young man) was frequently seen and heard at the residence known as Montpelier House; that fact was well substantiated by the accounts of many people—former vicars, wives of vicars, servants, and parishioners. One parishioner testified that on two occasions, though she saw no one at the organ, she heard the Silas Mass being played in the key of C.

There are innumerable stories similar to these. Not only are my files packed with clippings of this sort, but whenever I have spoken to a church audience on the subject of life after death, someone inevitably has approached me afterward and added to my collection. I have used only a few of the stories I have been told.

There are, after all, other aspects of parapsychological evidence, and the first of these has to do with visions near the time of death or during extreme sickness. George Gallup estimates that eight million Americans have had near-death experiences.[14] These experiences, almost as much as the sightings of spirits, continue to sustain popular belief in the afterlife.

A convincing account was told me by the grandmother of one of my students, during the days when I was teaching at Woodbury High School. Learning of my interest, Mrs. Carlton Tuttle invited me, together with my tape recorder, to her home in Waterbury. What she related took place in the late 1920s, when she was hospitalized for the birth of her sixth child. She was having a most difficult time of it, with tremendous pain. Quite unexpectedly, the pain ceased, and she found herself gently rising up from the bed. It was a little after ten o'clock in the morning.

"I had been watching the clock on the wall as I lay in bed," she explained, "but all at once I found myself watching that same clock from a much higher angle. I felt myself floating upwards, as if I were on one of those carpets you read about in the *Arabian Nights*. As I looked down, I could see myself lying in bed. There was also the clock, still farther below me. As I continued to float upwards, the ceiling disappeared, and yet I could still see the room, the bed with me on it, and the clock." Mrs. Tuttle explained that she had the clock so much in mind, because in childbirth one watches to time the duration of the pains and the intervals between them. "But the pain stopped completely," she continued, "and a most wonderful feeling came over me. I don't think there's a word in the English language to describe it.

"As I continued to watch the room, I saw the door open and a nurse entering. She took me by the hand—I mean the hand of my body that was lying in bed. I figured she was taking my pulse. She quickly dropped it and looked into my eyes. She rushed out of the room and a minute later came back with a doctor armed with a long needle. He jabbed the needle into my arm, and the next thing I knew I was back down there again, with the pain just as bad as ever. Eventually, I had the child, and completely recovered."

As we went on to discuss this experience, I probed for more details, but Mrs. Tuttle could do no more than reiterate, "I was just floating and seemed to be going off further and further away, though I could still see everything that went on in the room. It was such a feeling of peace . . . and, well, you just can't describe it. I've heard other people tell of seeing beautiful scenes and flowers and birds and all that. I read one time where someone who passed out like I did found herself walking in a garden. Someone else told me that when he was once given up for dead, he crossed a river and met his father and his mother. Though I saw nothing like that, I can tell you plainly it was the most wonderful feeling, and I didn't want to return to my body. But now that I'm back, I can tell you I'll never be afraid to die."

It does not always happen, however, that a person who has just quit this life is aware of his death. As Dr. S. Ralph Harlow, a retired professor of Smith College, points out, "When death comes painlessly or suddenly, as it often does, the surviving personality, . . . now free of the flesh, is not at first aware of the transition. . . . A soldier killed in combat by a shell explosion will attempt to help his comrades carry in his own shattered body. A woman suddenly finds herself standing by her bed and walks

The Universality of Belief in Life after Death

downstairs and wonders why her loved ones do not . . . see her."[15]

Such apparently was the case with Dr. George C. Ritchie, a practicing physician (later a psychiatrist) of Richmond, Virginia. Under the title of "Return from Tomorrow," Dr. Ritchie's account was first printed in the June 1963 issue of *Guideposts* (a devotional magazine published at Carmel, New York, by Norman Vincent Peale).

Stationed as an army private at the base hospital at Camp Barkeley, Texas, George C. Ritchie was about to take a train to Richmond, Virginia, where he was to enter medical school, "as part of the Army's doctor-training program." But before he was able to leave, he came down with double pneumonia and found himself in the army hospital, critically ill. After several days he was moved to the recuperation wing; it was there that an army jeep was to pick him up at four o'clock the following morning and drive him to the railroad station so he could get the train to Richmond. But he began to run a fever, and, although the details of what actually happened are not entirely clear, he remembers opening his eyes, lying in a little room he had never seen before. "All of a sudden," he writes, "I sat bolt upright. The train! I'd miss the train!" It was then that he experienced an incredible walk out into the night, not at first realizing that his body lay lifeless in bed:

> I sprang out of bed and looked around the room for my uniform. Not on the bedrail. I stopped, staring. Someone was lying in the bed I had just left.
>
> I stepped closer in the dim light, then drew back. The slack jaw, the gray skin were awful. Then I saw the ring. On [the] left hand was the Phi Gamma Delta fraternity ring I had worn for two years.
>
> I ran into the hall, eager to escape the mystery of that room. Richmond, that was the all-important thing—getting to Richmond. I started down the hall for the outside door.
>
> "Look out!" I shouted to an orderly bearing down on me. He seemed not to hear, and a second later he had passed the very spot where I stood as though I had not been there.
>
> It was too strange to think about. I reached the door, went through and found myself in the darkness outside, speeding toward Richmond. Running? Flying? I only know that the dark earth was slipping past while other thoughts occupied my mind, terrifying and unaccountable ones. The orderly had not seen me. What if the people at medical school could not see me either?
>
> In utter confusion I stopped by a telephone pole in a town by a large

river and put my hand against the guy wire. At least the wire seemed to be there, but my hand could not make contact with it. One thing was clear: in some unimaginable way I had lost my firmness of flesh, the hand that could grip that wire, the body that other people saw.

I was beginning to know too that the body on that bed was mine, unaccountably separated from me, and that my job was to get back and rejoin it as fast as I could.

Finding the base and the hospital again was no problem. Indeed I seemed to be back there almost as soon as I thought of it. But where was the little room I had left? . . . As I ran from one ward to the next, past room after room of sleeping soldiers, all about my age, I realized how unfamiliar we are with our own faces. Several times I stopped by a sleeping figure that was exactly as I imagined myself. But the fraternity ring, the Phi Gamma ring, was lacking, and I would speed on.

At last I entered a little room with a single dim light. A sheet had been drawn over the figure on the bed, but the arms lay along the blanket. On the left hand was the ring.

I tried to draw back the sheet, but I could not seize it. And now that I had found myself, how could one join two people who were so completely separate? And there, standing before the problem, I thought suddenly:

"This is death. This is what human beings call 'death,' this splitting up of one's self." It was the first time I had connected death with what had happened to me.

Dr. Ritchie, in this article, went on to describe other things that happened to him that night—how the room was lit up with the brightness of Christ, how his total life flashed before him, how he followed Christ out into the streets, and how, among other things, he got a glimpse of the heavenly city.

Dr. Ritchie maintains that he cannot fully fathom why he was permitted to return to life. "All I know," he says, "when I woke up in the hospital bed in that little room, in the familiar world where I'd spent all my life, it was not a homecoming. The cry in my heart that moment has been the cry of my life ever since: Christ, show me Yourself again."

Weeks later, when he was finally well enough to leave the hospital, George Ritchie sneaked a glance at the chart: "Pvt. George Ritchie, died December 20, 1943, double lobar pneumonia." Much later he talked to the doctor who had signed the report. The doctor told him there was no doubt in his mind he had been dead when he made the examination, but then, nine minutes later the soldier who had been assigned to prepare the body for the morgue detected a faint glimmer of life and came running to ask the doctor to administer a shot of adrenalin. This the doctor did—directly into the heart muscle, and the dead man was alive again. "My return to life, he told me, without brain damage or other lasting effect, was the most baffling circumstance of his career."

Dr. Ritchie feels that the reason he was allowed to return to this life was to become a physician and so carry out a life of service. At any rate, the experience changed him from an indifferent Christian into an active one.

The editors of *Guideposts* have in their files many fascinating stories similar to Dr. Ritchie's. They chose his rather than one of the others because it is completely supported by documentary evidence, affidavits from both the Army doctor and the attending nurse.[16]

A case similar to Dr. Ritchie's is told by Dr. Harlow. He tells of the experience of a medical doctor friend. Critically ill, this friend had been given up by his colleagues, as he lay in his hospital bed.

> "Suddenly," he told me, "I found myself outside my physical body. I cannot explain it in any other words." He observed his nurse leaning against the wall of the room sobbing, and he watched attendants pull a sheet up over his physical body lying on the bed. He left the room then and strolled down the hall. He saw a wheeled stretcher pushed into Room 30 and return with a patient. He entered Room 31 and watched a nurse help a patient out of bed.
>
> Then he heard a voice say, "You are not yet ready to come over. You must go back to your body." But he protested, he did not want to go back. And the voice said, "But you must. Your work on earth is not yet finished." With great difficulty he got back into his physical body, and some time later regained consciousness.
>
> His doctor and nurse were astonished. His colleague said, "By all tests you died, and now you are here again."
>
> "Perhaps so," my friend replied weakly, "but I must know some things." He called the nurse and asked her to take careful notes on what he was to say. He told her what he had observed in the hall and in Room 31, and he asked her to check if these events had indeed happened as he had seen them. Naturally his nurse suspected delirium, for she knew he could not have [seen] what he had reported. She herself was unaware of what had happened outside the room, for she had remained there with her patient. But to humor him she granted his request and found that his report checked in every detail.[17]

An impressive array of stories of this sort appears in a book *Life after Life*, written by another psychiatrist, Dr. Raymond L. Moody.[18] (In various translations, I have found this book on sale all over Europe.) Coming under the influence of Dr. George Ritchie and Dr. Elisabeth Kübler-Ross,[19] Dr. Moody decided to make a study of people who had been pronounced clinically dead but who for some reason had come back to life. In her foreword to the book, Dr. Kübler-Ross writes,

> Though he does not claim to have studied death itself, it is evident from his findings that the dying patient continues to have a conscious awareness of his environment after being pronounced clinically dead. This very much coincides with my own research, which has used the accounts of patients who have died and made a comeback, totally against our expectations and often to the surprise of some highly sophisticated, well-known and certainly accomplished physicians.
>
> All these patients have experienced a floating out of their physical bodies, associated with a great sense of peace and wholeness. Most were aware of another person who helped them in their transition to another plane of existence. Most were greeted by loved ones who had died before them, or by a religious figure who was significant in their life.[20]

In this first book of his, Dr. Moody reported that he studied 150 cases, fifty of them in detail. There are, he writes, "striking similarities among the accounts, [though] no two of them are precisely identical." As death takes over, there is usually a buzzing noise, a rapid movement through a long, dark tunnel, a knowledge of being out of one's body (though still being in the immediate area), the sight of one's own body, including attempts at resuscitation, the presence of others from the next world (usually loved ones) who come to help, a kind of judgment before a Being of Light (whom Christians usually identify as Christ), the facing of a gate or barrier beyond which the person cannot go, and finally the return to the physical body and the regaining of consciousness.[21]

Two decades after the publication of *Life after Life*, Dr. Moody published another book, *The Light Beyond*, reporting that he had interviewed more than a thousand people who had near-death experiences, which has given him more convincing evidence than ever of both the similarity of these cases and the assurance of life after death.[22] He mentions the Gallup Poll that found that eight million adults in the United States have had near-death experiences.[23] That same Gallup Poll listed ten traits that are characteristic of these experiences: (1) A sense of being out of the physical body, (2) accurate visual perception while out of the body, (3) the hearing of sounds or voices, (4) feelings of peace and painlessness, (5) the phenomenon of being surrounded by light, (6) a review of the person's life, (7) the sense of being in another world, (8) encountering other beings in the spirit world, (9) the experience of having gone through a tunnel exiting from this life, and (10) precognition ability in 6 percent of the cases. Though very few people have experienced all of these things, Dr. Ritchie has found several who did.

In considerable detail Dr. Moody provides evidence that effectively answers the skeptics who characterize near-death experiences as mental aberrations. His accounts also illustrate the ability of people having near-death experiences to observe what is going on in this life while they are apparently dead. First, an example of how the near-death experience cannot be just a hallucination:

> Some people postulate that NDEs [near-death experiences] are merely hallucinations, mental events brought on by stress, lack of oxygen, or in some cases, even drugs.
>
> However, one of the strongest arguments against the NDE as hallucination is their occurrence in patients who have flat EEG's.
>
> The electroencephalogram, or EEG, measures the brain's electrical activity. It records this activity by scribing a line on a continuous strip of paper. This line goes up and down in response to the brain's electrical activity when a person thinks, speaks, dreams, and does virtually anything else. If the brain is dead, the EEG reading is a flat line, which implies that the brain is incapable of thought or action. A flat EEG is now the legal definition of death in many states.
>
> For anything to happen in the brain, there must be electrical activity. Even hallucinations measure on the EEG.
>
> But there are many cases in which people with flat EEGs have had near-death experiences. They, of course, lived to tell about them. The sheer number of these cases tells me that in some people, NDEs have happened when they were technically dead. Had these been hallucinations, they would have shown up in the EEG....
>
> Sometimes, the brain can be alive at such a low level that the EEG doesn't register the activity. An example of such a case was given to me by a doctor at Duke University. He said that they had a little girl attached to an EEG who was showing no brain wave activity on the machine.
>
> The doctors thought she was dead and wanted to remove her from

the life support system but the family refused. They insisted there was going to be a miracle and they gathered around her bed for a week of prayer.

She came out of it. The doctor who told me this story said that she revived and had recently finished the first grade. He emphasized that she would have been dead had they relied upon the EEG. He discovered what many other doctors have discovered: brain activity can be going on at such a deep level in the brain that surface electrodes don't pick it up. [24]

Here is another account describing the ability of the person having a near-death experience to observe activity by the bedside:

A forty-nine-year-old man had a heart attack so severe that after thirty-five minutes of vigorous resuscitation efforts, the doctor gave up and began filling out the death certificate. Then someone noticed a flicker of life, so the doctor continued his work with paddles and breathing equipment and was able to restart the man's heart.

The next day, when he was more coherent, the patient was able to describe in great detail what went on in the emergency room....

He described [the emergency room nurse] perfectly, right down to her wedge hairdo and her last name, Hawkes. He said that she rolled his cart down the hall with a machine that had what looked like two Ping-Pong paddles on it....

When the doctor asked him how he knew the nurse's name and what she had been doing during his heart attack, he said that he had left his body and—while walking down the hall to see his wife—passed right through nurse Hawkes. He read the name tag as he went through her, and remembered it so he could thank her later.

I talked to the doctor at great length about this case. He was quite rattled by it. Being there, he said, was the only way the man could have recounted this with such complete accuracy. [25]

Since the publication of Dr. Moody's first book, a profusion of books dealing with near-death experiences has emerged. The most scientific of these is *Life at Death* by Kenneth Ring, in which the author systematically arranges and analyzes some hundred cases, complete with graphs and statistical tables, all laid out most objectively. [26] Not as scientifically presented, but convincing nonetheless, is *Beyond Death's Door* by Dr. Maurice Rawlings, a cardiac specialist. The author, who has resuscitated many patients after clinical deaths, discovered that if he interviewed the patient immediately upon his return to consciousness, he would hear both bad and good after-death experiences, including those which were quite hellish. He discovered that if there were a lapse of time prior to the interview, the hellish experiences were forgotten and no memory of them remained.[27] Another publication with an impressive array of interviews is *On the Other Side* by Marvin Ford. This book is very much Bible-oriented; it is well worth consideration, though it is less objective than the other books mentioned.[28]

Though all of the cases of leaving the physical body so far cited are connected with either death or near-death, there are others which have no associations with death. One is a book by Robert A. Monroe, entitled *Journeys out of the Body*. The author relates how accidentally on one occasion he found himself floating free of his body and later learned to cultivate the ability to leave his body and go off to distant places. He consulted psychiatrists about this "problem," and though some were naturally skeptical, others were most sympathetic and encouraged further investigation. What is more, this man was able to prove what he saw on many of his out-of-the-body experiences, since they were later checked and verified.[29]

A cassette recording, *Out-of-Body Experiences* by Charles Tart,[30] describes in some detail a laboratory experiment this psychologist conducted, in which he wired up a woman for several nights' sleep and discovered his subject actually could get out of her body and correctly read and remember a five-digit number placed out of view and out of reach elsewhere in the laboratory.

Robert Monroe, in his book, describes how one might initiate out-of-body experiences, but I feel such activity should be discouraged. It may well be that our Lord gives this gift now and then for some special purpose, but to cultivate it is to invite trouble. Also, Monroe admits that on two occasions in his out-of-the-body wanderings, he actually did get intercepted by a demonic personality who attempted to prevent his return to his body. I am impressed with the veracity of this book, but I am not impressed with the underlying thesis, which I find somewhat anti-Christian.

Jung makes the point that "there are indications that at least a part of the psyche is not subject to the laws of space and time. . . . Not only my dreams, but also . . . the dreams of others, helped to shape, revise, or confirm my views on life after death." Jung then goes on to describe a number of dreams which foretold a death and of others where he was able to communicate with the dead.

In one mystical experience, which Jung doesn't quite classify as a dream but which comes close to it, a dead friend beckoned Jung to follow him to his house. This he did in a mystical way. The friend then invited him into his house and conducted him into his study. There he saw a stool upon which his friend climbed, while he pointed out the second of five books with red bindings that were in the bookcase on the second shelf from the top. It was there that the vision faded. The next day Jung went to his friend's widow and asked to see the study, which in physical fact he had never before entered. "Sure enough," as Jung writes, "there was a stool standing under the bookcase I had seen in my vision, and . . . five books with red bindings. I stepped up on the stool so as to be able to read the titles. They were translations of the novels of Emile Zola. The title of the second volume read: 'The Legacy of the Dead.'"[31]

A theological college classmate of mine told of having dream communications with a friend who had died prematurely. This happened quite a number of nights in a row. One night, while still asleep and having this dream of communication, my classmate, actually conscious of the fact that this was all going on while he was lying in bed, said, "Why is it you speak to me only in dreams?" To this his departed friend replied, "Because that is the only time you will listen. You are too preoccupied during your waking hours."

Anyone who takes the Bible seriously should not be surprised at this kind of encounter. For example, it was during a dream that an angel appeared to Joseph and told him not to be afraid to take Mary for his wife, for that which was conceived in her was to be the Christ Child.[32]

A classic case of what might be thought of as separation of body and soul during sleep comes from F. W. H. Myers's two-volume work, *Human Personality and Its Survival of Bodily Death*, now regarded as a classic in this field. It was on October 3, 1863, that Mr. S. R. Wilmot, a Connecticut manufacturer, sailed from Liverpool, England, for New York, on the steamer *City of Limerick*. After two days of sailing a severe storm began, which lasted nine days. Mr. Wilmot gives us a vivid description of what happened:

> Upon the night following the eighth day of the storm the tempest moderated a little, and for the first time since leaving port I enjoyed refreshing sleep. Toward morning I dreamed that I saw my wife, whom I had left in the United States, come to the door of my state-room, clad in her night-dress. At the door she seemed to discover that I was not the

only occupant of the room, hesitated a little, then advanced to my side, stooped down and kissed me, and after gently caressing me for a few moments, quietly withdrew.

Upon waking I was surprised to see my fellow-passenger, whose berth was above mine, but not directly over it—owing to the fact that our room was at the stern of the vessel—leaning upon his elbow, and looking fixedly at me. "You're a pretty fellow," said he at length, "to have a lady come and visit you in this way." I pressed him for an explanation, which he at first declined to give, but at length related what he had seen while wide awake, lying in his berth. It exactly corresponded with my dream. . . .

The day after landing I went by rail to Watertown, Connecticut, where my children and my wife had been for some time, visiting her parents. Almost her first question when we were alone together was, "Did you receive a visit from me a week ago Tuesday?" "A visit from you?" said I, "we were more than a thousand miles at sea." "I know it," she replied, "but it seemed to me that I visited you." "It would be impossible," said I. "Tell me what makes you think so."

My wife then told me that on account of the severity of the weather and the reported loss of the *Africa*, which sailed for Boston on the same day that we left Liverpool . . . she had been extremely anxious about me. On the night previous, the same night when, as mentioned above, the storm had just begun to abate, she had lain awake for a long time thinking of me, and about four o'clock in the morning it seemed to her that she went out to seek me. Crossing the wide and stormy sea, she came at length to a low, black steamship, whose side she went up, and then descending into the cabin, passed through it to the stern until she came to my state-room. "Tell me," said she, "do they ever have state-rooms like the one I saw, where the upper berth extends further back than the under one? A man was in the upper berth, looking right at me, and for a moment I was afraid to go in, but soon I went to the side of your berth, bent down and kissed you, and embraced you, and then went away."

The description given by my wife of the steamship was correct in all particulars, though she had never seen it.[33]

Whether we call this incident a dream, a vision, or a case of bi-location, stories like this appear from time to time. They provide further evidence that death is not always necessary for a separation of body and soul.

There are other aspects of parapsychology which might also be considered—poltergeists, telepathy, extrasensory perception, clairvoyance, psychokinesis, and the like—but, while admitting these are related to our subject, perhaps they are rather far afield and as such are more properly the business of investigators such as the people at Duke University and the Society of Psychical Research.

One last point: I could easily have tripled (or more) the number of parapsychological accounts related in this chapter, for I heard many more than I have included. But a word of warning is necessary here. In the Parable of the Rich Man and Lazarus, our Lord makes it clear that this kind of evidence by itself is not convincing: "And he said unto him, 'If they hear not Moses and the prophets, neither will they be persuaded, though one rose from the dead.'"[34]

However, one constantly hears the jibe, "How do you know there is life after death? No one ever comes back to tell us about it." This chapter is part of the answer to that cynicism, but certainly only part of it. The real answer for the convinced Christian is that indeed one has come back to tell us about it, one no less than Jesus Christ. The Resurrection of Jesus, together with the account of the Transfiguration (the subjects of chapters 7 and 8), is the answer of the New Testament to this jibe. But at least the evidence of psychic phenomena from sources quite nonbiblical, and in some cases even nonreligious, should make it that much more impossible to say "No one has ever come back." The evidence may not be explained in terms of our present knowledge, but it cannot be ignored. It is far too plentiful and far too well-authenticated for any summary dismissal.

4

Old Testament Eschatology

*E**schatology* is a term very familiar to clergymen, though probably strange to laymen. As I shall explain, the word is used in the title of this chapter for a special reason. But first the definition, and it is a simple one. *Eschatology* comes from the Greek *-ology*, "the study of" and *eschaton*, meaning "end." Eschatology is that branch of theology which deals with *last things*—not only death, judgment, Heaven, and Hell (sometimes called "the four last things"), but the end of all life on earth and what the future holds beyond this earth—the end, the destiny, and the purpose of this life and this world.

Now, we are using the word *eschatology* in this chapter because from an Old Testament point of view it is a much more satisfactory term than something like *The Old Testament Doctrine of Life after Death*. The reason for this is that in the Old Testament little stress is laid on the individual as such, especially where his eternal destiny is involved. Generally the Old Testament is concerned with the final destiny of the Hebrew nation as a whole—first with its living destiny and then (perhaps after the fourth century B.C.) with its destiny after life.

Let us begin, though, with a consideration of what evidence there is in the Old Testament for belief in the individual's survival after death, and, after we are done, go on to what happens to the nation.

At first glance it would appear that there is no mention at all—anywhere in the Old Testament—of a belief in life after death for the individual, or at best not until the end of time. This conclusion, however, represents a superficial reading of the text. We should remember that the Old Testament, as it has come down to us, is a highly edited collection, with most of the primitive features sifted out or de-emphasized. Archdeacon R. H. Charles has pointed out that the Hebrew people originally were like all other primitives in their understanding of what happens after death and, like others, practiced ancestor worship. Most of the later editors of the Old Testament have tried to cover up these features of ancient Hebrew belief, and though they did a pretty good job of it, they failed to conceal all of the residuals.[1]

This critical understanding of the Old Testament is important, not only because it explains what seems to be a sudden new eschatological development that takes place when the New Testament period arrives, but also because it explains the beliefs of some fringe sects of modern Christianity. The refusal to accept the critical approach to the Old Testament and the acceptance of the literal interpretation is in large part the basis of the soul-sleep doctrine of such groups as the Seventh Day Adventists. It behoves us, then, to examine how the Old Testament concept of life after death develops and in the light of this development to judge for ourselves the deviations which would claim the adherence of modern Christians.

Here, then, in the Old Testament, are some of the residuals of ancestor worship: First, we have the instance recorded in Genesis 31:19. Jacob, with his two wives Rachel and Leah, escapes from his overpossessive father-in-law Laban, but one of his wives is unable to forsake her family cult, for, as we read, "Laban had gone to shear his sheep, and Rachel stole her father's household gods." Laban, who would retain Jacob as an unpaid hired hand, pursued and overtook his son-in-law, indignantly asking, "Why did you steal my gods?" These images were very important to Rachel, however; and, as the story goes, she "put them in the camel's saddle, and sat upon them," getting away with the theft. The King James version of the Bible translates the Hebrew used here as "images that were her father's," but the more accurate Revised Standard Version describes the objects of the theft as "her father's household gods." The word here in the Hebrew is *teraphim* (תרפים), a plural form which can also be used in the singular. These *teraphim*, R. H. Charles points out, are none other than images of the ancestors, which were traditional in the Canaanite houses of the well-to-do.[2] Moreover, possession of the teraphim implies headship of the family and control of the family inheritance. No wonder Laban was upset!

The same word occurs in the First Book of Samuel, where we read how Michal, David's first wife, laid a teraphim on David's bed and covered it to resemble her husband, thereby deceiving Saul (her father) whose jealousy impelled him to attempt the murder of the popular David.[3] These images of ancestors would, of course, vary in size from the ones which Rachel could hide in her camel's saddle to those Michal could place in a bed to resemble a man.[4] (One can see these small images unearthed from Mesopotamia in the British Museum in London and the Metropolitan in New York.)

The fact that these household gods were part of the equipment of the well-to-do family is well illustrated by chapter 17 of Judges, where we read of "a man of the hill country of Ephraim, whose name was Micah. . . . His mother took two hundred pieces of silver, and gave it to the silversmith, who made it into a graven image and a molten image; and it was in the house of Micah. And the man Micah had a shrine, and he made an ephod [an apron-like garment hung from the shoulders, worn by a priest at the time of sacrifice] and teraphim [a kind of collection of household gods], and installed one of his sons, who became his priest."[5]

Again, as Charles points out, the practice of these ancestor cults was more common than the later editors of the Old Testament would have us think. Every substantial family had one of these images at the front door, and always (except in later times) it represented an ancestor. We read in Exodus 21:2–6 that when a slave chose to become a member of the family he had been serving, the master of the house would take him before the teraphim and there, piercing his ear, make him a member of the family—not just the visible family, but the whole family, living and dead. Again, as with most primitive peoples (including other Semites), death did not separate one from the family unit, and (as with other Semites) there were always one or more images present to remind the living of the ancestors and to help in the ancestral cult.

The reason for ancestor worship among the primitive Hebrews is exactly the same as among other primitives: Everyone knew the ancestor lived on; he had seen him or felt his presence enough times to make that certain. Everyone also knew that the ancestor could do those remaining in the world a lot of good or a lot of harm. Hence there must be reverence for and submission to the ancestor. This awe is illustrated in the Bible by references to ceremonies such as the worshiper's removal of shoes (as when approaching something holy), girding himself with sackcloth (as a sign of servility), the removal of hair and beards (as an offering for the dead), and incisions in the flesh (for blood was used to make an enduring covenant).[6]

Equally important as the effect the ancestor had on the living was the ancestor's dependence upon continued sustenance by means of sacrifices. It is this need for sacrifices that is at the root of the levirate law,* as it is called, which required that if a man died before he had a chance to sire a child (or adopt one), any unmarried brother he might have remaining would be required to marry his widow and, hopefully, raise up a son who could carry on the cult.[7] (In ancient Hebrew life it became the responsibility of the eldest son to offer these sacrifices.)[8] The Sadducees, of course, make mention of this law when they approach Jesus with the hypothetical question of which husband a woman who had been widowed and married again might have in the afterlife.[9]

The fact that sacrifices made to the departed were common in ancient Hebrew life is illustrated by the many injunctions against the practice which appeared in later Hebrew life when monotheism gained a strong foothold, as for example in Deuteronomy 26:14, where there is an injunction to swear that no ancestral sacrifices are to be made.† And, though originally God's jurisdiction did not cover Sheol (the place of the departed), God, if he chose, could punish those dwelling there by cutting them off from the respect and worship they normally would get by the destruction of their still-living sons.[10]

Now, having mentioned Sheol, let us consider this subject for a moment and see how this figured in the development of eschatological thinking. Burial was regarded as an absolute necessity for the comfort of the departed, just as in the primitive religions of Greece and Rome. It would be withheld only in the case of a very idolatrous person such as Jezebel.[11] But, with or without burial, all without exception descended into Sheol.

Also, this burial, if possible, must be in the family grave, for that is how a man is "gathered to his fathers,"[12] for there he would be introduced to the society of his ancestors. In early times (and surely there are remnants of this thinking today) it was believed that the family grave was the ancestral home. But, inasmuch as no family was an isolated unit, as time went on it was believed that all in the clan or tribe, and still later the whole

---

* The word comes from the Latin *levir*, a husband's brother.

† The book of Deuteronomy was probably put into its present form between 650 and 300 B.C. and represents a fairly late development in Jewish thinking.

nation, occupied one subterranean passageway.[13] Hence the idea that prevailed on into New Testament times was that Hades was under the earth, and to it went all the departed—both good and bad.

Now, as we have already pointed out, descent into Sheol removed one from the jurisdiction of the God of Israel. Scholars well recognize that as early concepts of God developed in Israel, it was a god who had limited jurisdiction—a concept of deity which receives the name of *monolateralism* or *henotheism*, i.e., the worship of one god without denying the existence of other gods; or, to put it another way, the concept that there is one god for one people, but other gods for other peoples. In the Old Testament it was readily acknowledged that Milcom was the god of Ammon, Ashtoreth of the Zidonians, Chemosh of Moab, while, of course, Yahweh was the God of Israel. R. H. Charles underscores this idea by calling attention to the use of the term "strangers and sojourners with God" (Leviticus 25:23; Psalm 39:13). While the New Testament (Hebrews 11:13; Ephesians 2:19) speaks of us on earth as "strangers and sojourners" in the sense that our true citizenship is in Heaven, the Old Testament uses this term to mean that man on earth is only temporarily sojourning with Yahweh, and his eternal destiny is beyond Yahweh's domain.[14] This thinking is responsible for such passages as these:

> I am reckoned among those who go down to the Pit;
> I am a man who has no strength,
> like one forsaken among the dead,
> like the slain that lie in the grave,
> like those whom thou dost remember no more,
> for they are cut off from thy hand.
>
> Psalm 88:4, 5

> For Sheol cannot thank thee,
> death cannot praise thee;
> those who go down to the pit cannot hope
> for thy faithfulness.
> The living, the living, he thanks thee,
> as I do this day....
>
> Isaiah 38:18, 19a

There is only one step separating this line of thinking from the next. As the concept developed that the God of Israel was not only God of the people of Israel but God of all creation, then, of course, either he had jurisdiction over those in Sheol or, if they were beyond his jurisdiction, it was simply because they had ceased to exist. And, actually, the next step in the religious development of Israel was to choose the latter of these alternatives—"When you're dead you're dead."

Exactly where one step leaves off and the other begins is often difficult to determine in a religious development, but it would seem that the following are examples of an eschatology which preaches either extinction for the departed or at best eternal sleep:

> For the living know that they will die, but the dead know nothing, and they have no more reward; but the memory of them is lost. Their love and their hate and their envy have already perished, and they have no more for ever any share in all that is done under the sun.
> Ecclesiastes 9:5, 6

> Here my prayer, O Lord,
>   and give ear to my cries
>   hold not thy peace at my tears!
> For I am thy passing guest,
>   a sojourner, like all my fathers.
> Look away from me, that I may know gladness,
>   before I depart and be no more!
> Psalm 39:12, 13

> For there is hope for a tree,
>   if it be cut down, that it will sprout again,
>   and that its shoots will not cease.
> Though its root grow old in the earth,
>   and its stump die in the ground,
> yet at the scent of water it will bud
>   and put forth branches like a young plant.
> But man dies, and is laid low;
>   man breathes his last, and where is he?
> As waters fail from a lake,
>   and a river wastes away and dries up,
> So man lies down and rises not again;
>   till the heavens are no more he will not awake,
>   or be roused out of his sleep.
> Job 14:7–12

There are two factors involved in coming to think of the dead as extinct: First, and the more important for our purpose, is that this ances-

Old Testament Eschatology

tor worship, the ceremonies at the grave, and all forms of spiritualism came into an inevitable, irreconcilable conflict with the worship of the true God of Israel, with "Yahwehism," as the scholars are wont to call this worship.* "I am a jealous God"[15] implies no other gods of any sort are to be tolerated, including departed ancestors.† This new order of things, established by Moses and later proclaimed by the prophets in an uncompromising way, doomed ancestor worship with all its associations. Throughout the pages of the Old Testament (as it finally came to be edited) there is constantly reiterated the warning to have no truck with necromancy and to stay away from those "who have familiar spirits."[16] "Those nations, which you are about to dispossess, give heed to soothsayers and to diviners," said Moses, "but for you, the Lord your God has not allowed you so to do."[17] In fact, as the First Book of Chronicles points out, the reason why King Saul came to a tragic end was precisely because of his having sought guidance from the Medium of Endor.[18]

---

* Yahweh is the name for God used most of the time in the Old Testament. It appears some 6,800 times and is often called the covenant name, for it was introduced by Moses in connection with the covenant between God and his people, at the time of the Exodus. In Exodus 20:2, we read, "I am the Lord your God, who brought you out of the land of Egypt, out of the house of bondage." Here, and elsewhere for the most part, in the King James Version and the Revised Standard Version of the Bible, where the English rendering is *Lord*, the Hebrew is *Yahweh*. The name derives from the four Hebrew letters (יהוה), which, reading from right to left, is transliterated as YHWH, called the Tetragrammaton. In Exodus 4:14, God explains to Moses the meaning of his name—"I am that I am" or "I exist now and ever will exist." It is a name connected with the Hebrew root hayay—"to be." Later, this name becomes so sacred that it is never pronounced; a substitute term is used. In this book we have for the most part rendered *Yahweh* as "*The God of Israel*," and "*Yahwehism* as *The Religion of Israel*." The American Revised Version of the Bible (1901) renders the sacred name *Jehovah*, and this term is used four times in the King James Version of the Bible. Modern scholars, however, generally believe *Yahweh* is the correct pronunciation, though it is by no means certain. The confusion in pronunciation comes about because Hebrew is written entirely without vowels. In many Hebrew books, especially those designed for beginners, these vowels are indicated by means of what are termed massoretic points, developed when Hebrew ceased to be a spoken language. Since the personal name for God, *Yahweh*, had become too holy to be pronounced, a reader of the Scriptures would substitute for it the word *Adonai* (Lord), a practice still continued by most modern Jews. The Massoretes therefore inserted the vowels for *Adonai* among the consonants for *Yahweh*. If one tried to pronounce the result—but, of course, it was never expected that one should—it would be something like *Jehovah*.

† The departed ancestor, when he is thought of as in Sheol, is called a *nephesh* (soul). At other times the ancestors are termed *rephaim* (shades); when the departed ancestor is addressed, he is called *elohim* (as in Isaiah 8:19 and 29:4). This is significant, for *Elohim* is also one of the names used for God or for gods.

Removing all traces of ancestor worship, however, was not an easy matter. It would take centuries before such rites were entirely extinguished. Indeed, even at the height of Old Testament monotheism, there were some remnants of this worship still in hiding. That is why the condemnation of the cult is so often repeated, a condemnation which becomes the more severe as the understanding of one God for all creation develops.

The second factor leading to the conclusion that all the departed are extinct is a civilization trend common to Hebrew, Greek, and Roman religions (and perhaps many others), a trend away from the unquestioned belief in life after death and toward a more sophisticated approach which manifests itself in philosophical questionings and skepticism. Dr. John Baillie, in his book *And the Life Everlasting*, makes a most convincing case for the universal nature of this trend. All people, in their early stages of development, come by a belief in life after death naturally, through what Baillie calls "a lay philosophy of things" or "natural science." Unlike the religious understanding of life after death that developed later, this first stage, or primitive understanding, had nothing to do with the idea of justice or righteousness.[19]

As was pointed out in chapter 3, primitives are simply sensitive to spiritual presences. But it does not remain so. As the walls of civilization are built up, this primitive sensibility tends to be shut out—not entirely, but at least for the more educated persons.

Take Greece, for example. In Homer (before 700 B.C.) there is absolutely no doubt about life after death—though admittedly, as we shall see in our next chapter, it is not a life one would look forward to. But this simple acceptance of the afterlife then gives way under the scrutiny of the philosophers.

We see stage two of the universal trend beginning with Thales (c. 640–546 B.C.) whose idea of hylozoism (that all things are full of gods or all matter has something mental about it) tends to take away any personality of the gods and at the same time does away with any individuality of the human soul.[20] Heraclitus (c. 535–475 B.C.) continues the trend by questioning most of the then-current religious practices and by formulating the idea of a cosmic mind. Finally there come such men as Leucippus who developed the original atomic theory and the idea of materialistic necessity. The sophist Protagoras (c. 481–411 B.C.) was able to express the mind of the average thinker of his day by writing, "Concerning the gods, I am not able to know, neither how they are or how they are not, or whether they are or are not."²¹ It is well recognized that during this scientific period "there is no room for the immortal soul," and consequently religion became not something to be believed and followed, but rather "a ritual which should be performed correctly and in the proper frame of mind."²²

Stage three of Greece's religious development united a belief in life after death, with the idea that what happens in terms of one's eternal destiny depends in large measure upon how one's earthly life is lived. Or, to put it another way, this new belief was religious rather than psychological. In stage one, belief in the afterlife had little or nothing to do with religion or morality (and, indeed, spiritualism today—the modern counterpart of this first stage—frequently has little to do with faith in God, and many variants of spiritualism have little to do with ethics as well). But in the third stage of this development, the belief in the afterlife reappears as a religious concept.

Probably it would be correct to say that for Greece the full development of this third stage had to wait for the advent of Christianity. However, we can see the beginning of this development in the classical period. This religious understanding of the afterlife comes in through the mystery religions, such as Orpheism, and we find men like Socrates who are influenced by this new religious movement accepting the mystical element but also purifying it by an emphasis on the importance of right living and an understanding of deity which comes close to monotheism. The concept of a universe (as opposed to a multiverse or pluralistic creation) and a concept of one god seem to be tied to a concept of a god who is concerned about both how you live now and what happens to you later.

In his *Apology*, Socrates makes it clear that he is a religious man. He is guided by a spiritual presence (δαιμόνιον) which stops him whenever he is about to take a wrong course of action. Though he sometimes gives outward acknowledgment of one of the gods of the Olympic Pantheon,* it is obvious from the indictment laid against him by his accusers and by his defense that he had abandoned the popular religion of his day. In his defense he frequently refers to "God" (θεός) as if to acknowledge him as one, and he makes it clear that a truly religious person is also truly moral. He speaks of doing "God's will" and of "service to God" and "obedience to God."²³ And he claims, "It is God who has given me to Athens."²⁴

---

* As, for example, in his dying instructions to Crito, Socrates says, "I owe a cock to Asclepius; will you remember to pay the debt?" *Phaedo*, 118.

Life Here and Hereafter

Moreover, it is generally acknowledged, it is Socrates who "created the conception of the soul, which has ever since dominated European thinking."[25] "That soul," he says, "invisible, departs to the invisible world—to the divine and immortal and rational; thither arriving, she is secure of bliss and is released from the error and folly of men, their fears and wild passions and all other human ills."[26] Thus, we see that Socrates and his followers prepared the way for a new concept of the afterlife, one which is basically moral and religious.

In the development of the Hebrew religion this third stage reaches maturity not more than three centuries—perhaps two—before the time of Christ. But the beginning of the development is much earlier than that. It begins with the concept of the "Day of the Lord," as formulated by the great prophets of the eighth century B.C. And it is to this concept of the Day of the Lord that we now turn.

"The Day of the Lord," "The Day," "That Day," "The Days are coming," "The Latter End of the Day," etc. are the various ways the prophets of the Old Testament speak of a day when God's power will be vindicated. These are oft-repeated terms. The prophets constantly talk about *the* crisis in history, the great day when God will assert his power in the world.[27]

Originally the people of Israel thought of themselves as God's favorites. Israel was to worship God, and God in return was to protect Israel. Worship consisted in ritual and sacrifice, and the protection from the Almighty came as a matter of course.

Beginning with such men as Amos (c. 760 B.C.), the Day of the Lord departs from this supposition of favoritism and takes on the aspect of judgment. As the other great prophets and Christ would later expound, it is precisely because Israel is the chosen of God that more is demanded of her than of the other nations and that the judgment upon her is more severe:

> You only have I known
>   of all the families of the earth;
> therefore I will punish you
>   for all your iniquities.
>
> Amos 3:2

Judgment is, indeed, passed on Damascus, the Philistines, Tyre, and other peoples,[28] but the harshest judgment is upon Israel. Israel's highly nationalistic concept of the "Day of the Lord" is shattered:

> Woe to you who desire the day of the Lord!
> > Why would you have the day of the Lord?
> It is darkness, and not light;
> > as if a man fled from a lion,
> > and a bear met him;
> > or went into the house and leaned with his hand upon the wall,
> > and a serpent bit him.
> I hate, I despise your feasts,
> > and I take no delight in your solemn assemblies. . . .
>
> Take away from me the noise of your songs;
> > to the melody of your harps I will not listen.
> But let justice roll down like waters,
> > and righteousness like an ever-flowing stream.
> > > Amos 5:18–21, 23–24

Amos preached in the Kingdom of Israel, the northern part of the land we now know as Israel or Palestine, and his pronouncements were against that kingdom. Isaiah (c. 742 B.C.) in the southern Kingdom of Judah also points out that the Day of the Lord will be no picnic.* Isaiah seconds Amos's conviction that the northern kingdom will be punished:

> In that day men will cast forth
> > their idols of silver and their idols of gold,
> which they made for themselves to worship
> > to the moles and to the bats,
> to enter the caverns of the rocks

---

* For the benefit of those unfamiliar with the history of the two kingdoms of the Hebrews, a word of explanation is in order. All of Palestine was united as one kingdom under David and Solomon, but when Solomon's son Rehoboam announced, "My father chastised you with whips, but I will chastise you with scorpions" (I Kings 12:14), the northern kingdom carried through a successful revolt. From that time on the northern kingdom was known as Israel and the southern kingdom as Judah. However after many of the northern kingdom were carried away into captivity by the Assyrians and lost, and those who remained behind (probably most of the population) intermarried with others who were settled in the land, the term *Israel* was spiritually applied to the southern kingdom, the reasoning being that Judah had become the inheritor of the promises of God. Properly speaking, the term *Hebrew* is applied only when speaking of all of the Hebrew people, and the word *Jew* is used only when speaking of those from Judah (or Judea, as the area is called in the New Testament). Actually since the Greek *Ioudios* (Ἰουδαῖος) means either "Jew" or "Judean," its use in the New Testament is at times ambiguous.

> and the clefts of the cliffs,
> from before the terror of the Lord,
> and from the glory of his majesty,
> when he rises to terrify the earth.
> Isaiah 2:20–21

It would not be long before all this would come to pass. Then Isaiah's wife (whom he calls "The Prophetess") conceived and bore a son. God said to Isaiah,

> Call his name Maher-shalal-hash-baz [meaning "The spoil hastens, the plunder comes quickly"] for before the child knows how to cry "My father" or "My mother," the wealth of Damascus and the spoil of Samaria will be carried away before the king of Assyria.
> Isaiah 8:3b, 4

So it was that Israel was attacked by Assyria and in 722 B.C. destroyed, with the cream of its population deported to unknown destinations and lost to history.

But Isaiah foresaw bad days ahead for the southern kingdom of Judah as well. Though Assyria was defeated and its capital Nineveh leveled to the ground, a new empire of Mesopotamia was taking control. It was the sad lot of the kingdoms of the fertile crescent, as the land bridge between Egypt and Mesopotamia was called, to be tossed to and fro from one great power to the other. Isaiah warned rebellious Judah:

> Behold, the days are coming, when all that is in your house, and that which your fathers have stored up till this day, shall be carried to Babylon; nothing shall be left, says the Lord.
> Isaiah 39:6

As one reads the Prophets, one often gets the impression that this Day of the Lord is a time when the world is finished and time ends. True, all the Prophets see historical events in the light of eschatology, and all historical events are partial fulfillments of the great day when God will assert his power in the world. But these eschatological events must not be thought necessarily to refer to an end of history. Rather, they are partial fulfillments of God's day *in history.* Take the destruction of Jerusalem during the time of Jeremiah (627–580 B.C.). The Prophet delivers the proclamation from God of the destruction, as he is told to do; and as also he is instructed he dramatizes the destruction by taking an earthenware vessel and smashing it down upon the pavement as if to say, "There goes Jerusalem." The southern Kingdom of Judah, he tells the people, will be given "into the hand of the king of Babylon," who will carry off the inhabitants as captives.[29]

All of this prophecy was fulfilled in due course, and the so-called Babylonian Captivity began. This destruction and captivity was an *eschaton* for both Jeremiah and the people of Jerusalem, and the Prophet's descriptive language seems to indicate that with this destruction, history for his people would come to an end. But the fact that the world went on after the event did not disturb Jeremiah, for it was all seen as a partial fulfillment of God's purpose.*

As time went on "the Day of the Lord" gathered about it various other concepts. Through the eighth century B.C. the prophets saw the day primarily as a time of judgment, but after the exile in Babylon, they came to see God's day as one of hope, a day when God would save Israel. At times it was conceived of as a day when all those in captivity would be allowed to return home. Or it was a day when all those of Israel who had been scattered over the whole earth would be restored to the land.† In some contexts it was a day when there would be a conversion of the Gentiles. Eventually the idea of a messianic age emerged, when all would be restored to the peace of Eden, and in this connection the prophets sometimes wrote of the coming of a messiah. The well-known eleventh chapter of Isaiah incorporates both the messianic age and messiah:

---

* The Babylonian Captivity (or Exile) is usually dated from 587 B.C., when after another revolt Nebuchadnezzar destroyed Jerusalem, making it the object of derision. Nebuchadnezzar carried off into captivity the king of Judah and all but the very poorest of the population. The captivity ended in 538 B.C., when Cyrus the Persian granted permission for the people to return.

† The idea of the ingathering of the Dispersion (or Diaspora as it was called in Greek) figured very heavily in the thought of the Prophets, as, indeed, it does today. The Diaspora was usually thought of as beginning with the deportation of the ten tribes of the north (722 B.C.), despite the fact that those deported had been absorbed into the population, and lost, somewhere in Persia. After the end of the Babylonian Captivity, well-organized communities of Jews continued to remain in Babylon and to keep in constant touch with Jerusalem. There were also Jewish colonies in Egypt. Other deportations took place in the Roman period. The listing of the areas from which Jews had come, at the time of Pentecost (Acts 2:8–11), shows how widely dispersed the Jews of the New Testament period were. In fact, as Josephus points out in his *Antiquities*, vol. 14, 7:2, it was difficult to find a city where there were no Jews.

> There shall come forth a shoot
>   from the stump of Jesse,
> and a branch shall grow out of his roots.
> And the Spirit of the Lord shall rest upon him,
>   the spirit of wisdom and understanding,
>   the spirit of counsel and might,
>   the spirit of knowledge and the fear of the Lord....
>
> The wolf shall dwell with the lamb,
>   and the leopard shall lie down with the kid,
> and the calf and the lion and the fatling together,
>   and a little child shall lead them....
>
> They shall not hurt or destroy
>   in all my holy mountain;
> for the earth shall be full of the knowledge of the Lord
>   as the waters cover the sea.
>   Isaiah 11:1–2, 6, 9

This beautiful passage contains a number of looked-for blessings associated with the Day of the Lord, blessings that we find elaborated upon in subsequent Jewish literature—the peace of Eden, a descendant of David (Jesse's son) who would rule as God's anointed in the highest ideals of kingship, the holy mountain of Jerusalem from which the nations would be ruled, and the knowledge of God spread throughout the earth.

Though most prophetic utterances about the Day of the Lord do not have all these attributes, they do indicate at the least that God is in control of human events, that he is Lord of history, and, although he is not determining the details of history, he *is* determining the final outcome; for ultimately God's purposes triumph. Isaiah makes this control clear when he declares that what happened in the destruction of Jerusalem was God's will. Moreover, King Nebuchadnezzar was God's servant (Jeremiah 25:9) and he was commissioned to chastise God's people. But, of course, chastisement continues only for a period. Babylonia would serve the purpose of the Lord, but only that purpose, and when she would attempt to go beyond God's plan, she, like Assyria, would be destroyed:

> Then after seventy years are completed, I will punish the king of Babylon and that nation, the land of the Chaldeans, for their iniquity, says the Lord, making the land an everlasting waste.
>   Jeremiah 25:12

So, during the period of the exile, in the land between the Tigris and the Euphrates rivers, Israel is purified. As the purification process continues, a new hope arises, which is expressed by a later disciple of Jeremiah* in this way:

> Therefore, behold, the days are coming, says the Lord, when men shall no longer say, "As the Lord lives who brought up the people of Israel out of the land of Egypt," but "as the Lord lives who brought up and led the descendants of the house of Israel out of . . . all the countries where he had driven them." Then they shall dwell in their own land.
> Jeremiah 23:7–8

The Book of Jeremiah includes a messiah in this future blessedness:

> Behold, the days are coming, says the Lord, when I will raise up for David a righteous Branch, and he shall reign as king and deal wisely, and shall execute justice and righteousness in the land. In his days Judah will be saved, and Israel will dwell securely. And this is the name by which he will be called: "The Lord is our righteousness."
> Jeremiah 23:5–6

The great poet-prophet of the Exile, whose writings are contained in chapter 40 and following of the Book of Isaiah (the portion of the Book known as "Deutero-Isaiah")[30] rises to sublime heights in his understanding of the hope of Israel. There is first the sense of God's forgiveness expressed so beautifully by those lines which Handel chose to open his *Messiah:*

> Comfort ye, comfort ye my people saith your God. Speak ye comfortably to Jerusalem, and cry unto her, that her warfare is accomplished, that her iniquity is pardoned: for she hath received of the Lord's hand double for all her sins.
> Isaiah 40:1–2, KJV

Again, the fulfillment of these promises, and others, too, is possible because God continues to act in history, completing his purpose for his people. The man he has chosen to overthrow the Babylonian Empire (or,

---

* Most biblical scholars would agree that this promise did not come directly from the mouth of Jeremiah himself, but perhaps from what some would term "The School of Jeremiah," a later group of the Prophet's followers who, continuing in his discipleship, added to the prophecy as time went on.

more properly, the Chaldean) is Cyrus the Great, unifier of the Medes and the Persians and new ruler of the Middle East, the man described by historians as "a ruler with despotic power moved by a concern for all mankind":[31]

> Thus says the Lord to his anointed, to Cyrus,
>   whose right hand I have grasped,
> to subdue nations before him
>   and ungird the loins of kings,
> to open doors before him
>   that gates may not be closed:
> I will go before you
>   and level the mountains,
> I will break in pieces the doors of bronze
>   and cut asunder the bars of iron. . . .
> For the sake of my servant Jacob,
>   and Israel my chosen,
> I call you by your name,
>   I surname you, though you do not know me.
>   Isaiah 45:1–2, 4

If God is concerned for Cyrus and regards him as his anointed, God is also concerned for all humanity. This theology which we get in First Isaiah we find repeated in a more poetic way in Deutero-Isaiah, where there is stressed the mission of Israel to all peoples:

> Arise, shine; for your light has come,
>   and the glory of the Lord has risen upon you.
> For behold, darkness shall cover the earth,
>   and thick darkness the peoples;
> but the Lord will arise upon you,
>   and his glory will be seen upon you.
> And nations shall come to your light,
>   And kings to the brightness of your rising.
>   Isaiah 60:1–3

In this and other passages we see the high point of the Old Testament understanding of God the creator.[32] If God is in control of all things, it logically follows that he is in control of man from his beginning to his end—or if God so chooses—from his beginning on into eternity.

This universality of God and his control of man's destiny leads us next to consider the Prophet Ezekiel. As a young man carried off captive (in

598 B.C.) by Nebuchadnezzar, Ezekiel spent the rest of his lifetime in exile. He is the psychedelic prophet of the Old Testament, a man whose prophecy is full of strange creatures (1:4) and flashes of heavenly lightning (1:14). Despite his strange symbolism, he makes an important contribution to the theology of the Old Testament. His vision of the wheels within wheels (1:15–21) symbolizes God's mobility, his omnipresence; God's presence is not to be confined to the Temple in Jerusalem nor to anywhere else in Palestine; there is no place where he cannot be found. The four living creatures (1:5) with the four faces—a man, a lion, an ox, and an eagle—perhaps symbolize for Ezekiel God's reign over every area of human and animal life.[33]

Though Ezekiel at first directed his prophecies to those who remained in Jerusalem, later, after the destruction of that city in 587 B.C., he directed his ministry to the exiled congregation and changed his prophecies from judgment to restoration. He looked to the future with great hope, and it is in his prophecy of hope that we find another link between understanding the restored Israel as a purely earthly situation in history and understanding it as something above history. Well known is Ezekiel's vision of the Valley of Dry Bones:

> The hand of the Lord was upon me, and he brought me out by the Spirit of the Lord, and set me down in the midst of the valley; it was full of bones. And he led me round among them; and behold, there were very many upon the valley; and lo, they were very dry. And he said to me, "Son of man, can these bones live?" And I answered, "O Lord God, thou knowest." Again he said to me, "Prophesy to these bones, and say to them, O dry bones, hear the word of the Lord. Thus says the Lord God to these bones: Behold, I will cause breath to enter you, and you shall live. And I will lay sinews upon you, and will cause flesh to come upon you, and cover you with skin, and put breath in you, and you shall live; and you shall know that I am the Lord."
>
> So I prophesied as I was commanded; and as I prophesied, there was a noise, and behold, a rattling; and the bones came together, bone to its bone. And as I looked, there were sinews on them, and flesh had come upon them, and skin had covered them; but there was no breath in them. Then he said to me, "Prophesy to the breath, prophesy, son of man, and say to the breath, Thus says the Lord God: Come from the four winds, O breath, and breathe upon these slain, that they may live." So I prophesied as he commanded me, and the breath came into them, and they lived, and stood upon their feet, an exceeding great host.

Then he said to me, "Son of man, these bones are the whole house of Israel. Behold, they say, 'Our bones are dried up, and our hope is lost; we are clean cut off.' Therefore prophesy, and say to them, Thus says the Lord God: Behold, I will open your graves, and raise you from your graves, O my people; and I will bring you home into the land of Israel. And you shall know that I am the Lord, when I open your graves, and raise you from your graves, O my people. And I will put my Spirit within you, and you shall live, and I will place you in your own land; then you shall know that I, the Lord, have spoken, and I have done it, says the Lord."

Ezekiel 37:1–14

The primary purpose of this passage is to present a metaphor of the nation. Israel's hope as a nation in exile is as a field of dried bones. But if Ezekiel can prophesy, the Spirit of the Lord will return to the people, and they will once more become a great nation.

The idea of a resurrected nation is, then, the primary purpose of this passage; a restored Israel was uppermost in Ezekiel's mind. On the other hand, I feel there is a secondary purpose to this passage. Though scholars insist that the passage has no direct connection with the Christian doctrine of the resurrection, I cannot help but feel there is a double meaning here. As one writer points out, the line of demarcation between reality and imagery is much less definite for the oriental than for the westerner, and the transition from one to the other is easy.[34] Though the question of a general resurrection was not raised before Ezekiel's day, it certainly was raised after it. Also, perhaps the promise of opening the graves and raising the people from their graves (37:13) was inserted by a later writer, as some have suggested, but it could have been inserted by Ezekiel himself.

The big question that sooner or later had to enter the mind of the religious leader was this: Why should the present faithful of Israel live and die and perhaps enter oblivion without ever having a chance to participate in this future state of blessedness? If God is a God of justice and if he is the God of the whole creation, including both the heavens above and Sheol underneath—and this message was now coming through loud and clear—then there was only one conclusion that logic would permit: There must be some kind of a resurrection or some other kind of an afterlife so that those who have remained faithful to God in this very ungodly present will in a more godly future be able to enjoy a better life.

For a few, the idea of a blessed afterlife was chosen without any thought of resurrection. But for most of Israel, afterlife meant nothing less than a bodily resurrection. Shortly we shall take up the idea of an afterlife without resurrection, but first the matter of the bodily resurrection.

For the great majority of Jews, there was no dichotomy of body and spirit, and a truly living being consisted of both body and spirit, for both soul and body were created by God.[35] Remember also that too friendly an attitude toward Sheol bordered on necromancy and would, therefore, be objectionable in the light of Israel's strong monotheism. Furthermore, originally, all relationships to the God of Israel were confined to the material world.

The first unequivocal mention of resurrection in the Bible occurs in Isaiah, in what is sometimes called "the Little Apocalypse," chapters 24 to 27.[36] Though the Little Apocalypse is placed in the first part of this great book of prophecy, it is generally agreed by scholars that the passage is post-exilic, belonging perhaps to around the beginning of the second century B.C. Of course we cannot be sure, but it is quite certain that the passage does not come immediately from the hand of the Great Prophet himself but rather from his prophetic school. Chapter 24 contains much that is typical of judgment pronouncements, but this is followed by the great message of hope:

> And Yahweh of Hosts shall make
> For all people on this mountain
> A luscious feast,
> A feast of old wines,
> Rich meats well-marrowed,
> Old wines well-matured.
> And he will devour in this mountain
> The cover which covers all peoples,
> The web woven over all nations;
> He will engulf Death for ever!
> And the Lord Yahweh shall wipe away
> Tears from all faces:
> The reproach of His people He shall turn away
> Throughout the whole world.
> For Yahweh has spoken it.
> Isaiah 25:6–8[37]

Other passages in the Prophets have promised a future time when all will be at peace, but chapter 25 of Isaiah promises more. Not only will death be swallowed up, but also all the faithful of the past shall share in this blessedness. Other nations are included, too. The Prophet removes all doubt about the resurrection. He even answers the arguments of the opposition. As he puts it, some have said that the dead are dead; "they will not live; they are shades, they will not arise" (26:14), but the Prophet insists:

> Thy dead shall live, their bodies shall rise.
> O dwellers in the dust, awake and sing for joy!
> For thy dew is a dew of light,
> and on the land of the shades thou wilt let it fall.
> Isaiah 26:19

Thus in these chapters of Isaiah we get the first clear proclamation of an earthly messianic age enjoyed by both those dwelling on earth and those in Sheol.

Note also in the Little Apocalypse of Isaiah the forerunner of what later comes to be described as the "Messianic Banquet." References to "a luscious feast" or "a feast of fat things full of marrow" and "wine on the lees well refined" (RSV) indicate far more than the sacrificial rites referred to elsewhere in the Old Testament.[38] This is a joyful feast at which the Lord of Heaven is the host and the guests are all people, not just all Israel, for here the Gentiles are included in the festivities.[39]

At least two of the psalms support an idea similar to the bodily resurrection found in Isaiah, though, sadly, the festival emphasis is missing. Whether they come from a contemporary pen or from an earlier one we shall not concern ourselves. In Psalm 49 the Psalmist identifies himself with the pious Israelite or the righteous community. Though the wicked go down to death in Sheol and remain there for ever, there is more for the righteous man:

> Like sheep they [the wicked] are appointed for Sheol;
>   Death shall be their shepherd;
> straight to the grave they descend,
>   and their form shall waste away;
> Sheol shall be their home.
> But God will ransom my soul from the power of Sheol,
>   for he will receive me.
> Psalm 49:14–15

Psalm 73 is the other one which supports the belief in an afterlife for the righteous. It cannot be otherwise than that the God of justice who controls all things should be concerned about the future of the righteous, for as the first verse of this psalm tells us, "Truly, God is good to the upright, to those who are pure in heart." Also in this psalm Sheol appears to be a place of punishment for the wicked, and for the righteous perhaps only a temporary place. It may very well be that the wicked are prosperous, but eventually they perish (73:27). The righteous person recognizes that "God is the strength of [his] heart and [his] portion for ever" (73:26). He may, therefore, with reason hope to "be near his God for ever" (73:28). What earth has in store for the righteous, then, does not matter. What does matter is unbroken communion with God.

The need for understanding that life alone makes no sense, in terms of God's justice, is made all the more acute by the time the author of the Book of Daniel starts to write. When the empire of Alexander the Great broke up in 323 B.C. the territory was divided among his four leading generals, of whom only one concerns us here—Seleucius, who established his capital at Antioch, Syria, about 300 B.C. and whose dynasty (most of the time) controlled Palestine for the next hundred and fifty years. One of the successors of the Seleucid dynasty—Antiochus III (the Great), 222–187 B.C.—began a thorough policy of hellenization. Though Greek was already the international language then, this man wanted to make everything Greek. Whenever he found a local god that could not be uprooted, he gave it a Greek name. If a temple were to be rebuilt, it must be along Greek plans. The young responded with enthusiasm, taking up Greek customs and wearing Greek costumes.

The problem did not become critical until the next reign, that of Antiochus IV (175–164 B.C.). After disposing of his older brother Seleucius and another rival, Antiochus IV began what became a reign of terror for the Jews. As an ardent devotee of the Olympian Zeus and all things Greek, and as one of the cruelest tyrants of all times, he was determined to root out the Jewish religion completely. He took the name Epiphanes ("the manifest of God"), but his enemies quite appropriately called him Epimanes ("the mad one").

Antiochus announced that the God of the Jews was henceforth to be known as Zeus Olympus, and to reinforce that decision he had a statue of Zeus erected in the Holy of Holies in the Temple. On the High Altar, before this statue, he caused hogs to be sacrificed. (This event is called by

Daniel "The Abomination of Desolation"—Daniel 9:27, 11:31, 12:11). Any baby that was circumcised was to be killed along with the person who performed the rite. Copies of the Scripture were destroyed. In fact, it became a capital offence even to have a book of the Law. No one could observe the Sabbath any more. Any Jew refusing to eat pork was summarily executed. And, further to encourage the abandonment of the old faith, many of those who willingly accepted the new religion were politically rewarded.

This was the first completely religious persecution in Jewish history. Many political persecutions had previously taken place, but now, for the first time, men were put to death solely because they were righteous, and the more righteous the more terrible their deaths.

It is from this time onward that belief in the future life became an essential part of the Jewish religion. Up to this time there was still a great deal of the idea of "Be good and you will be happy and prosperous." Job's comforters expressed the orthodox position of the day. But Antiochus's persecution put an end to that.*

As we have seen, prior to 200 B.C., very few Jews believed in life after death *as part of their religion.* But now, with this persecution, such a belief soon became an essential part of the Jewish religion. The development was very rapid, so that by the time the Christian era opened there were very few Jews who did not believe in life after death. Actually, in our Lord's day, those making up the small priestly sect of the Sadducees were almost the only nonbelievers around. By the year 100 A.D. not to believe would excommunicate a man. The Jewish dogma, "God hath reserved a future for Israel," became amended to read, "For every individual good or bad, God hath reserved a future."[40]

The circumstances under which this new belief in the afterlife became part of the literature of Judaism center on the fierce and successful rebellion that took place (168 B.C.). This was led by Judas Maccabaeus and his family; they received support from everywhere. Eventually, Judas recaptured Jerusalem, tore down the Greek statues, and had the Temple rededicated (December, 165 B.C.), an event which has ever since become memorialized as the "Feast of Lights" or Hanukkah festival.

---

* Retribution did not always have to wait for the next world, however, for the account of the martyrdom of the seven brothers, to mention just one instance, reveals that at least some of the suffering was thought to be punishment for sins.

It was in the setting of Antiochus's persecution that the Book of Daniel was written. And, moreover, this same period spawned the whole apocalyptic literary trend, which we shall consider shortly.

In order to get the Book of Daniel accepted—for the author wrote long after the close of the canonical period—he resorted to the trick of pseudonymity. The writer purported to be a certain Daniel who was a young Jewish captive of the exile in Babylon, some four centuries before. Thus, his work became what R. H. Charles describes as "the first great pseudepigraph in Judaism."[41] In fact, it is generally believed that the author was a member of the Hasidean, the anti-Hellenistic, orthodox, heroic group of which we read in I Maccabees 2:29–38, the group that forsook all they had and, with their wives and children, took refuge in the caves of the wilderness in order to worship without hindrance.*

The Book of Daniel is not only one of many pseudepigraphs, it is also one of many apocalypses. And we must pause here to explain the meaning of that word, for apocalyptic literature did much to shape the eschatological thinking of the time of Christ. Literally, an apocalypse is an *uncovering*. The word is not to be confused with apocrypha, which means just the opposite, *things hidden*. All literature of the apocalyptic type involves strange symbols, grotesque characters, cosmic battles, and it is in large measure subversive. Its purpose is to cheer on those who are suffering for their faith and to assure them that, despite all the evidence to the contrary, God is in control of this world and ultimately his righteousness will be vindicated. The Book of Revelation is, of course, the greatest of all apocalypses, and we will look at more of this last book of the Bible in later chapters.

In chapter 7 of Daniel, in true apocalyptic style, we are introduced to four "great beasts" which represent the four successive world empires— Babylonia, Media, Persia, and Alexander's Greece (whose ruler at the time was Antiochus IV). The last beast has ten horns, which represent the ten kings of the Seleucid dynasty, the dynasty which inherited the Syrian part of Alexander's empire. "The little horn, . . . before which three of the first

---

* Josephus, the Jewish historian of the first century A.D., who gives us much information about this period, tells us that Antiochus, when he learned of this flight, went in pursuit of the Hasidim group and, when they refused to return and comply with his edicts, put one thousand of them to the sword. But many escaped and gave their support to the Maccabean struggle. For half a century or more the Hasidim disappear. When they appear again, oddly enough, they are known as the Pharisees. It is a strange twist of history that such a heroic group would later become leading opponents of the Christian movement.

horns were plucked up by the roots," is none other than the villain of our story, Antiochus IV, the man who by intrigue and murder removed others to place himself on the throne. But there is always hope in apocalyptic literature. After all the world empires are destroyed, we read of the coming Messianic Age and the new dominion given to the "Son of Man" (who in this case is Israel):

> As I looked,
> thrones were placed
>   and one that was ancient of days took his seat;
> his raiment was white as snow,
>   and the hair of his head like pure wool;
> his throne was fiery flames,
>   its wheels were burning fire.
> A stream of fire issued
>   and came forth from before him;
> a thousand thousands served him,
>   and ten thousand times ten thousand stood before him;
> the court sat in judgment,
>   and the books were opened....
>
> I saw in the night visions,
> and behold, with the clouds of heaven
>   there came one like a son of man,
> and he came to the Ancient of Days
>   and was presented before him.
> And to him was given dominion
>   and glory and kingdom,
> that all peoples, nations, and languages
>   should serve him;
> his dominion is an everlasting dominion,
>   which shall not pass away,
> and his kingdom one that shall not be destroyed.
>   Daniel 7:9–10, 13–14

Finally, at the end of the age, there is a culmination of events and one final battle, at which time Michael the Archangel shall deliver the people of Israel, "everyone whose name shall be found written in the book" (12:1). There is then the pronouncement of the last word in canonical Old Testament eschatology:

> And many of those who sleep in the dust of the earth shall awake, some

to everlasting life, and some to shame and everlasting contempt. And those who are wise shall shine like the brightness of the firmament; and those who turn many to righteousness, like the stars for ever and ever.

Daniel 12:2–3

Despite the comparison of the righteous with the stars, most biblical scholars agree that the resurrected kingdom pictured here is entirely an earthly kingdom, a purified realm of the Jewish people, though a realm that is, indeed, to last for ever.[42] And, oddly enough, though the details are not spelled out, some scholars believe that within this earthly kingdom, men are born and they die in the normal course of life's cycle. Assuming this hypothesis is correct, the point of the resurrection here is that the righteous who hitherto never had a chance, now have one. However my own belief is that the matter of what kind of resurrection is expected is intentionally left ambiguous. The idea of a resurrection in the body was in the air, so to speak, and the author is leaving the details an open question.

The new element that is brought in by this passage of Daniel is the idea that this is to be a resurrection of both good and bad. Though (by implication) for the good it is a life in the company of God, for the wicked it is a life of everlasting reproaches. Nothing is said about physical punishment; these wicked are simply objects of abhorrence.[43] Also note that it is an incomplete resurrection; perhaps Sheol continues to remain the abode of the majority. Again the question is left unanswered.

What is *not* left unanswered is the fact of retribution, a very important aspect of this apocalyptic period. No longer is the afterlife beyond the concern of God, for what a person does in life determines what rewards or punishments he is to receive in the afterlife.

The prayer life of the period seems to take for granted a resurrection that is a gift from God. This is made clear by this passage from the Jewish liturgy of the Shemoneth Esreh:

> Thou, O Lord, art mighty for ever. Thou revivest the dead. Thou art mighty to save. Thou sustainest the living with loving kindness, revivest the dead with great mercy, supportest the falling, healest the sick, looseth the bound, and keepest thy faith to them that sleep in the dust. Who is like unto Thee, O Lord of mighty acts who causest salvation to spring forth? Yea, faithful art Thou to revive the dead. Blessed art Thou, O Lord, who revivest the dead.[44]

In the setting of the Maccabean revolt and subsequent to it, there comes into existence an abundance of extracanonical, apocalyptic literature.[45] Most of these works are gathered up and published in the second volume of Apocrypha and Pseudepigrapha of the Old Testament.[46] These various works further develop understanding of the nature of the life beyond death and so set the stage for the eschatology of the New Testament. Of this literature, we shall consider just enough to demonstrate how it happens that there were conflicting ideas about the afterlife in New Testament times.

We begin with the Enoch literature, of which there are three books—Enoch I (The Ethiopic Enoch), Enoch II (The Slavonic Enoch), and Enoch III (The Hebrew Enoch).[47] The terms *Ethiopic, Slavonic,* and *Hebrew* indicate the language of the earliest versions in which the three works have survived, although probably all three were originally written in Hebrew, or at least Aramaic.* (The Slavonic Enoch is also called "The Book of the Secrets of Enoch.") As with most men after whom pseudonymous Hebrew literary works of this type are named, there is something mysterious surrounding their deaths, i.e., the idea that it was not really a death of the body. Elijah was taken up to Heaven in a chariot of fire (II Kings 2:11, 12). Of the body of Moses, it was written, ". . . no man knows the place of his burial to this day" (Deuteronomy 34:6). Of Enoch we read, "Enoch walked with God; and he was not, for God took him" (Genesis 5:24).

So the traditions about Enoch and his being allowed to view the supernatural continued to grow in the period between the close of the canon of the Old Testament and the beginning of the New Testament area. As Dr. Stanley Frost puts it, "Men who lived and worked in this tradition obviously received stories and instructions from their teachers, and in turn handed them on, to their disciples, in good faith that they had really come down from Enoch."[48]

Despite the fact that we are quite certain that the Enoch of Genesis 5 had nothing to do with the experiences written of him, who is to say that

---

* Aramaic was the language of the Arameans, a Semitic people who came in from the desert and settled in the Upper Euphrates Valley in the late Bronze Age. Because they were traders, their language became an international one. Somewhere around the time of the exile, Aramaic began to be used in Palestine and soon displaced Hebrew as the language of the people. Although Hebrew continued to be used as a written language and as a liturgical language, it was not until the time of Eleazar Ben-Yehuda (around the beginning of the twentieth century) that Hebrew was resurrected as a living language, and it is now, of course, Israel's official language.

the writings which bear his name are without inspiration of the Holy Spirit? For the most part they are of very high ethical content, the faith in the Almighty is unparalleled anywhere else, and the works reveal a genuine effort to draw back the curtain separating this world from the next. Certainly, such books as we find in the Enoch literature, despite some grand exaggerations, did much better than Daniel in strengthening the faith of the Jew in the afterlife. For example, the former contains the first written statement that there are seven levels of Heaven (II Enoch 3:3). Sheol, too, is subdivided into compartments[49] (a matter we will pursue in chapter 13).

We must not, however, expect consistency throughout the Enoch literature or, for that matter, throughout any of the literature of this period. Since this tradition existed in verbal form long before it came to be written down, and since, as R. H. Charles believes, the authorship is varied,[50] it could hardly be anything that might come under the heading of "systematic theology." Also, as W. O. E. Oesterley points out in his introduction to the Ethiopic Enoch, the writers of these apocalypses were, on the one hand, saturated with the traditional Old Testament thinking, and, on the other hand, exposed to and caught up into the "newer conceptions which the spirit of the age had brought into being."[51] As often happens with ancient Jewish writers, when there is a conflict of thought, both ideas are included without any attempt at reconciliation.

This unreconciled conflict of thought is well seen in both the geographical or cosmological setting of the new life that is to come and the nature of that life. First the matter of the geographical or cosmological setting: In the first part of I Enoch (24), the throne of God is on a high mountain on earth. Likewise the resurrected life is on earth, and that is the way it is in most of the early apocalypses. But, as time goes on, there is more and more disparagement for any hope in this present world, and more and more emphasis is placed on a hope for a new world. Thus we have in the latter part of I Enoch a new Heaven and a new earth:

> And the first heaven shall depart and pass away,
> And a new heaven shall appear....
>
> I Enoch 91:16

At other times, instead of a new Heaven and new earth, there appears to be an entire abandonment of things earthly. Or, as Sigmund Mowinckel would put it, "the boundaries between earth and heaven seem to disappear."[52] Sometimes there is destruction of the world by apocalyptic fire; literature generally pictures the end of our planet as catastrophic.[53] As we draw closer to the New Testament era, less emphasis is placed on the material, and more emphasis on the immaterial which is independent of this earth.

Consistent with this spiritualization of the afterlife and the development of the concept of a nonbodily life after death, there comes into this apocalyptic period less and less mention of a resurrected body. The New Testament is vague on this matter, a subject we shall discuss later in this book.

As we have seen, in primitive Hebrew life there was a firm belief in an immediate life after death—the life of the disembodied spirit in Sheol. But, under pressure from Moses and the Prophets, this personal spiritual survival was pushed underground—if you will pardon the pun—and the chief stress was placed on the future of the nation. The only way life after death and the future of the nation could be taken care of together was by means of a bodily resurrection in the Day of the Lord, when there would come an end, or *eschaton*, of this evil era. But, during this intertestamental, apocalyptic period, almost from the beginning, there is some teaching that immediately after death the afterlife begins, a conviction that continues into the first century of our era. Since God is a spirit and his angels are spirits, there is a logical connection between the concept of spiritual beings and a Heaven that is independent of earth.*

Despite the fact that I Enoch generally teaches a bodily resurrection, we find there, too, a statement that the souls of the righteous immediately upon death enter Heaven, and presumably they remain there until it is time for the general resurrection (I Enoch 39:4–7). Why they have to return to the earth for this general reawakening is not clear, unless it is for a final judgment upon the nation; and let us not fail to remember that righteousness, judgment, and retribution are all very important in apocalyptic literature.

In the later sections of I Enoch we find that the possibility of any resurrection at all is played down; the righteous just rise from the earth and are at once clothed with garments of glory, i.e., with spiritual bodies (I Enoch 62:13–16). Likewise, the Book of Jubilees (dated in the second

---

* I Enoch's rendering of the Trisagion illustrates this emphasis: "Holy, holy holy, is the Lord of Spirits: He filleth the earth with spirits" (39:12).

century B.C.)[54] gives no hint whatsoever of any bodily resurrection:

> And their bones shall rest in the earth and their spirits shall have much joy, and they shall know that it is the Lord who executes judgment, and shows mercy. . . .
> Jubilees 23:11

The Apocalypse of Baruch teaches the doctrine that the dead are raised exactly as they were in the earthly life for purposes of recognition, and are then transformed into the splendor of the angels, and they dwell with the angels in Heaven (II Baruch 51:10).[55] Likewise, II Enoch disconnects the righteous from Sheol entirely; the righteous, clothed with the garments of God's glory, enter Heaven immediately upon death. Thus when Enoch is about to be translated into Heaven, God directs the Archangel Michael to "go and take from Enoch his earthly robe, and anoint him with the raiment of my glory" (II Enoch 22:8). And, as Enoch reports, this is what Michael did:

> He anointed me and clothed me, and the appearance of that oil was more than a great light, and its anointing was like excellent dew; and its fragrance like myrrh, shining like a ray of the sun.
> II Enoch 22:9

It is generally believed that II Enoch is a product of Alexandrian Judaism. (There was a large and very influential Jewish colony in Alexander's famous city of culture and learning in Egypt.) Here there would be Greek influences, more emphasis on the spirit than on the body. Despite this and despite the late date of the work, it is remarkable to note the many parallels it has with the New Testament.

Another product of Alexandrian Judaism is the Book of the Wisdom of Solomon (one of the more useful books of the Apocrypha), where again we find no resurrection, since God "created man for incorruption" (2:23). A passage often read in churches during the Easter season expresses the confidence of the author of this book that for the faithful departed all is well in God's keeping:

> But the souls of the righteous are in the hand of God,
> and no torment will ever touch them.
> In the eyes of the foolish they seemed to have died,
> and their departure was thought to be an affliction,
> and their going from us to be their destruction;

> but they are in peace.
> For though in the sight of men they were punished,
> their hope is full of immortality.
> Having been disciplined a little, they will receive great good,
> because God tested them and found them worthy of himself. . . .
> Wisdom 3:1–5

This conflict of beliefs regarding the question of a physical resurrection continues even among the rabbis of the post-New Testament period. For example, there was a Rabbi ben Zakkai (c. 80 A.D.), who, on his death bed, spoke of his imminent appearance before the King of Kings, upon whose judgment his eternal destiny depended.[56] On the other hand we read that Rabbi Gamaliel II (c. 90 A.D.) had such a materialistic view of the resurrection that he believed a wife in the messianic kingdom would bear a child every day.[57]

Before leaving this whole period of eschatological development which came about between the closing of the Old Testament canon and the opening of the New, we should consider (but briefly) a very important aspect of apocalyptic literature which provides the explanation of the apparent triumph of evil in the world and the prosperity of the unrighteous. How can this evil condition be reconciled with the goodness of an all-powerful God? To this question there are a number of answers given in this literature. A rather good explanation is found in the Second Book of Esdras.* Here the answer is at least two-fold: In the first place, as Job so eloquently put it some centuries earlier,

> "Where were you when I laid the foundation of the earth?
> Tell me, if you have understanding. . . ."
>
> "Can you draw out Leviathan with a fishhook,
> or press down his tongue with a cord"
> Job 38:4, 41.1

---

* This book, found in our Apocrypha, is usually called by Biblical scholars "the Fourth Book of Esdras," the name deriving from St. Jerome's Latin Vulgate, where it first appeared. (In this figuring, I Esdras is the Book of Esdras which appears in the King James Version of the Bible, etc.; II Esdras is the Book of Nehemiah; III Esdras is material from II Chronicles, Ezra, and Nehemiah 8.) According to Robert C. Denton (*The Apocrypha, Bridge of the Testaments,* Seabury Press, Greenwich, Connecticut, 1954, pp. 94–95), this work was put together from material extending over a 200-year period, from the first to the third century A.D. Though this does not contribute to the New Testament, it reveals the climate into which the New Testament came.

This philosophy is worded by the writer of II Esdras in this fashion:

> You cannot understand the things with which you have grown up; how then can your mind comprehend the ways of the Most High? And how can one who is already worn out by the corrupt world understand incorruption? . . . For as the land is assigned to the forest and the sea to its waves, so also those who dwell upon earth can understand only what is on the earth, and he who is above the heavens can understand what is above the heavens.
>
> II Esdras 4:10–11, 21

The second answer is that, although this age is fast hurrying to an end, there are some more things which must be accomplished first. "Unless the living go through the trials of life, they cannot enter that which is destined for them" (7:14). Often, too, in apocalyptic literature, the end of time is predetermined (4:35); there must be a certain number of souls born into the world before the end comes; but, we are assured, when the time does come, we will see the souls of the righteous in Sheol released and the wicked punished (II Esdras 4:40).

Other explanations for evil are also found in this literature, such as the doctrine that this world is captive under a malevolent Power, who is allowed a free hand for a time. While the modern theologian has a lot more to say about the evils of life than we have here, at least this represents a beginning in the understanding that God does not willingly afflict man, and ultimately God's righteousness and justice will triumph.*

Having now reached the end of our discussion of both Old Testament eschatology and the development that took place subsequent to the closing of the Old Testament canon, I would like to make three concluding observations.

First, note that we have traced the Hebrew religion through three stages. We have examined Hebrew primitive belief in life after death and have seen how it had nothing at all to do with either religion or ethics (unless you want to call ancestor worship a religion). We have also noted, in stage two, that in the course of the growth of Hebrew civilization comes

---

* As, for example, in I Enoch 89:59, the evils that have come upon Israel are the doings of the seventy angels into whose care God committed Israel for the chastisement that was due the people, but these angels have exceeded their authority. As soon as their time is up they will be punished.

an abandonment of any belief in life after death or at best a belief that goes into hiding. Then comes stage three, in which the Hebrew people recognize that life after death can be no less than a gift from a God who is concerned about individual, world, and cosmic justice.

Second, a characteristic of this chapter which must have been quite obvious to the reader is the heavy emphasis on Hebrew history—from the time Moses led the people out of Egypt, through their settling in the land of Canaan, the threats from other powers, tyranny from the Assyrians, captivity by the Babylonians, freedom under the Persians, and finally religious persecution and revolt under the Greek dynasty of the Seleucids. This review of history came about as an inevitable by-product of the description of the eschatological development. As R. H. Charles put it, "This belief [in the afterlife] in Israel arose not in the abstract reasonings of the school, but in the moral strife of spiritual experience. . . ."[58] Charles describes this struggle as a "National Pilgrim's Progress . . . [for] in this progress from the complete absence of such a belief in Israel to a positive and spiritual faith in a blessed future life, all alike can read large in the pages of history from 800 B.C. to A.D. 100 a transcript of their own spiritual struggles as they toil up the steep ascent that leads to the city of God."[59]

Third, let us not neglect to pay tribute to revelations of God made outside the Jewish community. Mowinckel (and others) believe that Persian Zoroastrianism, with the idea of a cosmic conflict between the forces of light and the forces of darkness and also the idea of a resurrection, did much to shape Hebrew thinking in those directions.[60] Certainly, too, the Greeks and especially Socrates were responsible for at least some of the Jewish and Christian understanding of the immortal soul. Though the Almighty did, indeed, choose Israel for the ultimate pre-Christian revelation of himself, surely he did not limit his self-revelation to Israel alone.

5

This Is Life Eternal

*I*n the Upper Room in Jerusalem in what is generally believed to be the house of the mother of young John Mark,* Jesus and his disciples gathered following what has come to be known as The Last Supper. As St. John tells the story, after conversation was over, Jesus offered what is called the High Priestly Prayer. Almost at the beginning of this prayer is this definition: "And this is life eternal, that they might know thee the only true God, and Jesus Christ whom thou hast sent."[1]

Sometime before this—again another story related by St. John—Jesus and his friends Mary and Martha were approaching the tomb of Lazarus. In the course of the discussion, Jesus says, "Your brother will rise again." To this Martha replies, "I know that he will rise again in the resurrection at the last day." But Jesus means more than that. He corrects her: "I am the resurrection and the life; he who believes in me, though he die, yet shall he live, and whoever lives and believes in me shall never die."[2]

"This is Life Eternal" and "I am the Resurrection and the Life" have just about the same meaning in the Fourth Gospel.† They mean "Not only

---

* The Upper Room is generally considered to be the living room of a substantial home, though some commentators believe this could have been a dining room or even an attic. On a 1975 pilgrimage to the Holy Land, Canon Ronald Brownrigg, our guide, pointed out a number of "upper rooms" located on the second or third floors (American counting) which were accessible by means of outside stairways.

† Biblical scholars prefer to refer to "The Gospel according to St. John" as "The Fourth Gospel," since it is a matter of endless debate as to which John wrote it.

do you *not* have to wait until the last day before you have eternal life, but you don't even have to die." This "realized eschatology"* that dominates the Fourth Gospel has, then, this double implication: For the believer there is both an immediate entrance into life at death, and there is the opportunity of eternal life for those still living on earth and in the physical body. All life, both here and hereafter, can be eternal life, because Christ put new meaning into the whole of living. This is the essential difference between the Christian concept of life—both present and future—and the non-Christian concept.

The Greek term for *eternal* life and the Greek term for *everlasting* life is the same. The adjective in both cases is *aionios*—αἰώνιος. Yet, as the New Testament develops *aionios*, there is a big difference between the two concepts.[3] As we have seen, most people believe in some kind of life after death;[4] some believe in a limited extension of this life, while others believe in an everlasting extension of it. But for the Christian, life after death is not just a prolongation or even an everlasting extension of this life but something quite different. Dr. John Baillie makes the point most aptly: "I have often marvelled about the *naïveté* with which certain modern writers raise doubts about the desirability of an endless continuance of our present pilgrimage, as if they were arguing against the Christian hope."[5] This is a very important point, for what the Christian is hoping for is not a continuance of life as it has been but rather an intensification and perfection of life as it should be and can be now. "For my own part," writes a former Bishop of Oxford, "I can think of no prospect more terrifying than one of indefinite survival after death with no certainty of God and his revelation in Christ. This would simply mean the certainty or probability of what the Christian faith has always known as hell—everlasting life without God. Mere indefinite prolongation of existence is not in itself an object of hope. Extinction is a better and less dismaying prospect than that."[6] When my parishioner (mentioned at the beginning of chapter 3) said that all people believe in life after death and that there is nothing exclusively Christian about such a belief, he was thinking of a prolongation of this life—just more of the same. And, with few minor variations, this is how primitive man conceives of life after death.

---

* This is a term meaning the understanding of eternal salvation and judgment as realized in the present. The work of salvation is complete in Jesus Christ, and judgment takes place in Jesus' word and the response of faith to it. It is bringing the future into the present.

It may well be that there are *some* primitives who picture their spirits in the afterlife as passing their time "in feasting, dancing, and whatever occupations most agreeable to them,"[7] but these are exceptions, and even at best they are far from the Christian understanding of the afterlife. Rather, for the most part, primitive man expected to find in his afterlife what he found here, as we learn from Sir James Frazer's account of the Kai tribe of Papuans in New Guinea:

> Life in the other world goes on just like life in this one. Houses are built exactly like houses on earth, and there as here pigs swarm in the streets. Fields are tilled and crops got in; ghostly men marry ghostly women, who give birth to ghostly children. The same old round of love and hate, of quarrelling and fighting, of battle, murder and sudden death goes on in the shadowy realm below ground just as in the more solid world above ground.[8]

What is more, in many of these non-Christian beliefs, the social and economic distinctions of this world are perpetuated. We have seen how the king of ancient Ur of Mesopotamia must have his servants and others of the court buried with him so that he could be certain of being waited upon in the afterlife in the proper manner. Though this wholesale slaughter is not common, the principle behind it is. If a man is a servant here, as a rule he is a servant hereafter. Entirely lacking is our common appraisal of death as the great leveler.

Among the ancient civilized peoples of the west the afterlife is grim in another way. In Homer we discover that the *psyche* (ψυχή), which indwells man during his earthly sojourn, at death escapes to Erebus, the abode of King Hades, and there goes on to live its own dreary existence. Quite appropriately, those in that realm were termed shades, for existence in the underground region was indeed only a shadow of life enjoyed on earth.

In Book 11 of Homer's *Odyssey*, Odysseus (Ulysses) is sent on a mission to the realm of Hades. There the souls of the departed are spoken of as "airy phantoms," uttering "gibbering cries." Odysseus is asked why he has left the "light of day to come among the dead . . . to this joyless land?" The shades are even unable to converse with him until they drink the revitalizing blood of the sheep he brought with him.[9] When he finally gets to talk to his mother, Odysseus tries three times to embrace her, but, like a shadow or a dream, she slips through his arms. She explains that such is the way of death; "the soul slips away like a dream and flutters on the air."

Odysseus also finds his old friend and fellow-comrade Achilles, and in the course of their conversation suggests to him that he who had been so heroic a character on earth must have a position of prominence in Hades. To this Achilles replies, "Speak to me not of the dead. I'd rather be a hireling of the meanest man on earth than to rule over all the people of the Underworld."[10]

Now, it is true that at some point in the past a few humans were admitted to the Elysian Fields (to use Homer's nomenclature) or to the Isles of the Blest (to use Hesiod's nomenclature), where, in the company of some of the divinities, they enjoyed a kind of heaven—"There neither snow is nor wintry weather nor any rain and Oceanus sends forth only the gentle-blowing breezes of the west wind"[11]—but that kind of afterlife had been closed to mortals. Long ago, a few earth-dwellers—those who were semidivine or specially favored by the gods—had been translated in the manner of Enoch, but for all other mortals it was the gloomy life of the dark underworld.

Nor was the lot of the departed any better in Roman thinking. Ancestry counted for much among the ancient Romans, and this usually meant ancestor worship. Yet, as civilization and sophistication developed, this reverence for the ancestor diminished. The *manes* (the Latin equivalent of shades) dwelt in a dim and gloomy underworld, a land without sun.

Very much the same can be said of primitive Israel. It may well be that in very ancient time the Hebrews thought the soul had a measure of power and consciousness; but certainly long before the time of the Prophets, life in the Hebrew Sheol had become a mere subsistence. Sheol, dim and shadowy, over and over again is pictured in the most miserable terms. Job echoes the common concept of the place when he speaks of what awaits him there:

> Are not the days of my life few?
>   Let me alone, that I may find a little comfort
> before I go whence I shall not return,
>   to the land of gloom and deep darkness,
> the land of gloom and chaos,
>   where light is as darkness.
>   Job 10:20–22

Or, take Psalm 88, where Sheol is described as the nether world of *Abaddon* (destruction), a land where the shades *(rephaim)*, separated from God, dwell in "darkness" and "forgetfulness":

> Dost thou work wonders for the dead?
>   Do the shades rise up to praise thee?
> Is thy steadfast love declared in the grave,
>   Or thy faithfulness in Abaddon?
> Are thy wonders known in the darkness,
>   or thy saving help in the land of forgetfulness?
>   Psalm 88:10–12

Elsewhere in the Old Testament, Sheol is described as "a land of silence,"[12] a "pit,"[13] and a place of "dust"[14]—certainly a destination to avoid as long as possible. True, as the New Testament era approached, Sheol became segregated and a little more attractive for the righteous, but, except for the resurrected life promised in such passages as the Little Apocalypse of Isaiah and the heavenly visions of Enoch, anything like a happy expectation is completely lacking.

Standing in dramatic contrast to the old pictures of despair is the New Testament one of joyous hope. Two eschatological ideas dominate: First there is Christ's preaching of the Kingdom of God. Second there is the tremendous emphasis placed by the New Testament writers upon life in the Resurrected Lord. These two considerations fit together; treatment of both of them is necessary for our understanding of what is meant when Jesus speaks of "eternal life" or refers to himself as "the Resurrection and the Life." Let us now consider these two ideas, one at a time.

Shortly after the death of John the Baptist, Jesus appeared in the province of Galilee, in the northern part of Palestine, preaching "The Kingdom of God is at hand." As the crowds gathered about him, Jesus made it clear that this Kingdom must be prepared for; there must be repentance and remission of sins. Jesus agreed with John the Baptist on this matter, but, unlike the Baptist, he declared this to be a message not of doom but of joyful and happy news— "The Gospel" (*euangelion*—εὐαγγέλιον), as the New Testament writers call it.[15] All who would listen were invited to share in the joys and blessings of the Kingdom.

As the Synoptic Gospels* present the life of Christ, the good news of the Kingdom dominated his ministry. What did he mean by it? Although the Old Testament never uses the term *Kingdom of God* as such, we have seen how that portion of our Bible does provide the kernel of the idea.

---

* Matthew, Mark, and Luke are called the "Synoptic Gospels" because they present a synopsis (common view or order) of the life of Christ.

Beginning with Amos, the Prophets spoke of a future time on earth when God's rule would prevail. God would be the future King of Israel. The Prophets called this the Day of the Lord.

This prophetic Day of the Lord is now called the "Kingdom of God" or the "Kingdom of Heaven." Luke and Mark prefer the former, while Matthew prefers the latter. Matthew, the most Jewish of the three Synoptic evangelists, shares in the natural reluctance of Jews to make too frequent use of the divine name.* Regardless of who uses them, the terms *Kingdom of God* and *Kingdom of Heaven* are interchangeable. They both represent the old Day of the Lord, except that for Jesus this kingdom is not only a future expectation but at the same time a present reality.

Matthew is the evangelist who favors the future aspect of the Kingdom, though the others do not neglect it. All the evangelists (especially Matthew) use the appellation "the Son of Man," a title which, though frequently used in the Old Testament to mean simply a man, became developed by the apocalyptic writers to mean the Messiah who comes in the clouds of glory.† This expectation of the Messiah at the end of time is usually called "the Second Coming."[16]

This Second Coming aspect of the Kingdom is seen in many of the parables. The Parable of the Ten Virgins (Matthew 25:1–13) challenges all to be ready for this unknown time— "Watch, therefore, for you know neither the day nor the hour." Or, there is the Parable of the Talents, where Christ is compared to a man going away on a long journey and coming back at an unexpected time (Matthew 25:14–30). It is, moreover, made quite clear that the Son of Man will one day come as judge of the

---

* Here and elsewhere in this book we are using the word *evangelist* in a technical sense, meaning a writer of one of the four biographies of Christ. Though there is debate over the identity of the biographers, they are usually identified as Matthew, Mark, Luke, and John.

† Though, as I have pointed out, by "son of man" most of the Old Testament simply means a man, and Daniel means the people of Israel, it seems obvious that this term is picked up by the apocalyptic writers to mean none other than the Messiah sent from God. However there has been a great deal written to contradict this view. Compare T. W. Manson, *The Son of Man in Daniel, Enoch and the Gospels* (Manchester University Press, 1950). The argument of Manson is based on the meaning of *ben adam* as Ezekiel uses it, "a member of the human race." Despite this fact, this author maintains that all one has to do is to read such passages as I Enoch 46:1 and following to realize that often the original meaning of a term at best only slightly restricts its future development. In fact a multitude of English words could be cited to prove that often the modern meaning of a word bears practically no relationship to the original meaning. See also Alan Richardson's treatment of *Son of Man* in his *Word Book*, p. 230 and following. He shows that the *Son of Man* has other possible interpretations.

whole earth, when all the nations will assemble before him (Matthew 25:31–46).

The idea of a future rule and future world judgment also implies that one day this Kingdom of Heaven, which is not as obvious in this present world as it should be, will eventually become a reality for the whole earth. God is more than the King of Israel. He is King of all peoples. Both Judaism and Christianity look forward to the time when all secular powers will recognize the Most High. Christ speaks of his disciples sitting on thrones judging the twelve tribes of Israel,[17] but he also speaks of all the world's coming to the heavenly feast and dining with the patriarchs of Israel: "I tell you, many will come from the east and the west and sit at table with Abraham, Isaac and Jacob in the kingdom of heaven...."[18] The same expectation is proclaimed in the last book of the Bible, "The Kingdom of the world has become the kingdom of our Lord and of his Christ, and he shall reign for ever and ever."[19] This hope was also prayed for by the Jews in New Testament times and is still prayed for by them— "May He establish His Kingdom during your life and during your days, and during the life of all the house of Israel."[20] Likewise does the Christian pray, as Jesus taught us, "Thy Kingdom come."

This leads us to another aspect of the Kingdom: This prayer our Lord gave us is not just one for the folding up of this world and the Second Coming, but it is also a prayer for the spread of the Kingdom right now— "Thy will be done in earth as it is in Heaven." It is not to be denied that Jesus often talked about the future Kingdom and the coming of the Son of Man at the end of time, but he also affirmed the present reality of the Kingdom, and this is the main emphasis of the New Testament's teaching on the subject. The new age of the Kingdom was already at work in this world. The Fourth Gospel, with its strong emphasis on "realized eschatology" makes this present reality very clear— "This is life eternal" and "I am the resurrection and the life."

Realized eschatology is the idea of bringing the *eschaton* into the present. To a large extent, in the Fourth Gospel, the Second Coming is the coming of the Holy Spirit. Though this realized eschatology of John is not as obvious in the synoptic gospels, it is there by implication, for the *eschaton*, the end result of God's plan of salvation has broken through into the reality of the present. The ministry, the death, and the resurrection of Jesus—as the end revelation—have in the present arrived. This is not to say, however, that John has no futurist eschatology, for he speaks of "the

Last Day" seven times, and his is the only Gospel to use that term.

With regard to the present reality of the Kingdom, Jesus asks the question, "With what can we compare the kingdom of God . . . ? It is like a grain of mustard seed, which . . . is the smallest of all the seeds . . . ; yet when it is sown it grows up and becomes the greatest of all shrubs, and puts forth large branches, so that the birds of the air can make nests in its shade."[21] Or, at another time, Jesus compares the Kingdom to leaven, which permeates the whole dough and causes it to increase.[22] Surely, this new life in Christ would permeate and transform the whole of society.

In the eleventh chapter of Luke, Jesus sends out seventy missionaries. He instructs them to say to the people, "The Kingdom of God has come near to you."[23] Likewise, the exorcisms Jesus performs are signs of the arrival of the Kingdom on earth: "But if it is by the finger of God that I cast out demons, then the kingdom of God has come upon you."[24]

At one time during his ministry, Jesus was asked by the Pharisees when he expected that the Kingdom of God was coming. He answered them, "The Kingdom of God is not coming with signs to be observed; nor will they say, 'Lo, here it is!' or 'There!' for behold, the kingdom of God is within you."[25] A certain scribe declared that Love is the fulfilling of the Law; to this Jesus replied, "You are not far from the kingdom of God."[26] Likewise, St. Paul describes the Kingdom of God in present terms—"righteousness and peace and joy in the Holy Spirit."[27]

Whether it is in the present or in the future, this Kingdom is God's gift. There is the story of the rich young man who wanted to follow Christ.[28] To him Jesus explains that his followers must come to him without any encumbrances of property. The young man goes away sadly, for he possesses great wealth. Afterwards Jesus comments to his disciples, "How hard it is for those who have riches to enter the kingdom of God."[29] The disciples are astonished and ask, "Then who can be saved?" Jesus answers, "With men it is impossible, but not with God."[30] The followers of Jesus who had entered the Kingdom were not ordinary people, but were living under the new power of the Spirit. To put it another way, Jesus said in effect, "If you accept the gift of the Kingdom of God, then what is impossible for ordinary men becomes possible for you."

The growth of the Kingdom was even more obvious after our Lord's death and resurrection, and here we take up the other one of the two chief eschatological themes that dominate the New Testament. It is the life *in* the Resurrected Lord.

When Jesus died on the cross, the disciples knew he was safe in the hands of the Father. Did he not say to the penitent thief, "Verily today, thou shalt be with me in Paradise"?[31] The *today* came through very clearly—not at the end of time, but *today*. And were not the final words of Jesus from that cross, "Father, into thy hands I commend my spirit"?[32] The despair on the part of the disciples was not centered in a lack of faith that their Master had that day entered the afterlife. Rather the despair was that he had finished his life on earth without completing what he said he came to do—to establish the Kingdom of God. So it then seemed to the disciples.[33]

When they realized that Jesus had risen from the dead in the miraculous way that was his, the disciples rightfully regarded it as a victorious vindication of all that he had said and done. It was the victory of the Kingdom, if you will—though of course there had to be some adjustment in the thinking of the disciples as to the nature of this Kingdom. They now came to understand that this Kingdom was far more than an earthly restoration of Israel. (See Acts 1:6–7.) Jesus told Pilate, "My Kingship is not of this world,"[34] and by this he meant not a materialistic Kingdom, not one anchored on this earth or one which dealt with earthly territories. Yet elsewhere Jesus made it clear that the Kingdom was very much available to this world, available both now and in the future.

More than that, the events of that first Easter season infused into the community of believers a new life that made them very different people. We could say that the Resurrection made even more obvious than before the fact that the followers of Christ were living in the Kingdom, that they were now enjoying eternal life. Because Christ was raised from the dead, his followers were raised up into a new life, or—to put it another way—they were caught up into His eternal life. St. Paul exhorts his readers to realize the implications of this Resurrection:

> If you then are risen with Christ, seek those things which are above, where Christ sits on the right hand of God.
> Colossians 3:1 [my translation]

Baptism was the means of admission into this new life. Baptism—except in case of the infirm—in those days was normally by total immersion in the water.* Thus, it was logical and natural to compare a person's

---

* It was not until the second or third centuries that forms of baptism other than by immersion were adopted.

baptism with what happened to Jesus between that first Good Friday and that first Easter Day. The believer goes down into the water and rises to a new life in Christ, in the same way that Christ went down into the bowels of the earth and rose to his new resurrected life. Consequently, St. Paul writes:

> For if we have been planted together in the likeness of his death, we shall be also in the likeness of his resurrection. Now if we be dead with Christ, we believe that we shall also live with him.
> Romans 6:5, 8

> It is a faithful saying: For if we be dead with him, we shall also live with him.
> II Timothy 2:11

As life in the early Church progressed, the words spoken to Mary and Martha became increasingly meaningful, "I am the Resurrection and the Life," or the words spoken following the Last Supper, "This is Life Eternal." There may have been confusion in the minds of the followers of Jesus in the early days of the Gospel preaching concerning the meaning of eternal life, but as time went on, the members of the Church, looking back on this teaching, came to know what it meant. Even though the Christians were still looking forward to the imminent end of the world and the second coming of Christ, they also understood that the coming of the Kingdom did not have to wait for the end of time. Eternal life and the life in the resurrected Christ was to be *realized* now. His resurrected and ascended life was now indwelling the life of the Church, and when one came to believe and to be baptized into the Body of Christ he became a member of the Kingdom right then. The same thing may be said to the modern Christian: When we learn to believe—really believe, that is—in the resurrection of Christ, we find ourselves living in the eternal dimension, now.

This new life, it should be thoroughly understood, is to be realized in the fellowship of the Church. In the New Testament, with respect to both the concept of the life in the Kingdom and the life in the resurrected Lord, there is a tremendous stress on fellowship, the corporate life of the Church, mutual responsibility, and love for one another.

Many people are anxious to know, and they often ask the question, "What is going to happen to me as an individual when this life is over?" We might better ask, as did the early followers of Christ, "What does God intend for us, his children?" Viewed that way, this concern ceases to be one of selfish seeking after the occult and instead becomes one of fellowship in Christ through the power of the Holy Spirit.

The world-famous theologian Dr. Emile Brunner calls our attention to the fact that just as the prophetic message of the Old Testament was concerned not with the individual after death but with the nation, so, too, is the New Testament emphasis on the coming of the Kingdom.[35] It is a corporate, not an individual, reality; for all the resurrection experience is bound up with the Church. With only two exceptions—the appearance to Peter[36] and the appearance to Mary Magdalene in the Garden[37]—all appearances of the resurrected Christ during those forty days are to more than one person, and usually they are to the central group of his followers. And even these two appearances to individuals are tied in with the fellowship; immediately the two of them report what happened to the brethren.* Jesus promised his disciples, "Where two or three are gathered together there am I in the midst of them."[38] When he commissioned his disciples as apostles† and sent them forth into all the world with instructions to baptize into the fellowship, he undergirded them with the promise, "I am with you always even unto the end of the world."[39] Or consider the farewell discourses in the Fourth Gospel (chapters 13–16). There is the command to love one another, the exhortation to remain grafted into the life of the Vine, the need to be of service to others. And, of course, with all the farewell conversations, wherever we find them, there is the promise of the Holy Spirit's indwelling the life of the Church. Jesus' "presence is a living creative experience through faith and the Holy Ghost."[40]

All this emphasis on fellowship and concern for one another underscores the reality of the Body of Christ. Bishop J. A. T. Robinson, in an early monograph, *The Body*, reminds us that we have so taken for granted the use of the word *body* to mean a corporate reality that we fail to realize that it was quite an unfamiliar figure of speech to the people to whom St.

---

* Of course, it must be admitted that St. Paul's vision of Christ on the Damascus Road was to one individual. Acts 9:1–9, 22:4 and following, 26:12 and following. Though St. Paul rightly claims this confrontation was just as valid as the appearances to the others, it was of a different type, for it does not fit into the interval between the Resurrection itself and what is usually regarded as the Day of Ascension.

† The word *disciple* means a learner. *Apostle* means one sent forth. Though the two words are often used interchangeably in the Gospel narrative, strictly speaking the disciples did not become apostles until after the Resurrection, when they were commissioned by the Risen Lord.

Paul was writing.[41] It is a very important understanding of the nature of the Church, though, for the doctrine of what we call "the mystical body of Christ" is tied up with the Christian's hope of the resurrection and the renewal of one's own body. St. Paul writes in this connection, "Do you not know that your bodies are members of Christ?"[42] The implication is that the Church is the being of Christ himself, and what happened to Christ has happened and is happening to the Church. If the Old Testament's final message about eschatology is that there must be a resurrection, so, too, does the New Testament stress the fact that the life in the Church, permeated by the resurrected Christ and the Holy Spirit is, in fact, the "operation of the world of the resurrection breaking into the present."[43] Since Christ has "overcome the world" as the Fourth Gospel puts it,[44] the world to come is now a present reality. This means that the resurrection of the future has become a reality of the present— "Whosoever believes in me shall live though he were dead."[45]

It follows, then, that if life in Christ is the only true life, then death is something quite other than the cessation of bodily functions. Though, indeed, we die to sin through baptism, in that our old self is washed away and drowned,[46] there is another kind of death against which St. Paul warns us— "the wages of sin."[47] The person who gives himself to activities contrary to the purposes of God is dead even though he still survives physically. But the man who, in keeping with the spirit of Christ, devotes himself to eternal endeavors is very much alive—always.

As we have observed, primitive religions have a belief in an afterlife without any connection with any deity. Likewise many modern spiritualists can be certain of the afterlife without acknowledging the need of a personal God, but, as Dr. Baillie points out, "We must remind ourselves that the traditional Christian name for such endless existence without God is not eternal life but *eternal death.*"[48] If life is meaningless here and unrelated to the Eternal here, surely it would be just as meaningless and unrelated—perhaps even more so—after the cessations of bodily functions. St. Thomas à Kempis wrote, "I had rather choose to be a pilgrim on earth with Thee than without Thee to possess heaven. Where Thou art, there is heaven: and where Thou art not, there is death and hell."[49] John Greenleaf Whittier put the same thought this way:

> To turn aside from Thee is hell,
> To walk with Thee is heaven![50]

This Is Life Eternal

When I was an undergraduate at Sewanee (the University of the South) during the late thirties, we often had a visitor on the campus in the person of Dr. John Erskine, then a popular lecturer and writer of best-sellers. On one of these visits I heard him say, "The great mistake we make is to think that immortality begins just as soon as a person dies. Eternal life," he insisted, "is choosing to do now the things we are intended to do forever." So many of us, Dr. Erskine lamented, spend all of our time in only temporal things, when we should be spending our time on activities and relationships that endure forever.

This observation of Dr. Erskine's, while it is excellent from the point of view of the practical philosopher, might well be modified by the theologian to make clear that these "activities" include those pertaining to the good of all mankind and those pertaining to friendship with the eternal Christ.

That, then, is life eternal—a life of dedication to Christ as a personal savior, a life centered in the Christian fellowship as a member of the Body of Christ, an identification with Christian purposes in life. Such a life and such a relationship, instead of being broken off at death, will be intensified and perfected. Viewed that way, eternal life is a life of joy in an eternal, happy relationship.

In the most theological of all his writings—The Epistle to the Church in Rome—the Apostle Paul, after an involved discussion on the Law, bursts out into glorious poetry in his description of this eternal relationship:

> Who shall separate us from the love of Christ? Shall tribulation, or distress, or persecution, or famine, or nakedness, or peril, or sword? . . . No, in all these things we are more than conquerors through him that loved us. For I am persuaded, that neither death, nor life, nor angels, nor principalities, nor powers, nor things present, nor things to come, nor height, nor depth, nor anything else in all creation, will be able to separate us from the love of God, which is in Christ Jesus our Lord.
>
> Romans 8:35, 37–39

6

Life Here

An amusing anecdote is told of Thales, the father of western philosophy. The setting is the Greek island of Miletus, where Thales lived and taught during the sixth century B.C. As the account goes, Thales was walking along one day, gazing up into the sky, pondering the movements of the heavenly bodies. Not at all conscious of where he was going, suddenly he fell into a well. Humiliated enough by the experience, when he was finally able to climb out, Thales was further humiliated by an old woman who scoffed, "You are so engrossed with the heavens that you can't see what is at your feet."

Socrates, commenting upon this incident to his disciples, rightly observes, "Anyone who becomes a philosopher is open to similar mockery." [1]

If it is commonplace to reproach the philosopher for having his head in the clouds and not seeing what is in front of him, it is also commonplace—perhaps even more so—to reproach the theologian for the same fault, especially when the theologian places much importance on eschatology.

In the cotton mill districts of North Carolina serious industrial disturbances developed in 1930. Though the workers were nearly all pious religious people, reared in the fundamentalist tradition, they had reason to question the hypocritical attempts of the churches to justify the poverty in which they had become enmeshed. They expressed their bitterness with this doggerel:

> Hope and pray,
> Work all day,
> Live on hay.
> You'll eat pie
> In the sky,
> By and by.[2]

Communists for most of the twentieth century have accused Christianity—and other religions as well—of "pie-in-the-skyism," neglecting this world for the next. Oft-quoted is this statement from Karl Marx, the father of modern communism:

> Religion is the sigh of the oppressed creature, the heart of a heartless world and the soul of soulless conditions. It is the opium of the people.[3]

Although not all adherents of this political-economic philosophy would go that far, the general feeling of the Marxists is that religion dulls one's sensibility to the sufferings of this world by the illusionary hope of a wonderful world to come. Mindful of how the hierarchy of Russian Orthodoxy supported the Czarist regime, Lenin, the father of Russian Marxism, would describe religion as "one of the forms of spiritual oppression":

> The helplessness of the exploited classes in their struggle with the exploiters just as inevitably generates faith in a better life beyond the grave as the helplessness of the savage in his struggle with nature produces faith in gods, devils, miracles, etc. To him who works and is poor all his life religion teaches passivity and patience in earthly life, consoling him with the hope of a heavenly reward. To those who live on the labour of others religion teaches benevolence in earthly life, offering them a very cheap justification for all their exploiting existence and selling tickets to heavenly happiness at a reduced price.[4]

The Gospel record, too—on the surface at least—tends to support the evidence for this criticism. Throughout the New Testament there is tremendous emphasis on the last day, the *eschaton*. So, logically enough, St. Paul writes, "The day of the Lord is coming like a thief in the night."[5] Even though Jesus cautioned, "Of that day or that hour no one knows, not even the angels in heaven, nor the Son, but only the Father,"[6] the early Church to a man was certain that the end was not far off, even within the lifetime of that first generation of Christians. That is why we have this warning from St. Peter: "The end of all things is at hand; therefore keep sane and sober for your prayers."⁷ Or, that is why St. Paul writes to the Church in Corinth that, since there isn't much time left on earth for the human race, "everyone should remain in the state in which he was called. Were you a slave when called? Never mind. But if you gain your freedom, avail yourself of the opportunity."⁸

Along with this apparent hesitation to do anything about the social order in New Testament times, it has also to be acknowledged that no political or social or economic reform system was written from the time of Plato's *Republic* (c. 340 B.C.) to the time of Sir Thomas Moore's *Utopia* (1516 A.D.), despite the fact that a large part of this intervening period is always described as "the Age of Faith." Even in St. Augustine's *City of God* (413–426 A.D.), it is to be observed, there is not a word about social reform. All that St. Augustine expected civil governments to do was to keep an uneasy peace between wars.

This is only half the story, however; in fact, much less than half. The other part of the story is most surprising, for the facts support just the opposite point of view. Christianity throughout its history, up until modern times, has been the *only* voice in all the world for any kind of social reform. Christianity (together with its Judaistic background) has been the only philosophy or religion in all the ancient and medieval world concerned with the rights and needs of the common man; and, contrary to the impression one usually gets from looking at medieval history, Christianity has consistently been a propelling force for the amelioration of conditions of society. Moreover, as shortly it will become more apparent, the Marxists would never have thought of social reform if Christianity had not pointed the way.

Let's begin the investigation by another look at the New Testament. True, New Testament Christianity did stress the *eschaton*, but *never* did this stress on the *eschaton* lessen the faithful's responsibility for the *now*. It was pointed out in the last chapter that the Kingdom of Heaven is both present and future. When the Kingdom is compared to leaven, it means it is a force which permeates the whole of society—*this society on earth*—until the whole becomes leavened, until this world takes on the characteristics of the Kingdom. Despite the fact that the early Church expected an immediate end to this creation, in no case did the Church fail to teach social justice and brotherhood. In fact, it was the expectation of the end that stimulated concern for the present rather than retarding it. Keeping one's self in readiness for the return of Christ strengthens moral power instead of undermining it. In the New Testament, amid all this eschatological expectation, there isn't even the faintest sign of resignation to evil. On the contrary, Christians were exhorted to be good examples: "By well doing you put to silence the accusations of foolish men."[9] Christians were to be above defilement;[10] they were to live as examples of honesty and trustworthiness.[11]

Everyone admits that the unique contribution of Jesus' ethics is his stress upon the sacredness of the human personality. This is seen in countless examples in his life and teaching. Jesus begins his ministry in the synagogue of Nazareth where he reads what amounts to a keynote address, outlining the purpose of his ministry. It is from the Prophet Isaiah:

> The Spirit of the Lord is upon me, because he has anointed me to preach good news to the poor. He has sent me to proclaim release to the captives and recovering of sight to the blind, to set at liberty those who are oppressed, to preach the acceptable year of the Lord.
> Luke 4:18–19

To illustrate the Christian's concern for all kinds of people, Jesus tells the Parable of the Lost Sheep,[12] the Lost Coin,[13] and the Prodigal Son.[14] He demonstrates his concern for children and tells us that little children—or other little people—are just as important in God's eyes as the big and successful people.[15] He allows a woman of the street to anoint his feet and wipe them dry with her hair.[16] When seen in the company of sinners and the hated tax gatherers, he explains that his mission is to those who need him most.[17] He assures us of God's concern for each and every individual by telling us that the hairs of our head are numbered and that God knows when even a sparrow falls to the ground.[18] Likewise, St. Paul, when he sends back the slave Onesimus, writes to Philemon that he is sending back no longer a slave but a "brother beloved."[19] And, please note, all of this human concern was not in terms of a future Kingdom in Heaven, but of how members of the Kingdom are to live here and now.

The future and the present are tied up together, however, and we must not forget that. How a person behaves toward his fellows in the present shapes his future, and what a person expects of the future shapes his present. This is best seen in the Parable of the Last Judgment.[20] Here Christ is pictured on his throne as the supreme judge of all mankind. He separates the righteous from the unrighteous, as a Palestinian shepherd at sun-down separates the sheep from the goats. The righteous are sent into everlasting bliss, while the wicked are sent into damnation. The important aspect of the parable is not the pageantry or the harsh judgment, but the basis of the judgment: "I was hungry and you gave me food, I was thirsty and you gave me drink," etc. And when those judged ask when they ever saw the Lord in any of those situations, he answers, "Inasmuch as you have done it unto one of the least of these my brethren, you have done it unto me."

All this emphasis placed on the individual and those in need stands in sharp contrast to the accepted pagan standards of ancient times. You can't find a better appeal for teamwork than in Plato's *Republic*, but you look in vain for any emphasis on the individual's importance. Commonplace in the Greek-Roman world was the custom of exposing unwanted children to death: there was nothing precious about a child simply because he was a child. And, as for a slave, such a person Aristotle describes as merely a "living tool."[21]

The high standard of morality and concern for people in this world found in the New Testament continues throughout Christian history. I am indebted to Ray C. Petry, professor of church history at Duke University, more than to any other person, for the factual evidence to support this contention. In his very scholarly book *Christian Eschatology and Social Thought*, Professor Petry examines the first 1,500 years of the Christian era, demonstrating how writer after writer and preacher after preacher made unmistakably clear that the Church was very much involved with the human concerns of his age. Petry sums up his thesis this way:

> The realization dawns, however slowly, that in the first fifteen hundred years of Christian history, at least, eschatology provided the basic motivation and nucleating matter for Christian social thinking. Dawning, also, is the discovery that the ecclesiastical historian must play his part in reanalyzing and re-synthesizing the long ignored intimacy of eschatology and Christian social thought.[22]

Petry proves beyond any doubt that the Church in word and deed has consistently revealed a deep concern for the welfare of the individual here on earth, a responsibility for all levels of society. Throughout the centuries the Church constantly exhorts its members to care for the poor, the needy, the sick, and the downtrodden. Moreover the Church was the *only* institution in all of ancient and medieval society where one might begin from the lowest of the social strata and rise to the highest.

If, on the other hand, you are looking for models of the ideal society during these times, you will not find them; that kind of writing had to wait for Sir (and Saint) Thomas Moore's *Utopia* and its many successors. What you do find in the course of medieval Church history, however, is work among the downtrodden and poor, exhortations to treat all men as brothers, the building of hospitals, universities, and hostels; and you find all this social concern, not among the materialists or the Hindus or the Buddhists or the Shintoists or the primitive pagan religions, but among those who inherit the Judeo-Christian ethic. Evidence for what the Church actually did do in the care of the poor and the sick was dramatically and sadly presented for all of England to see when Henry VIII dissolved the monasteries (beginning in 1536) and unleashed upon the countryside hordes of the sick and destitute hitherto cared for by monks and nuns. The problem of these hapless creatures swarming over the land continued for years afterwards.[23]

We haven't space to go through the whole array of personalities and writings that Petry displays to prove that an eschatological orientation motivates social concern rather than hampers it. Two examples, typical of the many, will clinch the point, one from ancient times and the other from the early Middle Ages.

Our first example is St. Chrysostom (347–407), with whose prayer many are familiar.[24] As Petry puts it, "Chrysostom is under the firm impression . . . that the present may be most effectively served by turning its attention to that which is beyond."[25] In a homily on Matthew he voices this plea:

> Let us show forth then a new kind of life. Let us make earth, heaven; let us thereby show the Greeks, of how great blessings they are deprived. For when they behold in us good conversation, they will look upon the very face of the kingdom of heaven.[26]

Chrysostom insists that ". . . it is possible even while abiding here, to do all, as though already placed on high."[27] It is, as Petry observes, a case of the future pulling us forward rather than a case of the past pushing us. In other words, God's Kingdom on earth is not pushed on by a series of past events, but is rather pulled forward by the ideal Kingdom that is yet to be.[28]

Now for the second example: By looking at stone carvings on cathedrals, a favorite homiletic theme of the Middle Ages was the Parable of the

Last Judgment (Matthew 25:31–46). Thus these carvings and murals are saying that when Judgment Day comes at the end of time, it will be a social experience, based on what one did or did not do with respect to his responsibility to others. One example among many is a paraphrase of this parable from Cynewulf, the Anglo-Saxon poet who wrote around 750:

> Now with friends receive ye the Kingdom of My Father, that was prepared for you in winsomeness before all worlds, blessedness with bliss, bright beauty of home, where ye with well-loved men may see true weal of life, sweet heavenly joy. This have ye merited since joyfully ye received with gracious heart wretched men, the needy of the world; when in My name they humbly craved your pity then did ye grant them help and shelter, unto the hungry bread, clothes to the naked, and those that lay diseased in pain, enthralled of sickness, their souls ye softly stayed with love of heart. All that ye did unto Me what time ye sought them out with kindly love, ever strengthening their souls with comfort. Wherefore in blessedness with My beloved long shall ye reap reward.[29]

We do not want to infer that everything was well during the Middle Ages with respect to the Christian's concern for social amelioration. There were gross instances of injustice then as there are today, and some of those were in the name of Christianity. No one during the Middle Ages questioned either the stratification of society on earth or in Heaven; no one was interested in revolution or democracy, either within or without the Church; but there was a stress on mutuality within the Christian world not to be found anywhere else. Only by concern for others could one hope to gain the heavenly realm.[30]

Since the close of the Middle Ages, this has not always been so. With the dawn of the Renaissance, the Church has been at times a deterrent to social reform. At other times it has pioneered it. R. H. Tawney, in his classic work *Religion and the Rise of Capitalism,* demonstrates that, while the Church and the economic world were tied together in medieval times, during the sixteenth and seventeenth centuries a rift developed. The Church went one way and the economic world went another. Thus it was possible for a certain statesman of the early part of the nineteenth century to express amazement that a clergyman should wish to bring about social and economic reform. As this statesman expressed it, "Things have come to a pretty pass if religion is going to interfere with private life,"[31] and in his "private life," of course, he included the economic activities. But, Tawney acknowledges, the age when men believe the Church should "leave the present world to men of business and the devil" is drawing to a close.[32]

A man whose name all Anglican clergy will recognize as a great liturgiologist of the early 1900s is the Reverend Percy Dermer. But Percy Dermer was also a Christian reformer. He wrote, "Everyone who says the Lord's Prayer definitely proclaims himself a fellow-worker with God for a perfect social state: he prays for a heaven on earth, for God's will to be as perfectly done here as it is in heaven."[33] We are all familiar, too, with the tremendous leadership of Archbishop William Temple. In an address delivered during World War II, shortly before his untimely death, he said, "Let us become conscious of ourselves as a fellowship pledged to God and to one another to stand and contend for international and social justice...."[34] Those churchmen who desire no social change are, today, more and more in the minority. For every churchleader who would keep the status quo, we can point to ten who are working for a better society on earth.

It was the Church—all denominations—that led the resettlement of refugees when the need in our time called for it, whether European, Cuban, Hungarian, Vietnamese, Latin American, or whatever.

The ecumenical teamwork of Anglican Bishop David Sheppard and Roman Catholic Archbishop Derek Worlock formed what they called a "Christian partnership in a hurt City," the city being Liverpool. A book they co-authored, *Better Together*, describes how the two of them provided moral and spiritual leadership amid mob violence, a stubborn local leftist government which failed to understand the housing situation, and a conservative national government that was less than sympathetic to the city's adversity.[35] Everyone agrees that the most important thing the two bishops have accomplished is to give the city hope—and they have done that, for they are both men of God.

It is the Church in South Africa (Anglican, Roman Catholic, and some "Non-Conformist") that has lead a heroic battle against that government's apartheid policy. Well known in our day is the leadership of Desmond Tutu, first black Anglican Archbishop of Cape Town and winner of the Nobel Peace Prize, who as a man of peace had walked a tight-rope between the conservative South African ruling National Party and the radical African National Congress. Anyone who has come in contact with Bishop Tutu knows him as a deeply spiritual man of God, much involved in helping people on their way to Heaven, while at the same time working to make the world a little more like Heaven.

Another Nobel Peace Prize winner is Mother Theresa of Calcutta, India, a remarkably saintly woman who worked in the slums, ran a house for the dying, and ministered to lepers.

Though at one time the Roman Catholic Church in Latin America sided with the entrenched oppressive governments, wherever they were found, there are now no remaining churches that I know of which do not work hard for the rights of the common man, a work that often carries with it a great risk, for the Church is a serious threat to selfish land owners and oppressive politicians.

In this recitation of involved Christians, I should also point out that, although all the churches and all the leaders mentioned are concerned with the improvement of life here, none of them forgets that the work done here is work for the Kingdom which endures to eternity. I would, moreover, like to make the observation that some of the most successful churches in the social-reform movement are also the ones that stress the sacramental and prayer life and constantly assure their people that they are marching toward the Heavenly Kingdom of perfect brotherhood.

And, by the way, let it also be made clear in all this discussion that I am not advocating any one political-economic system over another, except insofar as we must make the observation that any political-economic system that is really Christian must be egalitarian or democratic in the true sense of the word, respecting the rights and needs of everyone.

The thought that a Christian government respects the rights and needs of all people brings us back to the subject of Marxian communism and its hostility to Christianity. Marxism has traditionally placed the impact of its opposition to Christianity on the Church's failure to involve itself in social reform. This, as we have seen, is sometimes true, but more often not. What disturbs the Christian about Marxism is not its failure to become involved in social reform—it does that quite effectively and efficiently—but the way the involvement is accomplished and what that involvement often ignores with respect to the sacredness of human personality.

Prior to the arrival of Mikhail Gorbachev, Marxist communism, as worked out in Russia, has not hesitated to indulge in organized terror, marauding, and depopulating of entire towns. The so-called Red Terror of the 1920s brought death to two million persons, and when the peasants revolted against forced collective farming, Stalin retaliated by killing thousands or shipping many more off to labor camps in Siberia. Purge after purge was repeated by Stalin. In fact it has been estimated that this communist leader was responsible for the deaths of thirty million of his own countrymen, making him the greatest butcher in all of history.[36]

Why is it that Marxist communism, though avowedly interested in the plight of the common man, could be so ruthless in its treatment of the very people it would help? The answer is that individuals, no matter how many, are not as important as the society. The reason this dichotomy can exist is that, oddly enough, Marxism is a Christian heresy.[37] A heresy, we should understand, is a corruption, a warping or a twisting out of shape of the original doctrine, usually an exaggeration of one element of the original at the expense of the other elements. Many of the churches during the period of the Industrial Revolution in England neglected the needs of the working classes. Marx pointed to this neglect and formulated a new political-economic system to cope with the situation—a system which, he believed, would produce a classless society in which the workers would be as well off as anyone else.

Marx's concern for the workers, however, would have been impossible had it not been for the Judeo-Christian ethic that intrinsically concerned itself with this area. It was, then, Christianity that provided the seedbed, the means of spawning Marxism. All the social reforms that Marx would promote were first promoted by Christianity—the need to regard all men as brothers, the hatred of war, the need to be free of bondage, and a wariness of too much wealth. Marx would have everyone produce according to his ability and consume according to his needs.[38] What monastic community is run any other way? That is also the way at least some of the early Christians managed their affairs, as we see by Acts 4:32 and following. Likewise it is the way the Bruderhof, that I came to know and admire in Norfolk, Connecticut, handle their affairs. Likewise it is the way of the New Creation Christian Community ("Jesus people"), a group of over a thousand who live in community, in England, manage their lives, sharing all things in common, yet working out in the world.[39]

During the course of my first writing of this chapter my wife Jane and I were invited to a tea in the neighboring town of Falls Village, Connecticut. Among those present were two retired faculty members of what was once called Yenching University, in Peking, China. We were interested to learn from them how their university came into existence. Originally there were a number of small Christian missionary colleges, of various denominations, scattered throughout China. Dr. Henry W. Luce (father of the American publisher) expressed the belief that if these small colleges could get together in one place and combine faculties and resources they could make a good university. Through Dr. Luce's efforts this was accomplished, and the university became the pride of China. After the Marxists took over, the university was re-named Peking National University. It still remains the pride of China, with many of the pre-revolutionary faculty members remaining in their positions. When U.S. President Nixon visited China on his much-publicized trip of 1972, his motorcade passed in front of the university's entrance. He couldn't avoid noticing the campus, yet no one bothered to point it out or otherwise identify it. Likewise no one in present-day China's government bothers to mention that this institution was put together as a result of Christian missionary activity. The government seems to be quite happy with the university but reluctant to acknowledge that had it not been for Christian missionaries it would not be there.

The story of Peking National University is a parable applicable to all the Marxist world, because all that they have by way of social reform was first pioneered by the Christian Church, and yet they refuse to acknowledge it.

The Communist world has done a great deal of good in a strange variety of ways, including shaming the democratic world into doing something about helping the "Third World." There are no more warlords in China, no more pyramiding of nobility in Russia. The man on the street in Russia or in China is better off economically than he was under the old system. Prostitution and vice are cleaned up in Shanghai. No one is starving, we are told, no one is unemployed.

But there is a sinister element here, even a demonic one. If only the ideal state is important, then the individual is unimportant. And it is this subtle difference between the communist reformer and the Christian reformer that makes *all the difference*. It would almost seem that this faceless god of humanism, like the pagan Moloch described in the Old Testament, demands human sacrifice.[40]

Marxism is a cruel doctrine. People are dying for a cause they will never live to enjoy. As the editor of the British *Marxism Today* candidly admits, a "Marxist feels identified with the common struggle even when as an individual he knows that he may not or will not see the end of it: yes, even when death is involved."[41] Indeed, in the past, millions have died for the communist cause.

And millions have died for Christianity, too, but, as St. Paul puts it, "not without hope."[42] That hope for the Christian is not just for a better society on earth, but also for a sure life to come in Heaven.

Those who are looking for *only* a Utopia on this earth will be concerned with only the claims of earth, and hence they will feel free to do the things that can never be allowed in Heaven; they can take away human rights, slaughter the innocent, and purge the opposition—all in the name of their Utopia on earth. On the other hand, those whose ultimate goal is the Heavenly Kingdom can do none of these inhuman things, for they are answerable to the Lord who created every individual in his own image.

It is not only social reform that should be of concern in this life; the wholeness of life for each person, the proper completion of this life for the individual, as well as for the whole, the full life, the happy life are just as important. This, I claim, Marxism has neglected. Christ said, "I am come that they might have life and have it more abundantly."[43] The coming of Christ into the world is the central theme of Christianity—"He pitched his tent and dwelt among us,"[44] for God loves the world so much that he saw fit to be born into it and live in it, thus sanctifying all life.

It is because of the Incarnation and the importance Jesus places upon this life that suicide has always been wrong for the Christian. Likewise wrong for the Christian is the disparagement of the worth of this world, or morbidness. Except under very unusual circumstances the Christian never looks forward to death as an escape from life. There is no demand, "Stop the world; I want to get off." Instead, as chapter 1 made clear, the Christian accepts life as a blessed gift from God to be lived to the fullest.

One last point for this chapter is the evidence from the near-death experience researchers. In his book *The Light Beyond*, Dr. Raymond A. Moody writes that of all the thousand-plus people whom he has interviewed following their near-death experiences he has "yet to find one who hasn't had a very deep and positive transformation as a result of his experience." Not only are these people transformed into more positive and pleasant individuals, but they become more active in grappling with this world.[45] Whether the cause of this is an assurance that there will be an afterlife or whether it is an exposure to a "higher being," Dr. Moody is not sure, but he is sure that these individuals have more concern for others than before the experience and that all have been changed for the better.[46] Dr. Moody cites the case of a con artist who made his living by cheating widows and running drugs. After his near-death experience he determined he was not going to face another life review like the one he had just been through. He ceased all his past nefarious activities and is now gainfully employed and doing well in an honest profession.[47]

Likewise persons who have had near-death experiences have learned the importance of love. Those who had led selfish lives lead outgoing lives after their experiences, lives concerned with the welfare of others.[48]

An interest in learning, too, is an outcome of a near-death experience, for knowledge is something you can take with you when you go on to the next world. As a consequence of these experiences, people often embark on new careers or take up serious courses of study.

Far from weakening human concern for life now, expectation of a Heaven to come strengthens it.

The previous chapter—"This is Life Eternal"—stressed that all life is or can be eternal life, if it is lived in the eternal setting. This chapter is a corollary to the last one, for if all life can be eternal life, then all life is important. If we don't have to wait until death to realize eternal life, then this life here matters very much. Likewise if we expect bliss and happiness in the future, we should expect happiness and at least some bliss in the present. The true Christian, then, never neglects this world for the next. Instead he constantly works to have the earthly world reflect the perfect society of the heavenly world. This world is part of eternity, and, although it is an imperfect world, the true Christian works in it, constantly striving for it to take on at least some of the characteristics of the perfect world of the future.

7

I Am the Good Shepherd

As the Fourth Gospel presents the life of Jesus, he and his disciples are in Jerusalem following the Feast of Tabernacles. One controversy follows another. Now it is time for Jesus to give his followers some reassurance. The cross is looming ahead; Jesus must prepare his disciples for that mystery. Part of that preparation is the analogy of the Good Shepherd who lays down his life for the sheep.

It was in the summer of 1975. Our pilgrimage was approaching the town of Bethlehem, and there before us were the sheep and the shepherds—various flocks scattered about the dry meadows, just as we had imagined they would be. We left the bus and stood by the roadside for a moment. As we contemplated the land where so much happened to shape the destiny of mankind, our pilgrimage leader—Canon Brownrigg—took the opportunity to explain Palestinian sheep-herding customs in terms of the well-known passage found in chapter 10 of the Gospel according to St. John. He explained that, at nightfall, a number of shepherds would combine forces and flocks. They would group behind the walls of a courtyard or behind an enclosure out in the field crudely made of the available stones lying about. Sometimes it would be only a very temporary wall made of a prickly bush called camel thorn. In any case, one shepherd would sleep stretched across the entrance way as a kind of human door. He could thus protect the flock from intruders, animal or human. (That is why Jesus could describe himself both as the "Shepherd" and as the "Door of the Sheep.") A man coming back into the circle of sheep and shepherds must identify himself, and when he does, the doorman lets him in.*

It was to this manner of keeping the sheep by night that Jesus referred when he said, "He who does not enter the sheepfold by the door but climbs in by another way, that man is a thief and a robber; but he who enters by the door is the shepherd of the sheep. To him the gatekeeper opens." Thus the flock is protected through the darkness. When the sun comes up again, each shepherd goes his own way. As he leaves the other members of the group, he utters his special call; the sheep know this call and will follow him, and no other. So Jesus says of the shepherd, "The sheep hear his voice, and he calls his own sheep by name and leads them out. When he has brought out all his own, he goes before them, and the sheep follow him, and they know his voice. A stranger they will not follow, but they will flee from him, for they do not know the voice of strangers."

Canon Brownrigg practices what he preaches, literally as well as figuratively. Throughout our entire Holy Land pilgrimage, he led us in a manner akin to the Palestinian shepherd. When we dallied long enough in any one particular spot, there would always come the "Cup, cup" that was our special call, and whether we happened to be out on some desert oasis or surrounded by many voices in a busy Jerusalem marketplace, we always heard that call and knew it was time to move on.

Not many days after our visit to Bethlehem we found ourselves just inside the Jaffa Gate at Jerusalem. Canon Brownrigg pointed to the Petra Hotel up ahead. "You see that hotel," he said. "Until only a few years ago, it was the custom for the Bedouin shepherd to bring his own little flock with him when he went to market. His sheep would follow him through the streets of the city, just as they would when out in the fields. Well, one day, I happened to be looking out of that hotel window up there, and right here in this street was a Bedouin with his sheep following. All of a sudden a lorry appeared speeding down the street. The sheep froze. The driver, with little respect for the Bedouin, drove, hooting hard, right up to the flock. Still the sheep didn't move. Then the shepherd reached out, touching the sheep on his right with his staff and those on his left with his rod. The flock relaxed, went around the lorry, and continued on their way."

It is an old story in the Holy Land—the shepherd and his flock. The

---

* This same figure, incidentally, has been carried over into Islam. Some Aramaists, however, think "door" is a mistranslation, and that "sheep" should be used throughout.

I Am the Good Shepherd

history of the Hebrews was considerably influenced by the pastoral life, because for centuries they had been a nomadic people, living off their flocks and herds as they traveled through the desert from one oasis to another.

The great King David was originally a shepherd. Many of the Old Testament prophets arose from life in the sheep country. Amos, for instance, introduces himself as one "who was among the shepherds of Tekoa." [1] And, as all of us are reminded every Christmas season, it was to the shepherds, watching their flocks by night, that the angel of God first told of the new-born King.

It is only natural, then, that the imagery of the Good Shepherd is an important aspect of the teaching of Jesus. "Good Shepherd" is one of the most popular titles applied either to our Lord himself or to the Heavenly Father. The Book of Isaiah declares, "The Lord God . . . shall feed his flock like a shepherd; he shall gather the lambs with his arm, and carry them in his bosom, and shall gently lead those that are with young." [2] Certainly, if there is only one psalm that a person knows, it is the Twenty-third—"The Lord is my shepherd. . . ." And if a home has in it any religious pictures whatsoever, there is a good chance that there is the portrayal of the shepherd who leaves his ninety-and-nine in the fold and goes out after that one sheep that is lost.

We quite rightly think of our Heavenly Father or of Jesus as the shepherd of the Twenty-third Psalm. Here it is in the King James version:

> The Lord is my shepherd; I shall not want.
> He maketh me to lie down in green pastures; he leadeth me beside the still waters.
> He restoreth my soul: He leadeth me in the paths of righteousness for his name's sake.
> Yea, though I walk through the valley of the shadow of death, I will fear no evil; for thou art with me: thy rod and staff they comfort me.
> Thou preparest a table before me in the presence of mine enemies: thou anointest my head with oil; my cup runneth over.
> Surely goodness and mercy shall follow me all the days of my life and I will dwell in the house of the Lord for ever.

As Christians interpret this Psalm, it is in terms of a personal God who watches over us through all of life. Green pastures, still waters, restoration of the soul—all these have to do with renewal and making over. He also leads us in the "paths of righteousness," i.e., down the right paths in life, if we will permit him. But there are also valleys of dark shadows through which the flock must travel. With his rod the shepherd beats off wild beasts, and with his staff he helps the sheep over difficult terrain. This is symbolic for us, for there are many dark areas of life through which we must pass from time to time. Still we need "fear no evil," for God is with us. His "rod and staff" comfort us. And, just as the Palestinian shepherd walls in his flock at night and tends them while wild animals howl outside, and just as he rubs oil into the head of each sheep at the end of the day, the Twenty-third Psalm is telling us that our Heavenly Shepherd gives us all we need until our "cup runneth over," and until finally we are able to "dwell in the house of the Lord for ever."

In chapter 3 I wrote of the Couples Club in St. Albans, Vermont. We were having a discussion on the subject of life after death. Seven of those twenty-eight members present were either sure there was no life beyond this world or they were very uncertain about it.

But what did they believe? I asked them, "Do you believe in God?" The answer was an unqualified "Yes." So I probed further.

"And *what* do you believe about God?" I asked. Surprisingly enough, they prayed to God, believed that God was with them every day, watching over them, helping them in life. He was their constant companion and was vitally concerned about what happened to them. But, they insisted, all this protection and care ends when life ends.

The Christian Church maintains that this kind of belief defies the test of logic. The Christian maintains that God could not be God and cease to be concerned about one of his human creations, either in this life or in any life to come. If we understand God as the Good Shepherd, we have to understand him as the giver and preserver of all life, temporal and eternal.

God is a spirit; his angels are spirits. God created the spiritual inhabitants of Heaven long before he created this material earth, and there is no reason why he who is himself a spirit and who created other spiritual beings could not make spiritual bodies of our physical bodies when the time calls for it.

Because we believe in God in the first place, because we believe he created us and sent his Son to redeem us and his Holy Spirit to sanctify us, because of what we believe about God in this world, we believe the same about him forever.

The synoptic gospels give us the image of the Good Shepherd in a way slightly different from the way the Fourth Gospel presents it.[3] Here a

I Am the Good Shepherd

shepherd loses one animal out of his flock of a hundred. Naturally, says Jesus, this shepherd leaves the ninety-nine sheep in the fold and goes out in search of the one animal that went astray. This would often involve dangerous wilderness country; many people have come to a sad end in the rocky hill country of southern Palestine.* So our Lord says by implication, if a man who has a large flock of sheep cares enough about one missing animal to risk his life by going out and searching for it and doesn't give up until he finds it, then we must realize how much more God is concerned about one of *his* lost sheep, about one of his human creations.

Or consider the woman who loses one of her ten silver coins (a drachma, equal to a denarius, worth about a day's work).[4] The coin has fallen somewhere amid the reeds that cover her dirt floor. She lights a lamp, sweeps out the house, and searches until she finds it. Again, our Lord says by implication, if this woman is concerned about one lost coin out of ten, realize how much more God is concerned about one lost person—actually, about any person, lost or not. And this concern, again we maintain, endures for ever.

Remember the time during the ministry of Jesus when the Sadducees came to him with a question about the resurrection of the dead?[5] The Sadducees were similar to the people in our Couples Club; though they believed in God, they were sure that there was no life after death. This small group of priestly aristocrats based their belief—or lack of it—on the Torah (the first five books of the Bible, in those days thought to have been written by Moses) which alone they regarded as the *absolute* part of the Bible, though they also used the Psalms. No doctrine was essential to their faith that could not be found in the Torah. Thus, they concluded, since there was nothing about life after death in the Torah, such a belief could not be substantiated. (As we know from our study of Old Testament eschatology, this conclusion is superficial, but it is understandable if one knows nothing of primitive Semitic beliefs.)

"Suppose," they said to Jesus, "a man marries and dies without leaving any children." As we know, the levirate law (as expounded in the Book of Leviticus, about which we read in chapter 4 of this book) demanded that any unmarried brother take the widow for his wife so that a posterity

---

* Diane Kennedy Pike, in *The Search*, describes the tragic death of her husband, The Right Reverend James A. Pike, who fell off a rocky ledge in Judea. His body was lost from view for many days (Pocket Books, New York, 1971).

might be raised up in the deceased brother's name. Again, as we know, the original reason for this ancient law was to provide male descendants who would be expected to offer sacrifices to the ancestor in Hades. But the Sadducees knew nothing about ancient Semitic cults. They just assumed that the purpose of the law was to provide a quasi-eternal life for one's descendants.

Now, in this hypothetical situation that the Sadducees concocted, there were seven brothers. So, they went on, "the second brother took this woman for his wife, and he, too, died without leaving any children. The third did likewise, as did also the fourth, fifth, sixth, and the seventh. Finally, the woman herself died." Now, the Sadducees wanted to know, if there is any such thing as a life beyond this life, how is this awkward situation going to be resolved? "In the resurrection, therefore, whose wife will the woman be, for all seven brothers had her as wife?"

Jesus tells the Sadducees that they know neither the scriptures nor the power of God. He tells them, "In the resurrection, they neither marry nor are given in marriage, but are like the angels in heaven."* (In chapter 9 we will discuss what we mean by "the resurrection"; suffice it to say here, sexual relations and the giving of birth, though they are a part of every normal marriage in this world, are neither necessary nor possible for spiritual bodies.)

But there is more to the answer than that. The important observation Jesus would make involves God's eternal relationship to his human creations. "And as for the dead being raised, have you not read in the book of Moses, in the passage about the bush,[6] how God said to him, 'I am the God of Abraham, and the God of Isaac, and the God of Jacob'? He is not God of the dead, but of the living...." There is no past tense here. Very

---

* This question still bothers many people. A second wife quite naturally wonders, "Who's going to have my husband in Heaven?" If one may be allowed to speculate on this subject, it would seem that, although friendships or relationships may vary during the first stages of development in the afterlife, in anything that we might label "Heaven" there can be no possessive relationships. This would mean that a couple married on earth may choose to continue a happy relationship in the afterlife, if it is continued in a nonpossessive manner. Or, if the relationship on earth was not as happy as it should have been, they may choose not to continue it. After all, the marriage ceremony contains only the promise "until death do us part." The primary purpose of marriage is for the procreation and nurture of children, and this task, however desirable, belongs strictly to the earthly realm. Also, we should remember that the Christian's goal is to have the mind of Christ (compare with Philippians 2:5), and the mind of Christ is to love all God's children with equal intensity.

clearly it is, "I *am* the God of Abraham. . . ." Despite the fact that Abraham had physically left the earth hundreds of years before Christ spoke, as had also both Isaac and Jacob, Jesus points out that God is still concerned about them. As far as God is concerned, "all are living to him." St. Paul makes the same point when he writes, "Whether we live or whether we die, we are the Lord's."[7]

Another New Testament passage that has considerable bearing on this theme of the Good Shepherd is found in St. Paul's first letter to the Church in the City of Corinth (I Corinthians 15:1–10). The Greek people in Corinth also had a problem with the idea of the resurrection (although it may be argued that they did believe in the immortality of the soul).* In answer to these people St. Paul makes it clear that he is giving to them the same gospel which he had received. After summarizing the resurrection appearances as he has come to know them, he asks this very important question: "Now, if Christ is preached among you as One who has risen from the dead, how is it that you can possibly say there is no resurrection of the dead?" "Surely," Paul reasons, "if you can say that the resurrection for us is impossible, then Christ isn't risen at all for us, and the whole Gospel that we preach is utter rubbish, and all your faith is vain."[8] Paul ends with the only logical conclusion for a Christian: "If in this life only we have hope in Christ, we are of all men the most miserable."[9] These followers of Jesus had given up everything they had for the cause of spreading Christianity—their friends, families, property, peace of mind, and all else that humans ordinarily seem to want in this world. If there is nothing in the future beyond a miserable death, why bother? It is like an investor's sinking everything he has into a stock he knows to be worthless. We have a hymn which summarizes the plight of the apostles of Jesus:

> They cast their nets in Galilee
> >Just off the hills of brown;
> Such happy, simple fisherfolk,
> >Before the Lord came down.
>
> Contented, peaceful fishermen,
> >Before they ever knew
> The peace of God that filled their hearts
> >Brimful, and broke them too.

* The difference between *resurrection* and *immortality* we will discuss in chapter 9.

Life Here and Hereafter

> Young John who trimmed the flapping sail,
>   Homeless, in Patmos died.
> Peter, who hauled the teeming net,
>   Head-down was crucified.
>
> The peace of God, it is no peace.
>   But strife closed in the sod.
> Yet, brothers, pray for but one thing—
>   The marvelous peace of God.
>   W. A. Percy, 1924*

To the person who does not believe in God—and a personal God at that—this chapter makes no sense; but to the person who believes in the God who is revealed to us through the pages of the Bible, and especially the New Testament, this chapter presents an appeal to logic. Once you have concluded that God was born into this life in the person of Jesus Christ and once you have come to recognize that he is to be identified with the Good Shepherd presented in the Gospel, then you have to realize that he cares now and cares forever, for "all are alive unto Him."

Some readers will remember a rather touching account that appeared in the 1951 best-selling biography of the late, much-beloved chaplain of the United States Senate, Peter Marshall. (The book was also made into a motion picture.) In a home described by Peter Marshall in a sermon there was a little boy who was slowly dying from what was then an incurable disease. As time went on, the boy began to realize that he was not going to get well. One day, after his mother had finished reading to him about the exploits of King Arthur and his knights and about the last battle in which so many "fair knights met their deaths," the boy sat silently for a while, and then asked, "Mother, what is it like to die? Mother, does it hurt?"

The mother turned her back and ran into the kitchen, pretending to take care of something on the stove. There she said a hurried prayer that God would help her with the answer, and here is the remainder of the story as Dr. Marshall told it:

> "Kenneth," she said as she returned to the next room, "you remember when you were a tiny boy how you used to play so hard all day that

---

* William Alexander Percy's poem provides the words to hymn, "The Christian Life," no. 661, *The Hymnal 1982* (The Church Pension Fund, New York, 1985).

when night came you would be too tired even to undress, and you would tumble into mother's bed and fall asleep?

"That was not your bed . . . it was not where you belonged.

"And you would stay there a little while. In the morning, much to your surprise, you would wake up and find yourself in your own bed in your own room.

"You were there because someone had loved you and taken care of you. Your Father had come—with big strong arms—and carried you away.

"Kenneth, death is just like that. We just wake up some morning to find ourselves in the other room—our own room where we belong—because the Lord Jesus loved us."

The lad's shining, trusting face looking up into hers told her that the point had gone home and that there would be no fear . . . only love and trust in his little heart as he went to meet the Father in Heaven.

He never questioned again. And several weeks later he fell asleep just as she had said.

That is what death is like.[10]

On this story we might well comment: "So the child fell asleep and was carried in the strong arms of Jesus, the Good Shepherd, carried into another room, another room in the Father's Eternal Mansion, and there he awoke in the daylight of eternal glory to find himself in the morning of a new life, heavenly life."

It will be the same with each one of us. There will come a time when we shall fall asleep, either through an accident or through sickness, and we shall never again awaken to this world. But we do not need to worry or to fear, because our Lord with his strong arms will carry us into his Eternal Abode where we may awaken as he wills it, after his likeness.

The Great Shepherd of the sheep, who cares for each and every one of his human creatures, cares for us not only in this life, but also on into the next. The relationship that is begun here is an eternal relationship and has no end. That love carries us through the "valley of the shadow of death," on to where we "dwell in the house of the Lord for ever."

8

The Transfiguration

The Transfiguration, which is often ignored or forgotten by the casual reader of the Bible, was an event of tremendous importance and is crucial to our subject. The old charge that nobody has ever returned from death to testify to the life beyond (discussed at the end of chapter 3) I hope has been repudiated by the evidence of parapsychology. This charge is also repudiated by the Transfiguration, an event that occured in the last autumn of our Lord's life when two men out of the Old Testament returned from the dead and were seen conversing with Jesus. One was Moses, the great law-giver who led the people of Israel out of slavery in Egypt. The exact dates of Moses' life are unknown, but no one places him later than 1200 B.C. The other Old Testament character in the Transfiguration was Elijah, a man who lived eight hundred and fifty years before Christ was born. He was traditionally held to be the greatest of the Hebrew prophets; he was also a champion of human rights who confronted King Ahab[1] and brought about the destruction of wicked Queen Jezebel, the woman who sought to beguile Israel away from the worship of the one true God.[2]

As the turning point of our Lord's ministry approaches, we find him and his disciples traveling up the Jordan valley in the northern part of Palestine. The Galilean ministry is over. The leaders of Jerusalem have begun an active persecution. The Pharisees and the Sadducees approach him, asking for a sign to prove his messiahship.[3] His fame has come to the attention of King Herod Antipas, who speculates that he is John the

The Transfiguration

Baptist risen from the dead.[4] On top of all this hostility, there is no peace from the people, for after the feeding of the five thousand, the crowd attempted to take him by force and make him a king.[5]

Consequently, it has become obvious to Jesus that a turning point in his ministry has arrived. When he would again go south and enter Judea, it would be to suffer and to die.

First, though, there had to be a retreat to prepare for that final battle. It was now past late summer. Leaving Bethsaida, on the northern shore of the Sea of Galilee, Jesus and his disciples journeyed still further north, into Gentile territory, though still under the jurisdiction of Philip the Tetrarch. Going up the valley they continued toward a source of the Jordan River, where they could look down on the whole of the northern Jordan Valley or look up to the snowy peaks of Mount Hermon. Finally the group reached the plateau there, 1,137 feet above sea level and 1,740 feet above the Sea of Galilee. The city below the plateau was called Caesarea Philippi, so named by Philip the Tetrarch, a name derived from his own and that of Tiberius Caesar. Here at Caesarea Philippi Peter made his famous confession of Jesus' lordship.[6]

"Who do men say that I am?" Jesus asked his disciples. The answers varied. Some, like Herod Antipas, said he was John the Baptist risen from the dead; others thought he might be the prophet Elijah; a few maintained he was the prophet Jeremiah or one of the other great prophets. These were the popular guesses of the day.

Then Jesus looked at the disciples and asked, "But who do you say that I am?"

Peter replied for the group: "You are the Christ, the Son of the living God."[7]

"That is right," our Lord assures them, "but," he adds by way of warning, "don't tell anyone about it now." He explains why: Christ is not to be an earthly ruler or a traditional king, as most of the Jews expected, for "the Son of man must suffer many things and be rejected by the elders and the chief priest and the scribes, and be killed, and on the third day be raised."[8]

The preparation for the final conflict was thus continued. Christ would indeed be the "Suffering Servant" whom the Prophet Isaiah had written about, one "despised and rejected of men; a man of sorrows, and acquainted with grief."[9]

So, we are told, at the end of the week following Peter's Confession,[10] the Lord chose three of the most trusted of his disciples—Peter, James, and John (the inner circle)* and he led them up a high mountain where they could be absolutely alone. The Gospel record doesn't say which mountain, though most scholars assume it was Mount Hermon, rather than the alternative suggestion of Mount Tabor above the Esdraelon plain. Mount Hermon is just fourteen miles north of Caesarea Philippi, and, unlike Mount Tabor which then had a fortress on its summit, Mount Hermon was a place where the group could be absolutely alone. Mount Hermon is 9,100 feet high and snow-capped most of the year; however, in late summer the top would have been clear, with snow only in broad patches running down the side.

There are three peaks on Hermon. My guess is that Jesus and his disciples went to the lowest of the three. There they would have had the back-drop of the snow-covered slopes of the other peaks.[11] Below would be the breath-taking beauty of the plateau, the lesser mountains, the river valley, the broad plains, on down past the Sea of Galilee. It was on this mountain top, midway up from the earth, surrounded by a heavenly beauty, that the Transfiguration took place.

We are told that our Lord was in prayer,[12] presumably prayer about the great agony looming ahead—the Cross. We gather that his praying began in the evening and continued on through the night into the morning hours. As the sun began to rise, the disciples looked up and were amazed to see that the Lord's whole appearance was completely changed; "the fashion of his countenance was altered."[13] Even his clothes became white and dazzling. Or, as Matthew puts it, "And he was transfigured before them, and his face shone like the sun, and his garments became white as light."[14] To this Mark adds that the clothes became "whiter than any earthly bleaching could make them."[15] The best way we can describe it is to say it was a spiritualization, a glorification of Jesus' whole being.

If my time speculation is correct, it was now early Sunday morning, the same time of week that would mark our Lord's resurrection from the

---

* The Essenes, who occupied the Qumran monastery by the Dead Sea and who were responsible for most of the Dead Sea scrolls, in all likelihood furnished the pattern for Jesus' organization of his disciples—except that, it should be observed, the number twelve was to parallel the number of the tribes of Israel (compare Matthew 19:28 and Luke 22:30). Among the Essenes the "Teacher of Righteousness" was surrounded by a council of twelve. From these twelve he would select an inner circle of three who would make up his executive committee. Emil G. Kraeling, in his *Bible Atlas* (Rand McNally and Company, New York, 1956, p. 94), speculates with good reason that Christ spent some of his "hidden years" at Qumran or a community very much like Qumran.

The Transfiguration

dead.[16] It would seem that the light of Heaven shone through him in such a way that his body took on the appearance of the glorified body that became his following that first Easter morning. The event was, in fact, a preview of the resurrected and ascended Christ.

While Jesus was thus clad in robes of heavenly splendor, two saints from glory appeared with him—the two great men out of Israel's past—Moses and Elijah. They appeared in their spiritualized bodies, for, indeed, they were in the Kingdom of Heaven beyond this world and returned to earth just for this brief moment. They were heard to talk with Jesus about the path he must follow to the end, the death that he must endure in Jerusalem.[17]

Peter was mystified by all this heavenly magnificence. It was a wonderful experience that he would have liked to preserve for all time—there on the mountain top. So he blurted out in child-like fashion, "Master, it is good for us to be here. Let us make three tabernacles, one for you, one for Moses, and one for Elijah." Of course, he didn't understand what he was saying.[18]

The word *tabernacle** was very much in evidence in the accounts of God's journeying with the children of Israel through the wilderness towards the Promised Land. The people built a tabernacle, a tent for worship, a kind of portable temple. This was to house the presence of God and keep him among them wherever they went. It was even at this time the Feast of Tabernacles, when Jews would go outdoors and live under shelters made of branches for a period of seven days, an annual re-enactment of the journey their forefathers had made through the desert. So Peter, in his child-like understanding of all this, wanted to house the presence of Jesus and his two companions up there on the mountain. Furthermore Peter could not be blamed for thinking about the connection with the Feast of Tabernacles, for that was the occasion when Jews concentrated their attention on their messianic hopes, and surely Jesus' messiahship had been made very clear to the three disciples.

No sooner had Peter finished talking than a bright cloud overshadowed them all. It has been observed of Mount Hermon that in a few minutes a thick cloud cap can form and just as quickly disappear.[19] Yet of this covering, we read, it was a "bright cloud,"[20] evidently miraculously illumi-

---

* *Tabernacle* is the King James Version translation of σκηνή [skene], "a tent or cloth hut." Revised Standard Version translates the word as *booth*, while both Phillips and the New English Bible translate it as *shelter*.

nated by the presence of the Almighty himself. Naturally, as the cloud came over the disciples, they were fear-struck, for it was an awe-inspiring experience. Out of the cloud came the voice of God proclaiming, "This is my beloved Son: listen to him."[21]

The disciples needed this reassurance, for much understanding would be required for the days ahead. Peter had declared just a few days before, "Thou art the Christ, the son of the living God." That fact the three of the inner circle now knew for a certainty, and they also knew that in that moment they had been caught up in eternity and had seen Christ's glory, the same glory that would be his forever following the Resurrection and Ascension. Thus, when they were reassured, the cloud moved on. Jesus was seen standing alone again, and in his natural form.[22]

The Transfiguration is a great mystery, yet a necessary step for both Jesus and his disciples. As they came down the mountain, Jesus instructed the three, "Now I want you to say nothing about what you have seen and heard—not until after I am risen from the dead,"[23] because, as we have seen, this was a foretaste of his life that would follow the Resurrection. At this point in time, neither the other disciples, let alone the world, could even begin to understand what it was all about. So down the mountain they came to face all the problems of the people waiting for them, and they said nothing more about the experience, as the Lord had instructed them, until after the Resurrection, when at last they would understand the Transfiguration in terms of Jesus' risen body.

To the early Church the Transfiguration was considered one of the most important events in our Lord's earthly ministry. This fact is attested to by the paintings frequently found over the altars in early churches, particularly Eastern Orthodox churches. Modern western Christians, by contrast, are seldom reminded of this event and make few attempts at trying to understand it.

Some church members are inclined to explain away this narrative. They say, "Maybe the disciples were dreaming; maybe they really didn't see Moses and Elijah come back from the dead; maybe it was only their imagination."

To this kind of talk the writer of II Peter replies, "We're not children who have been deluded by cunningly devised fables. We have been eye-witnesses of his glory."* He says in effect, "We were there—James, John,

---

* II Peter 1:16. Although most modern scholars believe that II Peter is not by Peter the

and I. We saw these things on the Mount." If this were evidence coming from one man alone, perhaps it would be right to question its veracity. But these were three practical men. Though promised nothing as they journeyed up this mountain, for them the curtains of time were drawn back and they were allowed this brief glimpse into eternity.

The Transfiguration is a well-attested fact. It cannot be denied in the face of the Biblical evidence, and, indeed, it is an essential fact in our understanding of our Lord's life and the eternal setting.

First, the Transfiguration was a necessary step on the journey to the Cross. Our Lord conversed with two great men of the Old Testament and so, it would appear, clarified his vision of the divine plan: the Son of Man must suffer for the redemption of the world. At the same time the inner circle of disciples was greatly strengthened. They now knew for a certainty who Christ was and what must happen for the fulfillment of his mission. Presumably this faith was to be passed on to the others.

Second, the Transfiguration is one of the best biblical answers to the claim, "Nobody has come back from death." The supreme evidence is, of course, our Lord's own rising from the dead (the subject of the next chapter). But if there is the temptation to put Christ's resurrection into a category all by itself, then we can point to the Transfiguration.

Third, the Transfiguration demonstrates as much as anything can that even in this mortal world we are in the midst of eternity.

The Transfiguration may also be compared to any spiritual experience we Christians might have in this world. Every Eucharist is a kind of transfiguration, when to some degree we can see the King in his Beauty. I have often come back from a thrilling church conference or a retreat and lamented, "That was so wonderful, why do I have to return to the ordinary things of life?" As with the Transfiguration, however, the pilgrimage, the conference, the meditation, the retreat, the service of worship, or the moment of exultation cannot go on forever in this life. After we have been refreshed, we must travel down the mountain.

So it is with all Christians. We do well to have these great moments of spiritual insight, however imperfect they may be when compared with the experience the three apostles had on Mount Hermon; and we do well to

---

Apostle but is a second century pseudepigraphon, John A. T. Robinson, in his *Redating the New Testament*, concludes that the Epistle was written between 60 and 62 A.D., prior to Peter's death (Westminster Press, Philadelphia, 1976, pp. 197–198).

meditate upon the King in his Beauty and realize that we are surrounded by the hosts of Heaven at all times, but for now must plod on our way. Then, finally, at the end of our lives, we will be given the opportunity to see fully the King in his Beauty. Then it will be unclouded, and we will never have to leave the Mountain.

9

The Evidence for the Resurrection of Jesus

"This resurrection of Jesus you talk about," once queried a bewildered woman, "happened so many, many years ago, how can we be sure it really ever happened at all?" This is the primary question confronting us in this chapter. And the answer is that we can test the authenticity of the report that has come down to us in a way that parallels the manner by which we can test the authenticity of any historical event.

There are three main arguments for the belief in the Resurrection of Jesus: (1) The evidence of the empty tomb, (2) the testimony of reliable witnesses, and (3) the existence of the Christian Church. These arguments we shall take up in the order given.[1]

"And they found the stone rolled away from the tomb, but when they went in they did not find the body."[2] So writes Luke, and the other three evangelists tell the same story in a similar way.

The theme on which the first Good Friday ends is the removal of the body of Jesus from the cross. Granted permission by the Procurator Pontius Pilate, Joseph of Arimathea, together with his friend Nicodemus, came to the scene at Calvary.[3] There wasn't much time to lose, for it was believed by all pious Jews that a body should not remain on the cross overnight and especially on the Sabbath; and, as is well known, the Sabbath would begin at sundown—about 6 P.M., on this particular day, believed by some to be in the spring of the year 33 A.D.[4] Carefully the two men extracted the nails and lowered the body to the ground. Nicodemus had brought 100 pounds of spices, that being the normal thing in those days for the preservation of a corpse. Reverently the two wrapped the body of Jesus in a large linen shroud, with spices between the folds. They then carried the body to the sepulcher in Joseph's garden. Out of solid rock in the hillside, was hewn a large, new tomb, apparently the one Joseph had intended to be used for his own family. After they laid the lifeless Jesus on one of the ledges, the two went to the entrance and, probably with the help of levers, proceeded to roll the large thick disk-shaped stone across the mouth of the tomb.*

The burial seemed to be complete; but the enemies of Jesus wanted to be more certain. Matthew reports that it had been noised around Jerusalem that Jesus had prophesied his rising from the dead on the third day. Consequently the chief priests and the Pharisees went to Pilate with the request that a detachment of soldiers be deployed to stand watch outside the tomb to make certain disciples did not steal the body and proclaim Jesus risen. Pilate gave his consent. The temple soldiers sealed the tomb and stood watch.[5] Friday night came and went. Saturday came and went. Then Sunday morning arrived and something tremendous happened.

We do not need to concern ourselves at this point with the spectacular details of the rising to life as Matthew tells it; all we need now concern ourselves with is what the women and the disciples found. Three or perhaps four women approached the tomb, carrying spices, planning to do the usual anointing of the body. Apparently these were spices in oil (unguents), a better preservative than the dry spices used on Friday afternoon. On their way to the tomb the women discussed the problem of rolling back the stone; this would require more strength than they had. The women expected nothing more of the garden scene than the way it was left on Friday evening.[6] Yet, looking up, they were amazed to see that the stone had been rolled back already. The tomb was empty. A little later, Peter and John came to the garden and observed the same thing—the tomb was empty. The most that anyone could see, besides the linen shroud and the head covering, was "a young man . . . dressed in a white robe" (as Mark tells it) or "two men . . . in dazzling apparel" (as Luke tells it). The body which they had come to tend was gone.

What a challenge the empty tomb was to the Roman and Jewish authorities! All they needed to do was to produce the body of Jesus and destroy the Christian faith right then and there. Even the smallest clue to the location of the remains would have crushed the enthusiasm of the

---

* This type of entrance stone was very common in Palestine; I have myself seen more than one example.

small group of believers. But that clue was nowhere to be found.

The evidence of the empty tomb by itself is not sufficient for belief in the resurrection of Jesus, yet it is supporting evidence, and, together with the other two items of evidence, it makes an irrefutable case.

Some have argued for alternatives to a belief in the physical resurrection, such as the possibility that the women went to the wrong tomb, or that Jesus had not actually died but only seemed to have done so, or that the resurrection appearances were only spiritualistic phenomena, or that the resurrection stories are only pictorial ways (perhaps myths) to portray the fact that Jesus' gospel was victorious. These alternatives have been argued by many brilliant men in almost every age.[7]

The second argument for the belief in the resurrection of Jesus is the evidence of reliable witnesses. When Peter preaches on the day of Pentecost, he proclaims that the apostles are all witnesses to the resurrection of Jesus.[8] At another time he says, "The Risen Christ did not show himself to everyone but only to chosen witnesses."[9] That was the way it went; whenever an apostle preached, he said in effect, "We are witnesses; we knew he was dead and we saw him alive again; and he lives for evermore."

All the apostles were witnesses; in fact, that was the main qualification for apostleship—having seen the risen Christ. When Judas, the betrayer, had to be replaced, two candidates were brought forward from among those "who have accompanied us during the time that the Lord Jesus went in and out among us, beginning from the baptism of John until the day when he was taken up from us—one of these men must become with us a witness to his resurrection."[10]

The story of what happened—how Christ rose from the dead—is told in various ways by the various authors of the New Testament. Different incidents appeal to the different writers. Yet all agree on this one truth: Christ did die, and he did rise from the dead.

Now comes the question: How reliable are these "reliable witnesses" to whose testimony the church has listened all these centuries? To answer this question, we must use logic. As Dr. George Caird of McGill University used to argue, we have to grant that the testimony of the Resurrection must be either true or false. Either Christ rose from the dead or he did not rise from the dead. If the resurrection evidence is false, then one of two conclusions follows: Either the apostles perpetrated a deliberate hoax or, if this is not the case, then it must be that the apostles were victims of numerous hallucinations. We have heard the leaders of the ancient Church accused of both these possibilities, so we will consider them both.

Suppose the apostles did perpetrate a hoax? We then have to ask, For what purpose? For jail? So that they could be crucified? So that they could be stoned to death? So they could be burned as human torches to light the Emperor's garden party? So they could be fed to lions in the Coliseum? Ridiculous. Nobody would endure excruciating pain and an ignominious death just to perpetrate a hoax.

Recall Paul's own account of himself. In a moment of rare boasting, he says that he has lived "with labors, . . . imprisonments, with countless beatings, and often near death. Five times I have received at the hands of the Jews forty lashes less one. Three times I have been beaten with rods; once I was stoned. Three times I have been shipwrecked; a night and a day I have been adrift at sea; on frequent journeys, in danger from rivers, dangers from robbers, danger from my own people, danger from the Gentiles, danger in the city, danger in the wilderness, danger at sea, danger from false brethren; in toil and hardship, through many a sleepless night, in hunger and thirst, often without food, in cold and nakedness."[11] All this Paul traded for his very respectable and comfortable life as an orthodox doctor of the Law. Could he possibly have made the change just to perpetrate a hoax? Would Peter have chosen to be crucified upside down because he wanted to deceive the world? And what about James who was clubbed to death, or Bartholomew who was skinned alive? Were they perpetrating a hoax? Typical of what happened is the line we read in Tacitus' description of Nero's garden party: "These [Christians] he executed exquisitely. . . . Some he dressed in skins of wild beasts and set wild dogs upon them. Others he soaked with oil to illuminate his grounds."[12]

You see, then, there could be no fraud. Fraud is perpetrated only when there is a selfish end to be gained. And a death by torture is hardly anything to be desired.

Let us now consider the other possibility—the possibility that the apostles were victims of hallucinations. Hallucinations have the effect of undermining the personality. We see this in the use of LSD or similar drugs, and we see it in mental illness. There is usually a downhill progression. The person who suffers hallucinations goes from depression to depression.

Is this what happened to the apostles? Was there any depression? Did their personalities become undermined? Quite the contrary. Instead of going downhill, they went upward, from strength to strength. Their personalities blossomed. Whenever you read how the followers of Jesus were confronted by the Risen Lord, there is at once apparent the note of great joy.[13]

Consider Simon Peter. Our Lord nicknamed him the Rock, and yet before the Resurrection he would be more accurately described as shifting sand. The reader will recall the night of the betrayal, how Jesus prophesied that everyone of his followers would forsake him. Simon Peter protested vehemently, maintaining that no matter what happened, he would remain faithful. Yet that very night, when Simon Peter was questioned about being one of Jesus' followers, three times he denied that he had ever heard of the man.[14]

Following the Resurrection, however, he did, indeed, become a rock. On the day of Pentecost, when the apostles would exhibit the strange phenomenon of glossolalia (speaking in tongues), it was Peter who was spokesman for the group.[15] Peter was the standard bearer when Christianity was on trial before the Sanhedrin in Jerusalem, where he spoke up boldly in the face of possible death.[16] He willingly suffered imprisonment. He risked his life every day until finally he endured death by inverted crucifixion.

Remember, also, the story of Thomas the Doubter: "I will not believe, unless. . . ." When he saw the Risen Lord and was invited to touch the imprint of the nails, and put his hand into the spear hole in Jesus' side, he came to believe, exclaiming, "My Lord and my God." Thomas became a new man, completely reversing his doubting. He was so much on fire with the resurrection news that he carried it all the way to India, so tradition tells us; there he met martyrdom by the thrust of a spear into his own side.[17]

Or there is the case of James, the brother of the Lord. During Jesus' earthly life, he wanted nothing to do with the disciples or with Jesus' ministry. After the crucifixion, however, and the Risen Lord appeared to him, he became a changed man. He remained at the head of the Church in Jerusalem until he was executed by being thrown from the Temple wall and then clubbed to death.[18]

Consider Paul, first introduced to us as Saul, the man consenting to the stoning of Stephen,[19] the man who made "havoc of the church," sending both men and women to prison.[20] He had been "extremely zealous for the Law,"[21] a "Pharisee" and "a son of Pharisees,"[22] "a Hebrew of the Hebrews."[23]

Then comes the journey up to Damascus, where Saul meets the risen Jesus, and everything is changed.[24] All the inner contradiction is gone. Paul accepts the commission to be the apostle to the Gentiles, and he goes from triumph to triumph in the power of the Risen Lord, traveling from city to city through the great Roman Empire, never ceasing to preach Christ Crucified and Risen.

Something more should be said concerning the possibility of hallucination. Dr. Easton of General Theological Seminary makes the point that following hallucinations over a protracted period there is, in unfavorable conditions, permanent mental derangement, or, if conditions are favorable, there is a *gradual* decrease of the conditions until they cease altogether. But the appearances of the Risen Christ were intensely vivid, large groups of people witnessed them, and they were in rapid succession. Furthermore just "at the climax the appearances ceased instantly and forever, leaving the recipients aware of the cessation and turning their energies into labor."[25] (Recall that the manifestation to Paul described in Acts chapters 9 and 22, and the one recorded in Acts 23:11, came after the Ascension and are of a different sort, along with all the other manifestations of the Risen Christ to the faithful throughout the centuries.) This sudden cessation of the appearances and the fact that they were never renewed is, again, contrary to everything psychiatrists know about hallucinations. It is also contradictory to everything known about psychic phenomena.

That's what we mean, then, by the testimony of reliable witnesses, witnesses who have all the symptoms of good mental health, witnesses who have everything in this world to lose and nothing to gain—nothing to gain, that is, except the tremendous joy of proclaiming Christ Risen. We call these people reliable witnesses not only because they are the kind of people who can be counted on to present reliable evidence, but also because of the positive changes brought about in their lives by their witnessing. The positive changes that happened to men like Peter, or Thomas, or Paul have happened to countless other people. Perhaps the best argument for belief in the Resurrection is that millions and millions of men and women have believed in the Resurrection and because of that belief have become new men and women.

This leads us to the third reason for believing that Jesus rose from the dead—the evidence of the Christian Church. Here is a Church which has existed for two millennia and now has a billion or more members scattered over the earth. How did the Church get here?

The Evidence for the Resurrection of Jesus

There is a principle of science that every effect must have a cause. Effects just don't come out of nothing. Likewise in history every event must have a cause; furthermore that cause must be of sufficient importance to account for the event.

Such is the case with the Christian Church. It was the Resurrection of Christ and nothing else that brought the Church into being. It wasn't the teachings of Jesus per se, however wonderful those teachings are. It wasn't the miracles of Jesus however spectacular they were. The 100th Archbishop of Canterbury, Michael Ramsey, underscores this: "We are tempted to believe that, although the Resurrection may be the climax of the gospel, there is yet a Gospel that stands upon its own feet and may be understood and appreciated before we pass on to the Resurrection. The first disciples did not find it so. For them the Gospel without the Resurrection . . . was not a gospel at all."[26] Or, again, with reference to the Book of Acts, the Archbishop points out, "The earliest speeches dwell upon the death and the Resurrection and say nothing of the preceding life and ministry."[27]

The little group of twelve disciples started to fall apart very rapidly at the time of the trial and crucifixion. When Judas and the band of Temple officials came out to the garden of Gethsemane to arrest Jesus, all of the disciples scattered like a flock of chickens. Denial and total absence of support surrounded the trial. When the time came for the execution, only one from among the twelve had courage enough to make an appearance.* What little organization there had been was completely dissipated by the time Jesus died on the cross.

It was nothing other than the Resurrection of Jesus, on that first Easter Day, that brought the Christian Church into being. Even if we had no account at all in the New Testament of how various people saw the Risen Lord, even if we had no account of the teachings of Jesus, and all we had was the fact of the Christian Church, we would have to postulate some great event to explain what happened. All of a sudden we have, penetrating the course of history, a group of people worshipping Christ as Lord, refusing to be silenced, compelled by the new life within them to tell everyone about this exciting news until the whole world would be told. Any honest historian, any psychologist or sociologist, would realize at once that something tremendous must have happened to produce this

---

*The apostle who is described by John 19:26–27 is generally thought to be the Apostle John, but some have disputed this identification.

mighty Church that soon made its appearance in every city and hamlet of the Roman Empire and beyond.

We have the historical record of the governor of Pontus and Bithynia in Asia Minor (what is now the area of northern Turkey), a man by the name of Pliny the Younger, writing to the Emperor Trajan, about the year 112 A.D. The governor is bewildered as to what to do with the Christians he finds in his province. They refuse to comply with the requirements of the state religion and insist upon worshipping Christ "as a god." He tells the emperor that if the official religion is to be saved, something must be done to stop these people, "for there are many of every age, of every rank, and of both sexes which are now and hereafter likely to be called up for trial . . . for this superstition is spread like a contagion, not only into cities and towns, but into country villages also."[28]

Since this Roman governor wrote, Christianity has continued to spread until it is now the leading religion of the world. It has shaped our modern civilization, and even nations and religions that refuse to recognize Christ are nonetheless influenced and shaped by Christianity. Our modern world may not be as truly Christian as it should be, but just the same, our democratic western civilization would be impossible had Christ not risen from the dead.

Now that we have considered the main point of this chapter—the evidence for the Resurrection of Jesus—there remain two questions that inevitably must be faced in any discussion of the Resurrection: First, what does the Resurrection prove? Second, what was the nature of the resurrected body? We will consider these two questions in reverse order, leaving the more important one to the conclusion of the chapter.

The nature of Jesus' resurrected body, first, then. Obviously the body possessed by Jesus during his earthly ministry was not the same that he had following the Resurrection. The Risen Christ was unlimited by space. Jesus could now enter a locked room, with doors and windows barred fast. He could all at once appear in the midst of his followers and could just as quickly disappear. He could withhold recognition for a time, as he did with the two who were walking along the road to Emmaus.[29]

On the other hand the Resurrected Jesus was the same Jesus that his followers had known before the crucifixion. The body he now had could be identified with the body he had beforehand. Luke tells us that Jesus even invited his disciples to touch his body and see for themselves that it was really a bona fide body. Moreover, according to Luke, Jesus ate a piece of broiled fish and some honeycomb to prove that he had indeed a body and was not just a spirit.[30] Then, as the Fourth Gospel tells us, Thomas was invited to feel for himself the imprint of the nails and the hole in the Lord's side.[31] John also implies that Jesus ate with seven of his followers by the Sea of Galilee.[32]

Perhaps there is no final answer that can be given in this world to these two sets of seemingly irreconcilable facts about the nature of Jesus' resurrected body. I think, however, that Leslie D. Weatherhead, in his book *The Manner of the Resurrection,* comes close to what may be found to be the truth, although I cannot totally agree with him. Dr. Weatherhead places great importance on the description of the *unresurrected* grave clothes that John and Peter found in the tomb when they first entered it: "He saw the linen clothes lying, and the napkin, which had been on [or around] his head, not lying with the linen clothes, but rolled up in a place by itself." [33] It would appear, Weatherhead observes, "that a process took place unknown as yet to modern science, by which the physical body of Christ completely evanesced, or evaporated, or dematerialized, so that the grave clothes, weighed down by their own weight and by the hundred pounds . . . of spices . . . just collapsed."[34] If someone had removed the body, Weatherhead further observes, that someone would have taken body and clothes together, and certainly no body snatcher would have been meticulous enough to have unwrapped the grave clothes and then folded them up again in order to make them appear as if they had never been unwrapped at all.* Weatherhead, furthermore, speculates on how this could happen in terms of what we know about the nature of matter and the fact that the speed of movement of molecules that form all matter, if increased or decreased, can transform that matter from one state to another. Solid wax becomes liquid simply by the application of heat, and liquid wax can evaporate by the application of more heat, and it is all simply a matter of the speed of the molecules that make up the wax. Weatherhead goes into

---

* The author Frank Morrison, on the basis of what he finds in the Apocryphal Gospel according to the Hebrews, reasons that it was one of the guards at the tomb—temple guards, not Roman soldiers, detailed to keep watch—who was really responsible for moving the stone *after* he saw the Risen Christ. He would prove to his commander that there was no point in remaining at the tomb and so removed the stone to demonstrate. I think Morrison has a sound argument, for, if the resurrected body of Christ were able to enter locked rooms and suddenly appear and disappear, there would be no need to have the stone removed for the resurrected Christ to escape from the tomb. (*Who Moved the Stone?*, Faber and Faber, London, 1957, p. 187 and following.)

some detail in this respect, and, while I can more or less agree with him, it is beyond the purpose of this book to repeat all his arguments.[35]

There are some Christians who have dismissed the idea of the materially resurrected body entirely. There are others, such as Rudolf Bultman, who speak of "the myth of the resurrection."[36] Yet if we fail to accept the material Resurrection at face value, we fail to take into account all the Biblical evidence; at the same time, we fail to explain the tremendous impact of the event on the lives of the followers of Jesus. Only a miraculous, material Resurrection could account for what happened. "The Christian begins," says an editorial in *The Living Church*, "by assuming that the Resurrection is wildly improbable, just as the scientific materialist does; but the Christian asserts that with God everything good is possible; . . .[for] supernatural causes can have natural effects. If they cannot, God never created the world in the first place."[37] I do not understand how human flesh can evaporate and coalesce in the manner suggested, but I also fail to understand many other phenomena that scientists at large take for granted.

Likewise I do not understand how it is possible for our own bodies to be resurrected, but I accept the assurance that it will happen, for the nature of the resurrected body of Christ also shows us something about our own resurrected body of the future. The Church has always proclaimed, "I believe in the resurrection of the body," and what that resurrected body will be for all of us is demonstrated at least in part by Christ's Resurrection. Christ is, as St. Paul writes, "the first fruits of those who have fallen asleep,"[38] of those who have died he is the first to have a completed resurrection.

The second question we must face is What does the Resurrection prove? Some have thought that its primary purpose was to prove the reality of life after death, alleging that before the Resurrection no one could be sure. Many an Easter sermon is based on this hypothesis. Certainly the Resurrection is supportive evidence for belief in life after death, and it surely is a pledge of eternal life in the true Christian meaning of the world; but, as we have already pointed out in this book, there was no question about the truth of the afterlife in the minds of almost everyone in the New Testament era. Rather than to say, then, that the Resurrection proves life after death, it would be more correct to say that, because of the Resurrection, we are now assured that everything Christ said is true. Or, to put it another way, because of the Resurrection, the apostles came to know beyond all doubt that this man Jesus was also the Christ, the anointed of

God, and what he taught them about this world and the next is what God had taught them. After proclaiming the Resurrection and Ascension in his homily on the Day of Pentecost, Peter declared, "Let all the house of Israel therefore know assuredly that God has made him both Lord and Christ, this Jesus whom you crucified."[39]

The impossibility of separating the Resurrection from the Lordship of Christ was very well put by Archbishop William Temple in an Easter Day broadcast: "If Good Friday had been the end of the story, the Victory, though won for [Christ], would have been fruitless for the world. For while the story of the cross would have laid hold on men's feelings wherever it was told, there is no reason to suppose that it would have been told more often or more widely than the story of any other hero's death; and though it would have stirred men's feelings, it could not by itself have persuaded very many to find in it the light of the knowledge of the glory of God. . . . The chief significance of the Resurrection of Jesus Christ . . . is the disclosure which it makes of the activity and character of God. For if the Gospel story ended with the crucifixion, it would be one more tale of heroic virtue crushed by brutal selfishness while the vast universe remained indifferent. . . . [But in the Resurrection] God acted and made His action known. . . . By the Resurrection of Jesus Christ, God not only gave us the pledge of our immortality, not only declared Jesus Himself to be the Son of God, but also vindicated His own Deity."[40]

In the trial and crucifixion of Jesus, man did his worst against God and his fellow man, but this worst was not enough to defeat the power of God's love, for no act of man is ever final against the purposes of God. The Resurrection proves that the universe is basically rooted in righteousness and justice and that, in the finality of things, right will win out. Yes, the Resurrection is a pledge of eternal life for all Christians, but it is primarily the victorious vindication of all that Jesus said and did during his earthly life. The corollary to the recognition of this victorious vindication is that because Christ rose from the dead *and* ascended into Heaven, he is now a living reality. Someone has pointed out that it would be very easy for all of us to be like Thomas the Doubter, were it not for the fact that Christ is alive right now—a present, living reality—in the life of the Church and in the life of each true member of the Church. For the convinced Christian the consciousness of the presence of the Resurrected Christ is essential. As the last verse of Matthew assures us, he is with us always, "even unto the end of the world."[41]

10

The Judgment

> And as it is appointed unto men once
> to die, but after this the judgment.
> Hebrews 9:27, KJV

*I*f it is unpopular to face the prospect of death, it is even more unpopular to face the prospect of judgment, for, although death is to be seen everywhere around us and must in some fashion be faced sooner or later, judgment is not so obvious. And when it comes to recognizing the Almighty as Judge, the average person easily identifies with Omar Kayyám's verdict on the subject, where he compares God to a pottery maker:

> Some there are who tell
> Of one who threatens he will toss to Hell
> The luckless Pots he marr'd in making—Pish!
> He's a Good Fellow, and 'twill all be well.
> *The Rubáiyát*, stanza 88

Or, as many of our day maintain, "I can understand that the God of the Old Testament is a Deity of Judgment, but certainly not the God of the New Testament."

So let us begin there, with the God of the New Testament, with Peter's address to friends at Caesarea, where he explains how the apostles were witnesses to the Resurrection: "They put him to death . . . but God raised

The Judgment

him ... and made him manifest ... to us who were chosen by God as witnesses.... And he commanded us to preach to the people, and to testify that he is the one ordained by God to be judge of the living and the dead."[1] This same phrase—"the living and the dead"—or, as the King James version words it, "the quick and the dead"—is found in two other places in the New Testament.[2] The idea of judging the "living and dead" was considered important to be used into the Apostles' Creed.

To what degree the average person hearing Jesus during his earthly ministry would have thought of him as judge, we don't know.* But after he had risen from the dead and had come to be known as Lord of Heaven and Earth, his followers soon recognized that this Lordship of necessity implied the role of judge—for all mankind. St. Paul, when he delivers his famous speech in the Areopagus, in Athens, also ties in the Resurrection of Jesus with judgment. God, he tells the Athenians, "has fixed a day on which he will judge the world in righteousness by a man whom he has appointed, and of this he has given assurance to all men by raising him from the dead."[3]

St. Paul in his epistles also makes this judgment role of Jesus quite clear: He tells the people in Rome that it is God, through Jesus, who judges the secrets of men.[4] Indeed Paul warns us to be careful about judging one another, and, he tells us, upon those who do indulge in this perennial pastime, "the judgment of God rightly falls"[5]—a goodly admonition in any age, for it is only unto Him that "all hearts are open and no secrets are hid." Later on in this same epistle, the Apostle again warns about passing judgment on one's brother, "For we all shall stand before the judgment seat of God."[6] There will come a time, St. Paul also says, when we all will have to give an account of ourselves.[7] Warnings about the judgment of God are also found in almost all the other epistles of the New Testament, and, of course, especially in the Book of Revelation.†

---

* On one occasion Jesus asks, "Who made me a judge or divider over you?" Luke, in 12:13–21, relates the account of the man who besought Jesus to bid his brother divide the family inheritance with him. The rabbis as interpreters of the Law were frequently called on to make decisions in this respect. But Jesus makes it clear that he is not a rabbi in any such sense.

† This last book of the Bible, recognized as the greatest of the apocalypses, was written by a Christian leader banished to the Greek island of Patmos (about forty miles off the coast of Turkey in the Aegean Sea) about the year 95 A.D., during the reign of the Emperor Domitian. The author identifies himself as John. He is carried up into a mystical experience on "The Lord's Day," and sees the cosmic conflict between the forces of good and evil, with the ultimate victory won by Christ as the "Lord of lords and King of kings" (17:14).

Though no doubt the Book of Revelation is extreme in its concept of judgment, the epistles of the New Testament only reflect what Jesus himself said on the subject. Regardless of whether or not the masses of people were fully aware of it, Jesus pictures either himself or his disciples as judges in the world to come. He tells his disciples that they shall "sit on thrones judging the twelve tribes of Israel."[8] Jesus often portrays himself as Judge of all humanity. The most obvious example is the parable of the Last Judgment, wherein he pictures himself as "the Son of Man [who] comes in glory, and all the angels with him," and from his throne of glory he separates all mankind into the saved and the condemned.[9]

In my Vermont parish, as Advent approached one year and the possibility of a sermon on Judgment came up during a conversation in one of our women's groups, one astonished member exclaimed, "You mean God is going to hold us responsible for our sins and judge us! That doesn't sound very much like the Sermon on the Mount!"

Well, if that didn't sound very much like the Sermon on the Mount to this lady, it was only because she hadn't read the sermon carefully. True, this great sermon of Jesus, as it is recorded in Matthew, chapters 5, 6, and 7, is a wonderful message of hope for the despairing, but it is also a sermon of judgment. For one thing, if people are blessed because they are "pure in heart" or because they "seek after righteousness," etc., then those who fail in such activities are not blessed. For another thing, very high demands are made on those who would be members of the Kingdom of God. Jesus tells his hearers that he has not come to destroy the Law and the Prophets; rather, he has come to fulfill them, to bring out their full meaning. This fulfillment of the Law is more, not less, demanding than the legalists would have it. The Pharisees had a very high standard, but it was an achievable standard. According to the Pharisees, one could actually achieve righteousness by adherence to a course of strict legalism. Jesus, however, teaches that we cannot achieve the righteousness of God. "Unless your righteousness exceeds that of the scribes and Pharisees, you will never enter the kingdom of heaven."[10]

This sermon also gives us much to consider when we are tempted to judge others: "Judge not, that you be not judged. For with the judgment you pronounce you will be judged."[11] Moreover in this sermon Jesus warns us that living one's life as God would have it is a task not to be taken lightly: "enter by the narrow gate; for the gate is wide and the way is easy, that leads to destruction, and those who enter by it are many. For the gate

The Judgment

is narrow and the way is hard that leads to life, and those who find it are few."[12] Finally this sermon on judgment ends with warnings of the precariousness of building a life upon the sands of this world's standards. When the floods of trial come, such a life will fall with a thundering crash.[13]

Actually Jesus preached judgment throughout the whole of his ministry, either in word or in deed. And, contrary to much popular opinion, there was even the element of fear: "I tell you, my friends, do not fear those who kill the body, and after that have no more that they can do. But I will warn you whom to fear: fear him who, after he has killed, has power to cast into hell; yes, I tell you, fear him!"[14] Jesus warned the two towns just north of the Sea of Galilee, Chorazin and Bethsaida, because of their failure to repent and to respond to the Gospel message: "I tell you, it shall be more tolerable on the day of judgment for Tyre and Sidon than for you."[15] He even threatened Hell for Capernaum, the town which he made the headquarters for his Galilean ministry.[16] In fact, Jesus passed judgment upon his whole generation: "The men of Nineveh will rise at the judgment with this generation and condemn it."[17] He reminded his hearers that the Queen of Sheba came a great distance to hear the wisdom of Solomon, "and behold, something greater than Solomon is here."[18] Those words surely provided a judgment on those who ignored or rejected God's Messiah.

Not only did Jesus threaten a judgment that would come in the future, but he also exercised in person a certain amount of judgment during his own earthly lifetime. He pronounced forgiveness when the occasion called for it, as the time he healed the paralytic who had been let down through a hole in the roof of the house where he was teaching: "'But that you may know that the Son of man has authority on earth to forgive sins'—he said to the paralytic—'I say to you, rise, take up your pallet and go home.'"[19] Jesus also passed judgment upon those who would blaspheme against the Holy Spirit, assuring them that there would be no forgiveness for that sin,[20] for those who refuse all spiritual guidance can hardly expect to develop spiritually.

On the other hand there is always hope for those who recognize their sins and ask for mercy; so Jesus on the cross promises an entrance into Paradise for the repentant thief.[21] Proverbial, too, in the ministry of Jesus is his condemnation of hypocrisy and legalism: "Woe to you, scribes and Pharisees, hypocrites! for you tithe mint and dill and cumin, and have neglected the weightier matters of the law, justice and mercy and faith."[22]

Jesus also passed judgment in action. On Monday of Holy Week he went into the Temple and "drove out all who sold and bought in the Temple and he overturned the tables of the money-changers and the seats of those who sold pigeons. He said to them, "Is it not written, 'My house shall be called a house of prayer for all the nations'? But you have made it a den of robbers."[23] This was a judgment on Israel's religion, a religion which had turned inward and failed to carry out its true purpose of mediating God to all peoples. On this same day Jesus passed judgment on a fruitless fig tree, a parable in action, symbolizing a judgment on all things which fail in fulfillment of the purpose for which they were created.[24]

It is, as has been pointed out, quite clear, too, that Jesus saw himself as judge of all mankind. This is obvious not only in his telling of the parable of the Great Judgment (Matthew 25:31–46), but also in his references to the Second Coming (the *Parousia*): "And then they will see the Son of man coming in clouds with great power and glory. And then he will send out the angels and gather his elect from the four winds, from the ends of the earth to the ends of heaven."[25]

It is certainly evident, then, from the whole of the Gospel record that Jesus regarded himself as God's judge of all humanity. It is likewise evident from the rest of the New Testament that his followers also regarded him as such, or, at least, they came to regard him as such.

Now, logically, comes this question: When does judgment come? The answer is at times confusing, for in the New Testament there are diverse ideas in flux; but as the historic Church has come to understand it, there are three judgments—the Particular Judgment, the Final Judgment, and the Ongoing Judgment. Let us consider these in the order given.

First, the *Particular Judgment*. This is the judgment all of us will have to face immediately when this life is over, a judgment of a particular individual at a particular time in his life, i.e., at the end of his life. It is often said that a drowning person has the whole of his previous existence flashed before him. So, too, the person entering the afterlife, entering the world immediately beyond this one, has flashed before him all that he is and all that he has been. This truth has been substantiated by the findings of death-experience research. Raymond J. Moody, M.D., in his *Life after Life*, recounts a common experience of those who have been pronounced clinically dead but somehow are revived. After the person leaves his physical body and meets a number of his relatives and friends on "the other

The Judgment

side," he encounters a "being of light" who asks him to evaluate his life and "helps him along by showing him a panoramic, instantaneous playback of the major events of his life."[26] This review of one's life is not, as some have suggested, a balancing off of this good deed against that sin. Our Lord does not operate a giant computer in the sky. Rather, this is a judgment on the quality of the life that a person has lived.

J. Patterson-Smythe, a popular Canadian Anglican writer early in our century, in his classic *The Gospel of the Hereafter*[27] (a book that was printed and re-printed many times and had much influence on subsequent popular writing in the field of eschatology), maintains that there is no judgment at all until the end of time. Those who have left this world, he says, are in what might be called "Hades," or "Paradise,"* or "Under the Throne," † and he quotes early Christian patristic literature such as Lactantius' *Divine Institutes*, to support his contention: "Let no man think that souls are judged immediately after death: all are detained in one common place of safe keeping till the time when the Supreme Judge makes his scrutiny."‡

The denial of the Immediate or Particular Judgement has not, however, been the belief of the main stream of Christianity. While we will frankly admit that there is ambiguity and perhaps difference of opinion on the subject in the New Testament, there is much pre-Christian belief in some kind of judgment at death, and certainly this thinking is one of the streams of thought that is present in New Testament times.[28] Perhaps the first Christian patristic writer to allow for this immediate judgment is Tertullian (160–220 A.D.), who admits that martyrs enter directly into Heaven, but we have to go forward to St. Augustine of Hippo (354–430 A.D.) before we find a definitive statement on the subject. Augustine writes that the soul is judged as it leaves the body.[29]

Certainly the idea of an immediate judgment makes sense. For one thing, the whole Christian doctrine of the Intermediate State (Purgatory or the Church Expectant or whatever else you wish to call it) depends on some kind of immediate judgment, since only those souls judged to have a potential hope of Heaven are allowed to enter a state of purgation. For

---

* There will be a more complete treatment of this term in chapter 13.
† Revelation 6:9 speaks of the souls of those who died for the Lord as "under the altar."
‡ Lactantius, *Divine Institutes*. Lactantius (c. 240–.330 A.D.) was a Christian apologist, described by one scholar as one "skilful in the Latin language, but very unskilled in theology." He was suspected of Arianism, a heresy which denied the full divinity of Christ.

another thing, waiting through the centuries for a final judgment at the end of time in a kind of suspended animation is far worse than the "soul sleep" doctrine of the Seventh Day Adventists (referred to in chapter 3). At least the soul sleep would mean oblivion as far as consciousness goes, whereas this suspended animation would be like waiting—for literally God knows how long—in what is comparable to the antechamber of the judge's office to hear what the verdict will be. The reason the people of the early Church had no problem in putting off all judgment until the consummation of the world was that they expected the world's consummation in their immediate future. As the last chapter of this book hopefully will make clear, the consummation of the world is eventually coming, but most of us, at least, don't expect it any day now.

Yet no matter how distant it may be, there will be an end to this world, for time will eventually run out and that brings us to the *Last Judgment*, the judgment at the end of time.

This final judgment is a favorite theme of medieval and Renaissance art. Most of us are familiar with Michelangelo's portrayal of this event in the Sistine Chapel, or with Hans Memling's great altarpiece in St. Mary's Church at Danzig, or Lucas Van Leyden's painting in Leiden, or Fra Angelico's triptych in the National Gallery in Rome. Not a medieval cathedral can be found without a stone carving of this dread subject. And, as we are all aware, this is the way judgment is pictured in Matthew 25—the Son of man seated on his throne, while before him are gathered all the nations of the earth.

The Last Judgment is put on an even grander scale in the latter part of the Book of Revelation, which pictures a judgment coming at the end of the Millennium,* and this time it is God (as Father), not Christ, who is the Judge:

> Then I saw a great white throne and him who sat upon it; from his presence earth and sky fled away, and no place was found for them. And I saw the dead, great and small, standing before the throne, and books were opened. Also another book was opened, which is the book of life. And the dead were judged by what was written in the books, by what

---

* Revelation 20:4–7. This is the only place in all the canonical Bible where there is mention of a millennium. Most Christians would interpret the millennium of Revelation symbolically, for since Christ came to earth, he has, in effect, bound Satan and limited his power. There will be more about the millennium in chapter 14.

they had done. And the sea gave up the dead in it, Death and Hades were thrown into the lake of fire . . . and if anyone's name was not found written in the book of life, he was thrown into the lake of fire.[30]

This terrifying prophecy is, of course, generally regarded by most Christians today as pictorial language. I don't think anyone—except, perhaps the most ardent fundamentalist*—believes that the five billion people now on this earth plus the five billion or so who have previously occupied this planet could ever be assembled in a physical sense before the throne of judgment.

We must not, however, dismiss the Last Judgment as an idea that belongs wholly to the fancies of an unenlightened age because of the vastness of it, or the logistical problems involved in such an assemblage, or because the apocalyptist has over-dramatized it. The idea of the Last Judgment over which the Almighty presides has always been basic in Christian theology.

If, then, we cannot rule out the Last Judgment, this question comes to mind: Why is it needed? If there has already been a particular judgment, and everybody leaving this earth immediately upon death passes under this judgment, why need there be another judgment at the end of time? The answer is that it will be God's judgment upon the whole of creation.

We must remember in this connection that we are not just individuals set apart from one another, for no individual lives or dies unto himself. Rather all of us are members of our community, citizens of our country, and part of the entire human race. This is the concept of the corporate person which the Hebrew people of the Old Testament took for granted—the idea that for good or for ill, we are all tied up together in one bundle of life. Man's triumphs and failures, his joys and sorrows are shared with his fellows. It is the idea that neither blessings nor misfortunes are meted out entirely according to individual deserts.

Though this is an Old Testament concept, we can see many examples of how this corporate person is a fact even in our modern world. The average German on the street had nothing to do with starting World War

---

*A Christian fundamentalist, by definition, is a Protestant who takes the Bible at face value. Though he allows for some symbolic expression in the Bible, he takes the whole of it literally, including the story of Adam and Eve, the Flood, and the Old Testament miracles. There is no room for the theory of evolution, critical analysis, or the possibility that a particular writer may be in error.

II, yet he was caught up in his country's fight and he suffered the ravages of war along with all his other countrymen, and when the war was concluded, he, along with all his fellow Germans, had to accept the responsibility for what his country had done. The same can be said of the Japanese or any other nation that carries along its people toward some particular end, be it good or evil.

Surely, too, the idea of the corporate person is carried out in the Christian understanding of the atonement. Jesus died for "the sins of the whole world."[31] Or, as Paul writes, "For our sake he made him to be sin who knew no sin."[32]

Again, in Christian theology, the idea of the corporate person is involved in our understanding of the Body of the Resurrection, which, as we discussed in chapter 5, means that all Christians through baptism become members of Christ's Resurrected Body.

And there is more to the concept of the corporate person than that. If man is tied to his fellow man, he is also tied to the total creation of God, for man is the product of a long evolutionary chain and is very dependent upon this creation for his sojourn upon earth.*

A time *will* come when this creation will have served its purpose, and God will judge it accordingly. At the end of this judgment the Kingdom of God and Christ's reign will come fully into existence. God will be all in all. A final, general judgment must come, then, when the Lord of the Universe will pass his verdict on the destiny of his creation.

There is yet a third type of judgment, and this one we might well have considered first, for it is the judgment in which all of us on this earth are now under. For want of a better term we call this the *Day-to-Day Judgment* or the *Ongoing Judgment of God*, the judgment that takes place in everyday life, day after day. The Fourth Gospel with its emphasis on "realized eschatology"[33] has much to say about this kind of judgment: "For God sent the Son into the world, not to condemn the world, but that the world might be saved through him. He who believes in him is not condemned; he who does not believe is condemned already, because he has not believed in the name of the only son of God. And this is the judgment, that the

---

* Romans 8:19–23 illustrates St. Paul's contention that all creation is tied up together. Because of Adam's sin, he argues, all creation has come under the sentence of condemnation. While modern theologians would have difficulty in going as far as St. Paul, our present-day ecological studies do demonstrate more obviously than ever before that man and nature are very interdependent.

The Judgment

light has come into the world, and men loved darkness rather than light, because their deeds were evil."[34] This means that every day is judgment day, and what that judgment is depends on how we respond to the light of Christ.

The Fourth Evangelist, then, shifts the judgment back from something that happens in the future to something that happens in the present. It is not that he discards the future judgment altogether, but that the primary judgment is what happens here and now, in this life. The judgment that determines a person's destiny he brings upon himself, and this he does by his response to the light of Christ, day by day. For that reason, the verdict at the end of life will in no way be a total surprise; it will merely corroborate what has already happened in life.[35]

This everyday judgment, of course, deals with sins of omission as well as sins of commission; it includes not only those actions or nonactions we are in the habit of labeling "sins," but also everyday omissions, such as opportunities to do good deeds ignored, kind words left unsaid, personal trials borne with impatience or anger. One who responds positively to the light of Christ will take advantage of every opportunity to follow in the footsteps of his Lord, not only in knowing him in the brother or sister with whom he comes in contact daily, but also in getting to know him through prayer, Bible reading, attendance at public worship, through participation in the sacraments, and all other God-ward acts. The person who rejects or ignores our Lord in all these ways rejects or ignores—to that degree—the light that has come into the world.

Every day, then, is judgment day, and every day is important, eternally important. We can use it either to get closer to our Lord or we can use it to get further away from him. J. Patterson-Smythe rightly words this everyday judgment in this manner: "Choice forms habit, habit forms character, and character forms destiny."[36]

This brings us to the very positive note about judgment, to the realization that Judgment is part of the Good News of Christ. I used to be disturbed by one of the Prayer Book's collects for Christmas, the one which asks God to "Grant that as we joyfully receive [Christ] as our Redeemer, so we may with sure confidence behold him when he shall come to be our Judge. . . ."[37] This intrusion of judgment into the tenderness of the Christ Child theme seemed to me an unnecessarily sour note, quite out of place with Christmas joy. But, properly understood, judgment does belong also to Christmastide. If Christ came down from Heaven to dwell among men and bring salvation, there must be judgment, for judgment has to do with how we relate to that coming down and the opportunity for salvation. Judgment is really *Good News,* for it tells of a God who cares, one who is very much concerned with how we live our lives. This *Good News* also assures us that the highest principles are used to determine our fate. Unlike the capricious gods of Greek and Roman mythology, with the Christian God, there is no favoritism, no special privilege, no vindictiveness, no loss of temper, no irrationality; but rather a destiny fixed in accord with the highest principles of equity, reason, and love, for as Psalm 25 (and many other passages of scripture) word it, our God is full of mercy and loving-kindness.

Moreover this judgment is dealt out by someone who has shared this human life with us, one who knows our weakness and temptations as well as our potentials, and that is, of course, why God's judgment—except in its final stage—is committed to Christ: he knows this life from first-hand experience.

So God cares about the way we live our lives, about the kind of people we are, and this is *Good News.* It means that the Lord of Heaven and Earth, the Ruler and King of the Universe, is concerned about each and every one of us. My life does matter, not only to myself and to those about me, but most of all to God.

11

Heaven

> Rejoice, because your names
> are written in heaven.
> St. Luke 10:20

*T*he setting for the text that introduces this chapter is the return of the seventy missionaries. As Luke tells the story, these missionaries were sent forth to carry the Gospel message "to every town and place where [Jesus] himself was about to come." They came back full of success, bubbling over with enthusiasm. Jesus told them he would give them power over the forces of evil, but he added, "Do not rejoice . . . that the spirits are subject to you; but rejoice that your names are written in heaven."[1] We have also the Beatitudes, which concludes with a similar promise, "Blessed are those who are persecuted for righteousness' sake, for theirs is the kingdom of heaven. . . . Rejoice and be glad, for your reward is great in heaven."[2]

At another time Jesus tells his followers not to worry too much about the material things of this world, but rather to "seek first his kingdom and his righteousness, and all these things shall be yours as well."[3] There is nothing wrong with "these things." It is a matter of priorities. Heaven must be foremost among our goals. Again, Jesus exhorts his disciples, "Do not lay up for yourselves treasures on earth, where moth and rust consume and where thieves break in and steal, but lay up for yourselves treasures in heaven, where neither moth nor rust consumes and where thieves do not break in and steal. For where your treasure is, there will your heart be also."4

That's the way it is all through the pages of the New Testament. Jesus is ever setting forth the Kingdom of Heaven as the goal of his followers. "The kingdom of heaven is like a merchant in search of fine pearls, who on finding a pearl of great value, went and sold all that he had and bought it."5 Nothing is of more value than Heaven, and nothing is to stand in the way of his followers' entering Heaven. As we saw in chapter 6, this Kingdom is at times a present reality, but it is also a promise of a future beyond earthly life, and it is this future—the ultimate Kingdom—with which we are primarily concerned in this chapter.

The Apostles' Creed ends with the assertion that we believe in "The Resurrection of the Body/And the Life everlasting," while the Nicene Creed says, "And I look for the Resurrection of the dead/And the Life of the world to come." The creeds, in a sense, say that because we believe in God the Father, in Christ, and in the Holy Spirit, we believe forever, and we can enjoy a fellowship with the Heavenly Hosts forever.

We must not attempt to localize Heaven, however, even though religious people from earliest times have tried to do so. In Old Testament days most men believed in a three-story universe. Underneath the earth was a cavern called Hades or Sheol, and above the solid sky over the earth (the firmament) was Heaven. This all changed with the spread of the Greek understanding of a spherical earth.* Ptolemy (c. 150 A.D.) placed the spherical earth in the center of the universe. Based on Ptolemy's geocentric cosmology, the scholars of the Middle Ages worked out the location of Heaven very "scientifically" and situated it in a series of nine crystalline spheres encircling the earth. First there was the lunar sphere, in which the moon was firmly fixed; that was the lowest stage of Heaven. But one could look right on through the lunar sphere to the next stage, where Venus was located. Then came the Martian sphere. It continued on like that until one got to the ninth sphere, called the Empyrean—the highest stage of Heaven. No planet or satellite was involved in the Empyrean; this was the motionless Heaven, where there was no "shadow of turning."6

---

* The Greek philosopher Anaximander (610–547 B.C.) was the first to conceive of the earth as a cylinder, floating in space. Pythagoras (died c. 497 B.C.) and Aristotle (422–384 B.C.) both maintained that it was spherical. The geographer Eratosthenes of Cyrene (275–200 B.C.) measured the circumference of the earth to within 200 miles of its actual dimensions.

Here God was seated on his throne, surrounded by his angels and his saints.*

Though we have long ago abandoned the geocentric universe, we still find with us today speculation as to the exact location of Heaven. A pamphlet on the subject of Heaven was given to me by a fundamentalist friend. The pamphlet postulates that there is a "place in the northern skies which is not filled with stars.... It is evident from Isaiah 14:13 that heaven is located beyond that empty place."[7]

I contend that all speculation as to the location of Heaven is fruitless, for Heaven does not depend upon place. Rather Heaven is better described as a state of being, a condition. In this book I frequently refer to Heaven, Hell, and the Intermediate State as places, but I hope the reader understands that the use of such a term is simply a handy way of speaking and that it is not my intention to fix the spot for these states of being. Also it may very well be that people in the afterlife localize their various stages of existence—a lot of mystical insight seems to point to this—but it is not the same kind of space relationship we use in this life.

We also often speak of *going* to Heaven. The *going* cannot be used in the same sense as we would speak of *going* to New York or *going* to London. There is no distance per se to be traveled. When we get to Heaven, it is simply a new life that we enter. If we must localize Heaven at all, perhaps it would be correct to say that Heaven is all around us, for it breaks in upon us from time to time. But to say that Heaven is all around us certainly does not mean that it is dependent upon this world or upon the solar system or upon the created universe at large.†

There is, indeed, a barrier between this world and the next, but it is not a spatial or physical barrier, since, as we have seen, for many human beings still living the veil of separation has at times been drawn back. Essentially that was what was done for the three disciples as they beheld the Transfigured Lord. In a different way the mystics also see beyond the veil.

---

* Dante, in his *Divina Commedia*, has his beloved friend Beatrice escort him through these nine stages of Heaven. In this great classic of western literature the poet presents a typical medieval view of things to come.

† The Book of Revelation ends with the prophecy of "a new heaven and a new earth" (21:1). It may well be that the end of earthly creation will be followed by a new heavenly creation. If in any way our present Heaven is dependent upon this material creation, then we can be sure that there will be a new heavenly creation, for God's Kingdom is "from everlasting to everlasting." (See Psalm 20:2, etc.)

In our discussion of Heaven we cannot be precise, nor should we be. A few things have to be accepted on faith; and besides all that, to be precise would be to impose our four-dimensional, space-time world upon a condition quite outside of space and time.

Our approach, then, to the subject of Heaven is to consider it under ten headings,* and the reader will at once discern that the characteristics listed, with minor exceptions, are none other than the characteristics of the Christian life here and now. The most accurate, general statement we can make about Heaven is that it is an intensification of the best that a Christian can know and do and believe during this life. The Christian in Heaven has fellowship with Christ, he experiences intense love, he enjoys reunion and fellowship with family and friends, he has great joy, he grows in grace and helps others to do the same, he is able to rest, he is immersed in righteousness or goodness, he worships God, he looks upon great beauty, and he meets his Lord face to face.

All these activities the Christian can do here, though in a limited way. Many a person reading the writings of the mystics has observed that, while they are very good at describing the horrors of Hell, they seem to be colorless when put upon to describe Heaven. At least part of this fault is that we are expecting something totally different from the good Christian life and fellowship that begins here, and we ought not to expect that—different and more wonderful, yes, but *not totally different.* Admittedly, too, the mystics have no words for what they see. The Apostle Paul, in the experience he relates in II Corinthians, chapter 12, candidly admits he is at a loss for words to describe his view of Paradise. (More about Paul's experience later.) But we do know what is expected of a Christian here, and we also know what our Lord and his apostles have promised us in the life to come.

Here, then, are the ten characteristics Christians generally associate with Heaven:

---

* This is an arbitrary number, and no particular significance should be attached to it. Another writer could just as effectively subdivide my headings and have more characteristics, or cluster the ideas and have fewer. St. Augustine, in his *City of God,* summarizes our life in Heaven under only five headings—"There we shall rest and we shall see; we shall see and we shall love; we shall love and we shall praise. Behold what shall be in the end and shall not end." (Book 12, chap. 30.) These five activities E. L. Mascall, an English theologian, uses for the outline of his excellent book, *Grace and Glory* (Morehouse-Barlow Company, New York, 1961).

Heaven

The first and most obvious thing we can say about our ultimate goal is that it provides an intensification of our *Fellowship with Christ*. We have an *earnest*, a down-payment of this fellowship here on earth, when we give our lives to him.* We have the completion of this fellowship in Heaven, when we are with him eternally and in the fullest sense of the word. In chapter 5 and elsewhere we made the point that the Christian does not seek never-ending life as such; instead, he seeks eternal life, a life of fellowship with Christ. That life begins on earth, it continues through the "Valley of the Shadow of Death," and it finds its fulfillment in Heaven.

The Book of Revelation, while it may have some awful shortcomings in terms of its vindictiveness, does have many glorious passages, wonderful promises that justify its being included among the canonical books of the New Testament. Among them are affirmations of this intensification of fellowship with our Lord and with God:

> Behold, the dwelling of God is with men. He will dwell with them, and they shall be his people, and God himself will be with them.
> Revelation 31:3b

> And I saw no temple in the city, for its temple is the Lord God the Almighty and the Lamb. And the city has no need of sun or moon to shine upon it, for the glory of God is its light, and its lamp the Lamb.
> Revelation 21:22–23

Or there is the passage that comes right at the beginning of the Book of Revelation, where the Heavenly Christ speaks to the Church in Laodicea. He has something good to say about all the churches of Asia, except to this one in Laodicea, the church that is "neither cold nor hot." But to the people there he gives this most gracious of all promises:

> Behold, I stand at the door and knock; if any one hears my voice and opens the door, I will come into him and sup with him, and he with me.
> Revelation 3:20, KJV

The fellowship that he promises may be compared to the fellowship that

---

* The word *earnest*, or its equivalent, is used in Romans 8:19; II Corinthians 1:22, 5:5, 7:7, 8:16; Ephesians 1:14; Philippians 1:20; Hebrews 2:1. For some time translators were unsure of this word *arrhabon*—ἀρραβών, for it is a word not found in classical Greek. It was only in fairly modern times that archaeologists dug up in the sands of Egypt documents where the word was used in business contracts; the *arrhabon* was a down-payment to seal the contract.

Christ had with his apostles at the Last Supper when he promised them his life, so that this life of fellowship would endure forever.

Fellowship with our Lord is rooted in *Love,* and that is the second characteristic of Heaven. "God is love,"[8] writes St. John in his first epistle, and he writes this after proclaiming the doctrine of Christian fellowship—"our fellowship is with the Father and with his Son Jesus Christ."[9] It is because God is love that he brought the world into being in the first place; it is because God is love that Jesus gave himself for us on the Cross. It is because God is love that he wants us to belong to him always. But the love that God has for us must also be shared with one another: "For this is the message which you have heard from the beginning, that we should love one another.... We know that we have passed out of death into life, because we love the brethren. He who does not love remains in death."[10] (That is, he who lacks this love, cannot go to Heaven.) "If any one says, 'I love God,' and hates his brother, he is a liar; for he, who does not love his brother whom he has seen, cannot love God whom he has not seen."[11]

Dr. Moody, in his *The Light Beyond,* has much to say about love. As he puts it, "'Have you learned to love?' is a question faced in the course of the episode by almost everyone who has had a near-death experience. Upon their return, almost all of them say that love is the most important thing in life.... Most find it the hallmark of happiness and fulfillment, with other values paling beside it."[12]

The Eucharist is often called an *agape* (ἀγάπη) or love-feast, though in ancient times the *agape* was not always identified with the Eucharist. This *agape* is the kind of love that St. Paul exhorts us to have in his famous sermon on the subject of love found in the thirteenth chapter of I Corinthians, the word that the King James version of the Bible translates as *charity.* The word *charity* comes from the Latin *caritas,* meaning a sense of the dearness of people. *Caritas* is listed by St. Thomas Aquinas as one of the three theological virtues, the others being faith and hope. Of these three virtues St. Paul writes, as the King James version translates it, "And now abideth faith, hope, charity, these three; but the greatest of these is charity."[13] This is the virtue, above all others, he says, that will endure through all eternity.

Heaven is filled with people who love and care for one another. There is no "flight of the alone to the Alone," as in Hinduism. "See how these Christians love one another," exclaims the patristic theologian Tertullian.[14]

Yes, goes a modern spiritual, "We shall know them by their love." After all, in the Parable of the Last Judgment, the basis for separating the sheep from the goats is whether or not those being judged have ministered to Christ out of their love for "the least of these . . . brethren."

Out of this love and affection Christians have for one another comes the need for reunion, the meeting of friends and members of one's family parted from each other long ago. *Reunion and fellowship*, then, is third in our characteristics of Heaven. In the Creed, we say, "I believe in . . . the Communion of Saints," and fellowship in Heaven is at least part of what we mean by the "Communion of Saints."*

The most common symbol of Heaven among the Jews during New Testament times was a huge messianic banquet, a fellowship of eating and drinking together, with Abraham at the head of the table. In chapter 4 we saw the beginnings of this idea in the "Little Apocalypse" of Isaiah. Jesus makes use of the banquet symbol when he tells the story of the Rich Man and the Beggar.[15] The same idea is conveyed by the Eucharist, which is an earthly counterpart of the Heavenly Banquet. When Jesus tells his disciples, "Truly, I say to you, I shall not drink again of the fruit of the vine until that day when I drink it new in the kingdom of God,"[16] he was thinking of the Heavenly Banquet, a feast in the presence of God with all the great and lesser saints who have lived and died in ages past.

In the last year of my mother's life, somewhere around her ninetieth birthday, she showed me a letter just received from one of her Glasgow girlhood friends. The letter read in part: "Like you, I often look back to the old days and think of the happy times we had at your home in Ure Place, when the McFarlanes were all together. How long ago that seems! And yet, so near and dear. And I remember well that time we had tea together in Sauchiehall Street and your telling me about your dear children. But some day soon there will be grand reunion of all of us in heaven. . . . It will be such fun!"

Most of us, to be sure, look forward to some kind of reunion like that, when we will meet old friends and members of our family long separated

---

* While not easy to define in a short space, essentially the Communion of Saints means an interaction involving all Christians living or dead. In this sense, the word *saint* means any baptized person, and the word *communion* means fellowship. Those in the afterlife can pray for us, as we can pray for them, and just as we can have fellowship with other Christians on earth, so, too, can those beyond this earth have fellowship with one another.

by death. Heaven, then, will afford an opportunity for a grand get-together.

Communication in the heavenly realm, however, will not be the same as communication in the earthly realm; it will be much better. A standard joke is told in theological seminaries to the effect that we must study Hebrew, so that when we get to Heaven we will be able to speak to God in his own language. Of course, nobody takes this admonition seriously, but it is always good for a laugh. The truth of the matter is that language of any sort will not be necessary in Heaven, not only to speak to God, but also when we speak to our neighbor. Again, consider Dr. Moody's findings: Auditory language will be superseded by a more direct form of communication. *"Hearing"* in the spiritual state, "can apparently be called so only by analogy," and most [of those interviewed by Dr. Moody] say that they do not really hear physical voices or sounds [in that moment when they have been allowed to leave this life]. Rather, they seem to pick up the thoughts of persons around them.[17] In heavenly communication the language barriers that separate one people from another here on earth will be missing; our fellowship will be truly without racial, national, or cultural barriers.

Fourth in our understanding of Heaven comes *Joy*, for joy naturally emerges from fellowship, love, and believing. The word *joy* (*chara*—χαρά) appears over and over in the New Testament, usually in connection with the reception of the Good News—actually over fifty times, in addition to many other forms and synonyms.

A parallel word is *blessed* (*makarios* μακάριος). In the Beatitudes of Matthew 5:1–12, in both the Revised Standard Version and the King James Version of the Bible, we read, "Blessed are those who. . . ." An equally good translation would be, "Happy are those who"—those who are poor, those who mourn over the evil conditions of the world, those who are meek, those who are merciful, those who are pure in heart, etc. All these people are happy because they are participating in activities which belong to the Kingdom of Heaven.

The idea of joy or happiness in one form or another is found throughout the Gospel message. The angels announced Christ's birth to the shepherds as "good tidings of great joy."[18] In Luke's version of the Sermon on the Mount, Jesus tells his disciples to "rejoice and leap for joy."[19] In telling the Parable of the Lost Sheep, Jesus says, "Joy shall be in Heaven over one sinner that repents," and "There is joy in the presence of the angels of God."[20] Or, as St. John remembers the farewell address of Jesus in the Upper Room, despite the betrayal of that night and the imminence of the death on the Cross, we have a dominant theme of joy: "These things I have spoken to you, that my joy might remain in you, and that your joy might be full,"[21] and "Your sorrow shall be turned to joy. . . . So you have sorrow now, but I will see you again and your hearts will rejoice, and no one will take your joy from you."[22]

The other writers of the New Testament likewise manifest the theme of joy, especially St. Paul. His prayer for the Church in Rome is typical: "May the God of hope fill you with all joy and peace in believing, so that by the power of the Holy Spirit you may abound in hope."[23] And it is clear through all these wishes and promises that the joy available here will continue and intensify in the heavenly realm.

"Did Jesus ever smile?" someone asks. "Did he have a sense of humor?" Many good cases have been made for answering this question in the affirmative.[24] One answer comes from a letter to the *Living Church:* "I'd be certain he did if there were no evidence in scripture, for love smiles often and on many. Anyone who has been God's child for any length of time knows deeply that Jesus . . . has a magnificent sense of humor which pours forth abundantly and personally in, for example, the answering of prayers."[25]

Psychologists tell us that a sense of humor is tremendously important in all human relations: it is often the key to a happy marriage, it is important in the instruction of children, it is the basis of good social relationships, and it is the essence of good personal adjustment to the world that surrounds us. John Donne argues:

> *Ride, si sapis, o puella ride*—If thou beest wise, girl, laugh; for since the powers of discourse, and Reason, and laughter, be equally proper unto Man only, why shall not he be only most wise, which hath most use of laughing, as well as he which hath most of reasoning and discoursing?[26]

Consider, too, this item from *Christianity Today:*

> Everyone knows that death did something terrible to Christ, but not everyone knows he did something wonderful to death. . . . No one knows how he did it. But the deed was mighty enough to dry Mary Magdalene's tears, transport desolate disciples into an upper room of unspeakable

joy, and send them out stammering with faith in jail and out, living or dying. After five terrible beatings and two horrible stonings, Christianity's most jubilant apostle got up and dusted off the opposition with a shout, "Rejoice, and again I say unto you, rejoice!" After wading through inquisition, torture, blood, and hell, the Book [of Revelation] ends with a great host no man could number singing "Hallelujah!" As Dr. Fosdick [formerly of Riverside Church in New York] has said, "There is . . . enough tragedy in the New Testament to make it the saddest book in the world and instead it is the joyfullest."[27]

In view of all this emphasis on the joy of the Gospel message, it is not surprising to find theologians arguing that a sense of humor belongs in Heaven itself. Dr. Burnett Streeter, a great Anglican theologian of about two generations ago, has this to say in support of such a thesis: "In a society of real friends humor is the solvent in which egotism, the root of all unsocial thought and action, is insensibly dissolved. . . . The highest form of humor implies the unerring perception of reality which sees at once through shams, pretences, and self-deceptions."[28] To this we say "Amen." Although humor can be vulgar or coarse at times, a Christian sense of humor has no such quality. A proper sense of humor springs from the ability to look on life as a whole—from birth on into eternity—and see the individual components of life in their varied perspectives. It is the difference between seeing the whole forest as opposed to seeing only the individual trees. Further Dr. Streeter points out, humor "In another aspect . . . is an expression, the most spontaneous perhaps of all, of the joy of life. It is essentially thanksgiving though not consciously realized as such."[29]

Number five in our list of the characteristics of Heaven is *Growth and Constructive Activity*—both self-fulfillment and doing work for others. We will talk more about the process of personal growth in chapter 13, when we consider the doctrine of the Intermediate State, but what should be underscored at this point is that creative activity belongs to the very nature of God himself and, therefore, cannot be separated from Heaven. "My Father is working still, and I am working," said Jesus to those who objected to his healing on the Sabbath.[30] Creation is not to be thought of as something God did once and for all; it is an ongoing process. Every creative activity of man is a sharing in the creative activity of God, and surely opportunity for creative activity continues in the heavenly realm.

Heaven

Heaven is not a "Scottish Sabbath" where inactivity and boredom prevail.*

The Christian concept of Heaven is quite different from the Moslem one, too. The Moslem would imagine his eternal abode as a lush oasis, a haven of perpetual leisure, shade from the desert sun, ample fruit, fountains of water, and exotic plant life. In this Heaven the *men* who have arrived lie about on couches, in beautiful gardens, eating and drinking (fruit juices, of course) to their hearts' desire, while beautiful, black-eyed maidens wait upon them.[31] It is this concept of the Moslem Heaven, I suppose, which caused Sir Thomas Moore to write, though somewhat unfairly:

> A Persian's Heav'n is easily made,
> Tis but black eyes and lemonade.[32]

My Vermont mystic friend (whom I introduced in chapter 2) wrote of being granted a vision of her grandson in his new life beyond the grave. After a period of about a year's development, he was shown in his heavenly home seated in a room with a little girl. This girl, he later explained to his grandmother, had become his charge. He had been given the responsibility for her nurture as she continued to "grow" in the heavenly realm. Heaven, then, involves helping others, just as life with Christ on earth involves helping others.

To what extent God permits people in Heaven to help those still in their earthly pilgrimage is a debatable subject, but surely the doctrine of the Communion of Saints has relevance here. This implies that not only the great saints are permitted to help us here but many of the lesser saints as well. A case in point is the story of Archdeacon Hudson Stuck (mentioned in chapter 3). He returned from the other world to encourage a would-be mission nurse, timid and afraid as she was about to begin her work in the wilds of Alaska. Another case I read about some time ago is that of the "Surgeon with a Kitchen Knife," the amazing but well-authen-

---

* In case the reader is not aware of what is meant by a "Scottish Sabbath," I remember hearing my Scottish Aunt Elizabeth (my mother's sister) saying how liberal her father was with respect to the Sabbath, compared to some of their neighbors in Glasgow, because "he never pulled down the blinds so we couldn't look out on the streets or make us spend the entire Sabbath indoors reading the Bible." Of course, in my grandfather's family, games and play of all sorts were forbidden, but the children were permitted to go walking outdoors. During my early boyhood, before my parents became "corrupted" by American customs, it was much the same in my own family.

ticated account of Jose Pedro de Freitas, a Brazilian peasant, who performed thousands of painless miracles of surgery with no other instrument than an old kitchen knife. This was possible, he would explain, because from time to time he was possessed by the spirit of Dr. Adolpho Fritz, a German surgeon who died during the First World War. There was one stipulation on the part of the man who worked through Jose Pedro de Freitas: the gift of healing was his just so long as he did not profit from it.[33]

In addition to these two and many other dramatic accounts others have cited, there are many less dramatic ones—help or guidance often not perceived at all by the receiver—but which happens in time of need, often in answer to prayer. All of this is quite in keeping with the doctrine that the Church on earth and the Church in Paradise are in "one communion and fellowship." Again I quote Dr. Streeter on this point:

> What exactly the work will be which we have to do [in the afterlife] we cannot even profitably guess; but there will surely be different kinds of work for different kinds of people. And for some, if not for all, we may suppose that part of it will consist in labour for souls of those who have entered the next life lower down in the moral scale than themselves. And why may not the work of some be to watch over and inspire the lives of loved ones still on earth?[34]

Growth in Heaven also means self-fulfillment, the completion of one's personality and the fulfillment of God's plan for the individual. Again we must contrast Christianity with the other great religions of the world. The eastern religions—Hinduism and Buddhism in particular—look forward to eternal bliss as an absorption of the personality into the Godhead. Until that final absorption takes place, according to these religions, the soul is something to be tossed about from one body to another, from one incarnation to another, until finally it reaches the point where it relinquishes all desire. When that time comes, these religions would say, the soul merges with the Godhead as a drop of water returns to the ocean and loses all identity. Nirvana for the adherents of these eastern religions means for the individual to become less and less. In contrast, for the Christian, Heaven is the opportunity, in a sense, to become more and more oneself. Of course, "more and more" does not mean more egocentric or more separated from one's fellows; rather, it means fulfillment, development, completion, an opportunity for the real "I" to emerge as God has planned for that "I."

This is, *in part*, what we mean by "The Resurrection of the Body," and, although this doctrine was discussed to some extent in chapter 5, at this point I must say something more about it. St. Paul writes to the Church in Philippi, "Our citizenship is in heaven and it is from heaven that we look for our Savior, the Lord Jesus Christ, and when the time comes, he will change this body of ours [with all its troubles and all its limitations] into a heavenly body that it may be conformed unto the body of his glory, according to the working whereby he is able to subject all things unto himself."[35]

This means that ultimately our bodies are to be transformed, glorified, made similar to the body which Our Lord had after he rose from the dead. About the nature of this body-to-come, the Apostle has something to say in his First Epistle to the Corinthians: "What you sow does not come to life unless it dies. And what you sow is not the body which is to be, but a bare kernel, perhaps of wheat or of some other grain. But God gives it a body as he has chosen, and to each kind of seed its own body. . . . So it is with the resurrection of the dead. . . . It is sown a physical body, it is raised a spiritual body."[36]

The theologians of the early Church believed that the resurrection involved a re-assembling of all the particles that once made up the human body—and this had to be accomplished before there was to be any bodily glorification[37]—but we now realize that such a re-assembling of the chemicals that once made up our earthly bodies would constitute too much dependence on the material. It is also true that for the early Christians (with certain exceptions) this resurrection of the body had to await the consummation of the world. This, again, we cannot follow literally—at least, most of us—except that we must acknowledge that our resurrection remains incomplete until the whole Body of the Church is resurrected at the end of time; for we are inextricably tied in with that Body.*

Despite the fact that we have had to modify some of the views of the

---

* The orthodox Christian doctrine with respect to the resurrection of the body and the immortality of the soul is that at death body and soul are separated. The soul (with the exception of those of the great saints) goes into a stage of waiting (Purgatory for Roman Catholics and something like a state of heavenly rest for the others). When the last day arrives at the end of time, the body is resurrected and the soul reunited with the resurrected and glorified body. This doctrine is reflected in the 1928 Book of Common Prayer and its predecessors, in both America and England, in such prayers as the one where we ask that the departed "may rest in him" and "at the general Resurrection in the last day . . . be found acceptable in [our Lord's] sight" (p. 335).

early Church, we must not be tempted to abandon the doctrine of the resurrection of the body in its essential truth. Dr. Moody gives us important corroboration of some kind of bodily existence immediately in the afterlife: In describing the experience of the person who has just "died," he writes, "He notices that he still has a 'body,' but one of a very different nature and with very different powers from the physical body he had left behind."[38] As one patient told Dr. Moody, "I could feel my body and it was whole. I know that. I felt whole, and I felt that all of me was there, though it wasn't."[39]

The body following death, properly understood, means an entity of all that the person has been in this world—body, mind, and spirit—but unlimited by space and time.

This mention of a body unlimited by space or time suggests to some people the idea of no body at all. But that is not the case, and we can illustrate the difference between the theology of the resurrected body and the theology of a disembodied spirit by reference to the Greek thinking on the subject. To the Greeks of New Testament days, *body* and *spirit* were two irreconcilable elements. Plato would describe man's life in this world as a constant battle between body and soul. The body, with its carnal lusts and appetites, is constantly trying to pull man down toward this earth. The soul, on the other hand, is attracted only to the heavenly. The body, according to the Platonists, is essentially evil. Man's soul, for the duration of this physical life, is incarcerated in the body: it awaits liberation.[40]

This Greek thinking stands in contrast to that of the Hebrews. To the people of the Bible there is nothing essentially evil about either this world or the body, for, as the Book of Genesis records it, "God created [it] and saw that it was good."

Because man is both body and soul, the "resurrection of the body" means the resurrection of the total personality, not just half of a man or a woman, but all of a person, even all that has ever happened to that person in the course of his or her life. When we enter into the Heavenly Kingdom, then, we don't enter it as pure spirit, but as a personality that has been indelibly stamped with the events of this earthly life. Our Lord pointed out that we are not married in Heaven, but that does not mean we fail to carry over into Heaven the fact that we have been a man or a woman in this life. Further, we carry over into Heaven the psychology and the personality that belongs to our particular sex. We also carry over the psychology of the stage of this life where it ended for us—the psychology of a child, or of a middle-aged adult, or of an elderly person. Our racial and cultural background, too, shape the heavenly body. Also, if our body has chanced to cause us a great deal of suffering in this world, the *effects* of that—for good, we can be sure—are also carried over, so that anyone who has known us here will know us there.

But just as there are no tears in Heaven, there are also no sufferings either—of any kind. We are assured by the mystics and by the evidence of parapsychology that the body it pleases God to give us in our resurrected life will be the best for us.[41] Dr. Moody, along with Dr. Maurice Rawlings and others, gives us more than one good example of how the near-death body is free of its earthly malfunctions. Dr. Moody, for instance, tells of a Long Island woman of seventy who had been blind since the age of eighteen:

> [This woman] was able to describe in vivid detail what was happening around her as doctors resuscitated her after a heart attack.
>
> Not only could she describe what the instruments used looked like, but she could even describe their colors.
>
> The most amazing thing about this to me was that most of these instruments weren't even thought of over fifty years ago when she could last see. On top of all this, she was even able to tell the doctor that he was wearing a blue suit when he began the resuscitation.[42]

There are also cases like that of Caroline Larsen of Burlington, Vermont, who in the early part of the twentieth century, found herself breaking free of her physical body which was relaxing in her upstairs room. Her husband and some friends were rehearsing a Beethoven string quartet downstairs. As she continued to hear the music, she walked in what some have called an "astral body" out into the upstairs hallway and into the bathroom, where she faced a large mirror and was astonished to see that, instead of a middle-aged woman, she beheld the figure of a girl of about eighteen and immediately recognized the beautiful form she had as a girl of that age. As she later wrote, "My face appeared as if it were chiseled out of the finest alabaster and it seemed transparent, as did my arms and hands when I raised them to touch my hair. . . . My eyes, quite strong in the physical body, were piercingly keen now. . . . My hair, no longer grey, was now, as in my youth, dark brown and it fell in waves over my shoulders and down my back. And to my delight, I was dressed in the loveliest white shining garment imaginable—a sleeveless one-piece dress, cut low at the neck and reaching almost to the ankles." She was unable to continue this experience, for she was soon directed to return to her physical body and resume her normal life.⁴³

In view of what the New Testament tells us, we can expect such "making whole" in the future life. Our Lord does desire to make all things perfect, and, as we read in Philippians 3:21, the Lord will "change our lowly body to be like his glorious body."

This means that all earthly disorders will vanish as we enter Heaven. The elderly person who leaves this life a vestige of the former self will enjoy a heavenly body resembling his or her prime of life. The inarticulate infant will be a beautiful child. The bent and weary will be made straight. The retarded and the incomplete will be made whole. The deformed body will be perfected. There will be healing of all physical and mental maladies, for completion is the goal of Heaven. All of this is logical when we remember our Lord's promise to make all things perfect.

One other important aspect of the Christian understanding of the resurrection of the body is the impossibility of reincarnation. We haven't space to give this subject proper treatment, but, inasmuch as the doctrine of reincarnation is a popular heresy of our day, we cannot neglect to say something about it. The credence of the reincarnationists is based on the non-Christian belief that soul and body are totally independent of each other. This soul, the reincarnationists would claim, can occupy one body in one generation and quite a different body in another generation, a male body at one time, a female body at another time, one race this incarnation, another race next incarnation. In fact, some reincarnationists go so far as to subscribe to the doctrine of the "transmigration of souls," believing that the human soul can occupy a subhuman form of life for a time, should it be deemed necessary to punish that soul.

This whole doctrine of reincarnation, however, runs counter to the Christian principle of the uniqueness of the individual. Christians believe that the individual is precious in God's sight, a once-only creation with a once-only sojourn on earth. The individual is not to be defiled, disguised in subhuman forms, or trapped in circumstances unworthy of a God of mercy and loving-kindness.

That, then, is what we mean by growth and development in the Heavenly realm, the completion of the individual in accordance with God's plan for that individual.

Number six in our list of the characteristics of Heaven is *Rest*, and this is the other side of the idea of growth and development. Growth does not mean ceaseless struggle.

Dr. Burton Scott Easton would point out that the Church has overdone the rest theme in its prayers for the dead. He contended that the "Grant unto them rest" comes from the medieval idea of Purgatory, where those being purified of their sins are being tormented. (There is much of this in Dante's *Purgatorio*.) So, Dr. Easton would argue, "Grant them rest" means "Grant them respite from those purgatorial torments." Much better, Dr. Easton felt, was to use the type of intercession that asks that the departed "may go from strength to strength."

Dr. George B. Caird of McGill, in his lectures on the Epistle to the Hebrews, also warns us about a misunderstanding of the word *rest*. In Hebrews the writer speaks of entering into the "rest of God." The word used here is *katapausis* (κατάπαυσις), meaning ceasing from strenuous activity, the power to stop, relaxation. The word comes from the Psalms and is defined as a true Sabbath, as in Hebrews 4:9–10: "So, then, there remains a sabbath rest for the people of God: for whoever enters God's rest also ceases from his labors as God did from his."[44] But Dr. Caird is quick to make clear, this "rest" does not mean inactivity, for God's Sabbath "proceeds from all creative action. God's rest as it is found in Genesis chapter 1 is the rest that can be described not as a rest of inactivity, but as one of achievement."[45] To enter into God's rest, then, is to enter into a divine experience, to become partakers in Christ. Jesus, Dr. Caird would remind us, pushed aside the pharisaic notion of the Sabbath as a time for inertia and put in its place the idea that the Sabbath is the day for doing the works of God.

Let us not forget, however, that there is a legitimate, genuine place for rest following strenuous activity. Consider this paragraph by Dr. Donald Coggan, former Archbishop of Canterbury, in his preface to Dr. Mascall's book, *Grace and Glory*:

> A leading ecclesiastic said the other day that he would like to abolish the word "rest" from tombstones, and substitute the word "work." I felt the remark to be one more instance of that secularizing of our ideas of religion which is so sadly popular. Bustle and activity being the characteristics of our age, a superficial mind can suppose that these must be the characteristics of heaven also. But the Christian hope, so far from endorsing our mental habits, challenges them sharply, and nowhere more than by telling us that "rest" is what God has in store for us.[46]

Canon Theodore Wedell of the College of Preachers in Washington also protested against this idea of ceaseless activity and endless development. During a week's stay at the college, sometime in the fifties, I recall his saying something like this: "The idea of growth and 'going from strength to strength' is well and good, but I don't think we should do away with the idea of rest entirely. I'm getting old, and I'm tired, and when I'm through with this life I hope there will be a little rest in store for me before I start work again."

Perhaps the key to the solution of these divergent opinions lies in the difference between rest and idleness. Most of us have at one time or another indulged in just plain loafing. A lot of people misuse Sunday that way, making it a day of idleness instead of a day of rest. When you come to the end of a day of loafing and continue to relax, there is no sense of refreshment, no sense of accomplishment, but only a hollow feeling. If anything, after a day of loafing, one feels more tired than ever. On the other hand, when you work hard all day—whether it be in your vocation, avocation, or just wholesome recreation—and you relax at night, it is a wonderful feeling, for it is a rest after accomplishment. That is like God's rest, a heavenly rest, a rest that comes following a life of usefulness and achievement.

Seventh in our characteristics of Heaven is *righteousness (or goodness)* and *truth*. Righteousness is tied up with the preaching of the Kingdom all the way through Christ's ministry; the two are inseparable, and this is so regardless of whether the Kingdom is of the present or of the future: "Seek first his kingdom and his righteousness," Jesus tells us.[47] "Blessed are those who hunger and thirst after righteousness" is one of the Beatitudes.[48] In fact, Jesus is sent into the world to "convince" or "reprove" the world of righteousness.[49] That is, he is sent into the world to reveal the true meaning of righteousness. The righteousness and the goodness of God is, moreover, set forth all the way through the Bible as the goal of all religious people.

It is to be expected, then, that righteousness (or goodness) is one of the characteristics of Heaven. It is no coincidence that the creeds tie up forgiveness of sins with the idea of eternal life. The clear implication is that only those whose sins are washed away or forgiven are able to enter Heaven.

Moreover, in the Lord's Prayer, we pray, "Thy will be done, on earth as it is in heaven." We are acknowledging, in effect, that God's will is done perfectly in Heaven. Those in Heaven have come to love God, to honor him, to obey him, and this means doing his will. Because God is a God of righteousness, of justice, and of truth, Heaven is a place where those qualities are obvious. God is not to be mocked. His righteousness must be vindicated, and surely, of all places, it is vindicated in Heaven.

John of Patmos's description of the New Jerusalem also makes clear that righteousness and holiness preclude all that is contrary to that goodness. We read that through the gates of the New Jerusalem "nothing unclean shall enter . . . nor any one who practices abomination or falsehood."[50] Likewise in Heaven "there shall no more be anything accursed."[51] "Everyone who loves and practices falsehood" remains outside the gate.[52]

So truth and justice and righteousness will, indeed, make up the pattern of Heaven. Nothing will be hidden, no sham can exist, no false fronts, no deceit. Every Sunday at the Eucharist we address our Creator thus, "Almighty God, unto whom all hearts are open, all desires known, and from whom no secrets are hid . . ."[53] In Heaven our hearts will be open not only to God but also to one another—no secrets hidden from anyone. If the truth makes us free on earth,[54] surely it will complete our freedom in Heaven.

Does this openness and truth mean that Heaven will provide us with the answers to all our questions about the universe? Canon Streeter thinks this is a good possibility: "It is precisely because [St. Paul] rates knowledge of the truth so high that in praise of love he says that love is higher *even* than knowledge. And what he looks for in the world to come is, not the abolition of the interest in truth, but its full and complete fruition."[55] With this, however, a modern American theologian disagrees: Peter J. Kreeft, professor of philosophy at Boston College, writes, "There are two reasons [why this is not so] . . . the first one is simply a confusion between Heaven and divinity. We will remain human in Heaven, therefore finite, therefore our knowledge will remain finite. . . . The second reason [is that] . . . by the standard of the *infinite*, inexhaustible perfection of God, we remain children forever."[56] Perhaps this is so, yet Dr. Moody is quite sure that in the afterlife learning abounds. He tells of a woman who "described this place as a big university, where people were involved in deep conversations about the world around them."[57] We can be sure that Heaven implies an increase in knowledge, but whether it implies an answer to everything we cannot yet know. As Christians we do believe, however, that the truth about the universe which is gradually being revealed to men of science has its source in the Almighty Himself. I am inclined to believe, therefore, that as we move on through eternity, our understanding of the ultimate nature of all things will also move forward.

Worship is eighth in the list of heavenly characteristics of Heaven. Yet worship must be understood in its basic meaning. When we say that worship is a characteristic of Heaven, we do not wish to imply that Heaven is a perpetual Sunday or an interminable church service, or a constant droning of plainsong, or even a place where everyone is continuously strumming his golden harp. Instead, we would remind the reader that the term *worship* comes from two Middle English words, *worth* and the suffix *ship*. It is an activity that has to do with the worth of a person. When we worship a person, we treat him with the reverence due to his honor or merit or worth. When we use the word in a religious sense, we mean we are recognizing the worth of God and giving him the honor that he alone is worthy to receive. Pure worship is not asking God for anything. Pure worship is the adoration of God because of his worth.

Worship is important, both here and hereafter. We can see this importance by analogy. When we ask whether it matters if a child is polite or not, or whether or not a child has any love and respect for his parents, most parents agree that it matters a great deal. A good parent will teach his child to say "thank you" not because the parent needs it, but rather because the child needs to say it. Children learn to be thankful by expressing their thanks. And unless they are thankful and courteous they become spoiled and self-centered.

It is the same with us in our relationship to God. In spite of the fact that we worship entirely because of the goodness of God and the honor due him, worship is the fulfillment of our true selves. "What is the chief end of man?" asks the Scottish Westminster Shorter Catechism, and the answer is given, "To glorify God and enjoy him forever." In other words, in worship, we achieve the end which God has planned for us. By worship we grow away from self-centeredness or man-centeredness toward God-centeredness and all that this implies. Without worship, we are incomplete beings.

Worship also develops our love of God. The importance of this love is also illustrated by a parent's relationship to his child. A child learns to do well because of his parent who teaches him to do well. No matter how much a parent lectures, no matter how much he scolds or spanks, a child will not learn right conduct unless there is a positive love which keeps pace with positive teaching. You know, too, that a school teacher's effectiveness lies not so much in his or her knowledge as in his or her personality. The educational psychologists tell us that learning speed is in direct proportion to the pupil's attraction to those who are teaching.

So it is that by our worship we develop a love toward God, and with that love, it naturally follows that we do God's will.

We can be sure that in Heaven there will be worship in the pure sense of the word, or, if you wish, we can be sure that there will be time (if we may use that word) set aside for the singing of praises as such—surely the picture of Heaven we get in the Book of Revelation is that there is "time" for worship or, even more than that, there is a perpetual singing of praises—but in Heaven all our activities in the broader sense will be worship. Indeed, when you get right down to it, when a man or a woman does a useful job in this world, he or she has spent a lifetime in worship. Yes, there will be something analogous to church worship as we now know it, but that will be only part of it. As one of our hymns puts it,

> There are no tears within their eyes;
>   With love they keep perpetual tryst;
> And praise and work and rest are one
>   With thee, O Christ.[58]

Beauty certainly has to be considered in any contemplation of Heaven, so we place it as ninth in this list of characteristics of Heaven. We often think of beauty as one of the highest achievements of which humans are capable, and rightly so, for beauty is of the nature of God himself. As man becomes civilized, more beauty enters his life, and the higher the civilization, the higher the place of beauty in the culture's priorities. We speak of "the beauty of worship" or "the beauty of holiness;" no worship can be devoid of it. No architecture, no matter how functional it is, serves a proper purpose if it lacks beauty. It is also expected, of course, that music should be beautiful, and likewise all the arts. But more than that, speech should be beautiful, and all our daily relationships. If all this is true in this world, then it is logical to believe that beauty will be even more a part of the world to come.

One element that comes through loud and clear in the findings of parapsychology and mysticism is beauty. I mentioned it in chapter 3 that those who have died in the clinical sense of the word and come back to tell about it almost always speak of this beauty. Many see such wondrous beauty on the other side of life that they don't want to come back.

One Sunday summer afternoon during my days in Waterbury, Connecticut, I was calling on all the patients of our faith at one of the local hospitals, for most of the other clergy were on vacation at the time. I came across a Mr. Gilbert Hitchcock, a member of our neighboring church of St. John's. While he was with the Army in Korea, he had contracted malaria. As often happens with that disease, the attacks come and go for some time. One day, following his discharge from the military, Mr. Hitchcock found himself in the Veteran's Hospital at Rocky Hill. The malaria had set in again. "My temperature shot up to 105 or more," he told me, "and I lost consciousness.

"It was then I got a glimpse of what must have been Heaven. There was Christ: I saw his features quite clearly. He was holding me by the arm, helping me across this rounded up bridge. The side of the bridge from which I had come was covered by complete blackness, but the other side was bathed in a glorious light, showing the most beautiful country scene you ever saw. There were meadows and rolling hills, with grass so trim and neat it looked as though everything was covered with lawns. There were trees, too. It was the prettiest sight man could see, peaceful and wonderful."

Not everybody has had quite the same kind of experience as this, though I've had many people tell me of something similar. Some people see the city we usually call the Heavenly Jerusalem. This was what happened to Dr. Ritchie, whose story was told in chapter 3. Dr. Ritchie saw a city constructed of light where even the walls, buildings, streets, seemed to give off light.[59]

St. Paul, in the well-known passage where he obliquely refers to his own mystical experience as "the man caught up into the third heaven,"* mentions this beauty. Speaking of himself, he says, "And I know that this man was caught up into Paradise—whether in the body or out of the body I do not know, God knows—and I heard things that cannot be told, which man may not utter."[60] And again, St. Paul writes, quoting what is gener-

---

* In an effort to refute the charges of his opponents who were attacking his authority, St. Paul indulges in a little boasting, which he readily admits. Yet he does not want to give the appearance of being egotistical, so, in relating this experience, he avoids the use of the pronoun *I* and, instead uses this oblique reference to himself. As for the *third heaven,* both the Slavonic Enoch and the Testament of the Twelve Patriarchs (Levi chapter 3) have

ally believed to be a lost apocryphal or pseudepigraphical[†] source, "But as it is written, 'What no eye has seen, or ear heard, nor the heart of man conceived, what God has prepared for those who love him.'"[61]

The last book of the Bible dares to be a little more precise than St. Paul. In chapter 4 of John of Patmos's mystical vision, we are introduced to the "present" Heaven, where God is portrayed in splendor as he "who sits upon the throne," one likened unto "jasper and carnelian."[62] Around the splendor of God and his throne is a rainbow, the symbol of the covenant, and before the throne is a "sea of glass, like crystal."[63] The picture of the ceaseless worship of Heaven, too—the "four and twenty elders . . . clothed in white raiment . . . [with] crowns of gold," the "seven lamps of fire burning before the throne," the singing of "holy, holy holy, Lord God Almighty," and the proclamation of "worthy is the Lamb"[64]—ring of wondrous beauty.

At the end of the book, when "a new heaven and a new earth appear,"[65] we find all traces of the sea gone:[66] instead, there is a city, shaped as a tremendous cube.[67] The walls are of jasper, the foundations of various jewels, and the streets of gold. A river—the water of life—flows from the throne of God, and beside the river grows the tree of life.[68] This is, most moderns believe, symbolic language, but surely something like that is there. It is a case of the writer's suffering from the poverty of language, a vain attempt to describe the indescribable. John Mason Neale, in his rather free translation of Bernard of Cluny's twelfth-century *De Contemptu Mundi*, gives us one of our popular hymns, of which I will quote only four stanzas:

> Jerusalem the golden,
>   With milk and honey blest,
> Beneath thy contemplation

---

seven stages of Heaven; note, however, that not all these stages are what we usually associate with the word *Heaven*. In fact some of them are clearly *Hell*. The third Heaven, though, is to be identified with *Paradise* or the heavenly counterpart of the Garden of Eden, a place of great beauty.

† This word *pseudepigraphical* we used in another form in chapter 4. *A Practical Church Dictionary* defines the word *Pseudepigrapha* as "anonymous Hebrew religious books of the centuries immediately before and after Christ, ascribed to someone other than their real author, which were excluded from the Canon of the Greek Bible . . . but which were at various times thought to be divinely inspired: Book of Enoch, Assumption of Moses, Psalms of Solomon, and others" (by James M. Malloch, Morehouse-Barlow Co., New York, 1964).

> Sink heart and voice opprest:
> I know not, O I know not,
>   What joys await us there;
> What radiancy of glory,
>   What bliss beyond compare!
>
> O one, O only mansion!
>   O Paradise of joy!
> Where tears are ever banished
>   And smiles have no alloy
> Thy loveliness oppresses
>   All human thoughts and heart,
> And none, O Peace, O Sion,
>   Can sing thee as thou art.
>
> With jasper glow thy bulwarks,
>   Thy streets with emeralds blaze;
> The sardius and the topaz
>   Unite in thee their rays;
> Thine ageless walls are bonded
>   With amethyst unpriced,
> The saints build up the fabric,
>   And the corner-stone is Christ.
>
> The cross is all thy splendor,
>   The Crucified thy praise;
> His laud and benediction
>   Thy ransomed people raise:
> Upon the Rock of Ages
>   They built thy holy tower:
> Thine is the victor's laurel;
>   And thine the golden dower.[69]

To say the least, St. Bernard's poem employs the most extravagant language—especially as Neale has translated it—but it is possible even so that it falls short of what joys await us there. Again, as St. Paul affirms, "No eye has seen . . . what God has prepared for those who love him."

Finally, in our description of Heaven we come to what is known as *The Vision of God* or *The Beatific Vision*. The sixth Beatitude promises, "The pure in heart . . . shall see God,"[70] and the First Epistle of John promises, we shall see the face of Christ:

> Beloved, now are we the sons of God, and it does not appear what we shall be: but we know that, when he shall appear, we shall be like him; for we shall see him as he is.[71]

John is telling us that when Christ appears at the end of time, we will be made like him—having a glorified body like unto his—and *we shall see our Lord face to face.* This vision of Jesus, or, more accurately, the vision of the Divine Being or the Holy Trinity, is what is generally called "The Beatific Vision," the *summum bonum,* the highest goal of man, and it is obtainable, in the proper sense of the word, only in the highest Heaven. In fact, sometimes Heaven is defined as the place "where the redeemed rejoice in the vision of God."[72]

Dr. Kenneth E. Kirk, in his classic work on the subject, makes the observation that the doctrine of the Beatific Vision has its beginnings in ancient times; for it was Irenaeus (c.130–200 A.D.), "the first of a great line of post-apostolic theologians," who declared, "The glory of God is a living man; and the life of man is the vision of God."[73] In fact, as Dr. Kirk puts it, "Christianity had come into the world with a double purpose, to offer men the vision of God, and to call them to the pursuit of that vision."[74]

The doctrine of the Vision of God, however, is no simple one and is subject to many interpretations. During the Middle Ages a great deal of controversy surrounded the doctrine. On the one hand there was the question of when this vision would be obtainable—did it have to wait for the General Resurrection at the Last Day or was it available to those worthy of such a sight before the final consummation? On the other hand there existed the controversy between the Dominicans and the Franciscans as to the nature of this Beatific Vision. The Franciscans taught that the love of God is the real principle involved, while the Dominicans stressed the knowledge of God.[75]

With respect to all this controversy—and much more which is not mentioned—I am inclined to agree with Dr. Streeter, who believes that the ideas and associations that have clustered around the term *Beatific Vision* have actually "exercised a misleading and demoralizing influence on religious life and practice on earth."[76] Toward understanding what is meant by this term, then, Streeter would define the essence of "Eternal Life" as "the knowledge of God and of His Son Jesus Christ," which, as we have already pointed out, is something every Christian strives for in this world, and that knowledge is intensified and brought to fulfillment in the world to come. This means, then, that the Beatific Vision for the most part, but not entirely, is another way of expressing what is listed as the first characteristic of Heaven, except that this fellowship with Christ must be expanded to include the other two persons of the Trinity.

But not entirely, as we say, is this Beatific Vision to be equated with fellowship with the Divine Being. There is everything to be said for actually looking at the face of our Lord or even—if it be possible—on the face of God Himself. We become like the person we admire, and to admire is the first step on the way to adoration.

Nathaniel Hawthorne's classic story of "The Great Stone Face" helps to illustrate what we mean. In view of the character Ernest's home, in the White Mountains of New Hampshire, there was a mountainside rock formation which, when seen at the proper distance, gave the appearance of a great stone face. This face, moreover, embodied all that was good and noble, an "expression . . . grand and sweet," seeming to embrace "all mankind in its affection." Now, there was a long-standing prophecy in this area that "a child was to be born . . . who was to become the greatest and the noblest personage of his time, and whose countenance in manhood, should bear an exact resemblance of the Great Stone Face. . . ." Since Ernest's cottage commanded an excellent view of this face, he was wont to gaze upon it for hours. Even after he matured, when his day's work was complete, he would spend an hour or two in contemplation of this great figure. In the course of time Ernest became a kind of local philosopher. People from all walks of life came from near and far to see and converse with him. Often he would stand in the open, in view of the great face, and speak to the people gathered about him. One evening when he was talking in this manner, someone from the crowd exclaimed, "Behold! Ernest is himself the likeness of the Great Stone Face!" "This is true," everyone agreed. The personality of that great face had stamped itself upon Ernest and shaped his character.[77]

Something comparable to this, we suggest, will happen in Heaven. We will be given the opportunity to come face to face with our Lord and become like him.

On the other hand, let it be frankly admitted, one can go too far with the idea of the contemplation of the person of the Divine Being. The danger is reflected in some of our hymnody, such as this stanza by Frederick William Faber:

> Father of Jesus, love's reward!
>   What rapture will it be
> Prostrate before thy throne to lie,
>   And gaze and gaze on thee![7]

Had Ernest spent all his time gazing upon the Great Stone Face and not done any practical work in the world, he would have become a ne'er-do-well instead of a great man. Adoration of God must include both praise and work, or, to put it another way, the whole idea of the Vision of God involves a life of doing God's will.

To what degree we can actually see God or really come to know him must always be debatable. Belief in a personal Creator God implies that he knows us as persons, and because he knows us, we on our part can know Him. Whether you call this knowing of God as "seeing" or "loving" or as "intuitive knowledge" does not matter. Actually, too, we should make the point that seeing with eyes that respond to light stimuli in the same way as we see here is impossible in a spiritual body. Instead, we see with spiritual eyes. In fact, Dr. Moody, to whose books we have so often referred, cites case after case in which a person's vision after death is much more powerful than before, and no amount of light hurts the spiritual eyes.[79]

Dr. E. L. Mascall reminds us of the long-standing desire on the part of religious man to have a vision of God, yet man in his physical body finds this impossible.[80] He cites two well-known examples: In classical mythology, Zeus wooed Semele in his human form, but Semele wanted proof of the person he claimed to be: she wanted Zeus to prove his divinity by appearing to her in all his splendor. When her wish was finally granted, the maiden was struck dead and burned to ashes by the unbearable blazing majesty of the appearance.

In the Bible we have the story of Moses who begged God to show him his glory. The reply was "I will make all my goodness pass before you, and will proclaim before you my name 'The Lord;' . . . but you cannot see my face; for man shall not see me and live."[81] And while Isaiah is given a vision of God in the Temple,[82] and Ezekiel sees God veiled under the likeness of a man,[83] these are simply visions.

When we come to the New Testament, however, we do get closer to the fulfillment of this desire. The sixth Beatitude, as we have already pointed out, tells us that the "Pure in heart" shall "see God." The Fourth Gospel modifies this by saying that we can see God *through* Christ. As that Gospel reports the conversation at the time of the Last Supper, Philip makes the request, "Show us the Father." To this Jesus replies, "Have I been with you so long, and yet you do not know me, Philip? He who has seen me has seen the Father. . . ."[84] Whatever the vision of God might be in the eyes of Jesus, he put it forth as a present reality for those about him. If Philip and the others around Jesus might look upon him and see God, so can all other Christians.

St. Paul, too, is not without hope of this promise. In his great sermon on love, the Apostle admits that our present perception of spiritual realities is comparable to looking through a darkly colored glass: but when the time comes, when we enter the heavenly realm, he says, we shall be able to see "face to face."[85] Also, St. Paul tells us, we are very bold in our hope of seeing Jesus.[86] And, he assures us, this face of Christ reveals none other than the light of God, "For it is the God who said, 'Let light shine out of darkness,' who has shone in our hearts to give the light of the knowledge of the glory of God in the face of Christ."[87]

In Heaven, will it be possible to see and understand the Power that is behind all creation? I leave it an open question. Jesus, speaking of children, said, "Their angels do always behold the face of my Father who is in Heaven."[88] Surely, too, as promised, we will one day be like the angels; we will see our Lord as he is and through him we will be able to comprehend the other persons of the Trinity.

Let us conclude this chapter on the same theme with which we began. After Jesus greeted the return of his seventy missionaries, he told them, "Do not rejoice . . . that the spirits are subject to you; but rejoice that your names are written in heaven." This goal of Heaven we seem to have lost in our modern world—not only in our secular society, which might well be expected, but in our churches as well. This is unfortunate, because, having lost our goal, we have forgotten our purpose in life. As the Book of Proverbs warns us, "Where there is no vision the people perish."[89]

There is no intention to disparage the importance of this world—chapter 6 is entirely concerned with this subject—but we must remember that this life is good for how long?—fifty, sixty, seventy, at the very best, a hundred years. What comes after that is forever. If we forget our eternal purpose, we are leaving out the most important directive in this life. As our hymn reassures us,

Heaven

> We are traveling home to God,
> In the way the fathers trod:
> They are happy now, and we
> Soon their happiness shall see.[90]

Again, as St. Paul tells us, "Our true citizenship is in heaven." It is not a question of pie-in-the-skyism; rather it is a question of the terrible temptation to sell our heavenly birthright for a mess of earthly pottage. There is an old Gaelic saying, "We should often be mindful of the place where we're longest to be." Heaven to the young man or the young woman seems a long, long time off—something we needn't bother about in this practical world, at least not for the present. But Heaven or its opposite is much closer than we realize—timewise and otherwise. In fact every day brings us one day closer to that ultimate goal. "The night is far spent," St. Paul reminds us, "the day is at hand. Now [while we have time] let us cast off the works of darkness and put on the armor of light."[91] So, St. Paul admonishes, "Put on the Lord Jesus Christ," for it is now time to be thinking of Heaven and making plans to get there—before it is too late.

"Our destiny is beyond all imagining," Dr. Easton of General Seminary once said, "for it will bring us the open vision of God, and he who can endure the sight will be like the angels."

12

Hell

Hell is a controversial idea. Though it is a concept accepted since ancient times, and everyone was sure who would go there, we hear more and more Christians arguing that there is something wrong with the traditional view of Hell, that it is out of character with a merciful God. Many Christians are determined to reject any belief in Hell. Others simply would cool it down a bit.

The old-fashioned Puritan Hell is described in the famous sermon delivered by Jonathan Edwards. "To help your conception [of eternal punishment]," he said to his congregation,

> imagine yourself to be cast into a fiery oven, all of a glowing heat, or into the midst of a glowing brick-kiln of a great furnace, where your pain would be as much greater than that occasioned by accidentally touching a coal of fire, as the heat is greater. Imagine also that your body were to lie there for a quarter of an hour, full of fire, all the while full of quick sense; what Horror would you feel at the entrance of such a furnace! And how long would that quarter of an hour seem to you! If it were to be measured by a glass, how long would that glass seem to be running! And after you had endured it for one minute, how over-bearing would it be to you to think that you had to endure the other fourteen! But what would be the effect on your soul, if you knew you must lie there enduring that torment to the full for twenty-four hours! And how much greater would be the effect if you knew you must endure it for a whole year; and how vastly greater still, if you knew you must endure it for a

thousand years! O then, how would your heart sink, if you thought, if you knew, that you must bear it forever and ever! That there would be no end! That after millions of millions of ages, your torment would be no nearer to an end, than ever it was; and that you never, never should be delivered.[1]

Shocking though Hell may be in this description, Edwards is in good Calvinistic company. Here is the way the preacher in one of Robert Burns's poems threatens his flock:

> A vast, unbottom'd, boundless pit,
>   Fill'd fu' o' lowan brunstane
> Whase raging flame an' scorching heat,
>   Wad melt the hardest whunstane.[2]

Or we have Milton's description of Hell in *Paradise Lost:*

> A dungeon horrible on all sides round
> As one great furnace flam'd yet from those flames.
> No light, but rather darkness visible,
> Serv'd only to discover sights of woe,
> Regions of sorrow, doleful shades, where peace
> And rest can never dwell, hope never come.
> That comes to all, but torture without end.[3]

If these are typical descriptions of Hell, there is small wonder that many modern Christians are certain Hell does not exist. Surely we cannot think of the God that Jesus presented as one who would commit to a fiery, eternal torture the soul of even the worst of his creatures. Is there, then, any place for Hell in a modern Christian's belief? Or do such concepts belong to the cruel and distant past?

I contend that, despite the bad press Hell has received in our day, the doctrine still has a rightful place in sound Christian theology. Further, I believe that God *in his mercy* has provided Hell—as a refuge for those who refuse to love him. As emphasized in chapter 11, the primary characteristic of Heaven is a situation in which we can increase our fellowship with the Lord. It is also one where we enjoy the fellowship of other God-centered souls. Heaven, moreover, does involve worship. It is a place where there is justice, goodness, truth, brotherhood, and love. But must everyone fit into this pattern of worship and work for God?

On the contrary, God, in creating mankind, gave us a choice. A basic feature in both Jewish and Christian theology is the concept of free will. God loves us, for he created us in the first place. He wants us to return that love to him. In the person of Jesus he died for us. He pleads, he is always ready to welcome us back, *but* he does not demand that we respond. So those who do not want to respond to the love of God have a sanctuary—if we may use that word in this connection. They have a hiding place, or a seclusion, or dungeon, separating them from God. Canon Theodore Wedell, late warden of Washington's College of Preachers, used to say, "Hell is God's mercy to the sinner." Or, as Cardinal Newman once wrote, "Heaven is not a place of happiness, except for the holy."[4]

I am of course using symbolic language here, space-time terminology. We know that it is not possible to separate one's self from God, for God is everywhere. What we can say, though, is that, insofar as it is possible, Hell is a condition where God's presence and his love are not to be perceived.

Once I made the mistake of becoming involved in an eschatological discussion with a woman of the Jehovah's Witnesses sect. She maintained that the doctrine of Hell has no place in scripture; she claimed that it had been thought up by the medieval Church to scare the populace into submission to the hierarchy. "The word *Hell* doesn't once occur in the New Testament," she pointed out. "So there is no Hell."

In one sense the woman was right. The word *Hell* is not once mentioned per se in the original New Testament, and, for that matter, it is not once mentioned in the whole Bible. *Hell* is a German word, and it is used in our translation of the New Testament for either *Gehenna* or *Hades*. (Sometimes *Hell* is used in the King James Version as a translation for *Sheol*, as in Psalm 6). Regardless of what words are used, though, the concept of Hell is very much present in the New Testament, and you cannot get rid of it unless you also get rid of the New Testament.

The concept of Hell that emerged in our Lord's day grew up during the apocalyptic period in Israel's religious development. It will be remembered from chapter 4 that Sheol was originally conceived of as a cavern under the earth, the dwelling place of all the departed. And originally, too, there was no moral judgment involved in going to Sheol. Man simply lived in this world under the watchful eye of the Almighty and then departed to Sheol to be seen by God no more. But, as the understanding of God developed and it was realized that he is in charge of all creation, it came to be understood that his jurisdiction extended over Sheol as well as the rest of the cosmos. And jurisdiction on the part of a righteous God inevitably meant judgment at the end of life and segregation in Sheol of the good and the bad. Hence we get the concept, as shown in such apocalyptic literature as I Enoch, of different areas in Sheol and a compartment roughly resembling the early Christian concept of Hell.[5]

When the time came to translate the Old Testament into Greek, producing what we call the Septuagint, the word *Sheol* was rendered *Hades* (ἄδης), the standard Greek word for the underworld, the home of the departed. The word *Hades* is used in the Greek New Testament eleven times, and this word, with one exception, is translated by the King James Version of the Bible as *Hell*. But there is another word used by the Greek New Testament that is also translated as *Hell*, and that is *Gehenna* (γέεννα), a word which also appears eleven times.

South of Jerusalem there is a ravine which in Old Testament times was called "The Valley of the Son of Hinnom," or "The Valley of the Sons of Hinnom," or just "The Valley of Hinnom" (בי א הנם). The Greek and Latin form of this is Gehenna. There in the days of the apostate kings Ahaz and Manasseh children were burnt in sacrifice to Moloch, the Tyrian Baal.[6] As time went on, no doubt in large measure because of these idolatrous associations, the place became a huge rubbish dump, where a fire was kept constantly burning to consume the refuse. In the first century B.C. this fact was given eschatological significance, and the term *Gehenna* was used metaphorically for the place of the damned, a destiny that implied fire or burning, a never-ending burning. The beginning of this thinking goes back to Isaiah 66:24: "And they shall go forth [from Jerusalem] and look on the dead bodies of the men who have rebelled against me; for their worm shall not die, their fire shall not be quenched, and they shall be an abhorrence to all flesh."[7] Consequently, in time—by at least the first century B.C.—Gehenna had become Hell, the Hell of fiery torment for the wicked either immediately after death or before the final judgment day.[8]

This development continued. Sometime around the New Testament period the terms *Hades* and *Gehenna* had become interchangeable for the Jew; though in the New Testament itself *Gehenna* has more fearful overtones than does *Hades,* because the destruction of the body by fire, as implied by *Gehenna,* was abhorrent to the Jew, the worst fate that could befall a man or woman. When Jesus tells the Parable of the Rich Man and the Beggar (Luke 16:19–31), he uses the word *Hades* (or, more exactly, the

Aramaic equivalent of this word) for the afterworld, because both the selfish rich man and the beggar are there. In this parable, consistent with what we find in apocalyptic literature, "a great chasm" separates the two. The rich man, who was completely oblivious to the earthly plight of the poor beggar, ended up in that part of Hades where there is fiery torment, but he could easily look across the yawning gap to the Messianic banquet and see Lazarus seated at Abraham's right, in the place of honor. In contrast, when Jesus is quoted using the word *Hell* in the judgment sections of the Sermon on the Mount, it is *Gehenna* (as in Matthew 5:22, 5:29, 30). We might add, too, that there are other equivalents for Hell in the New Testament, such as "the pit," "Abaddon," "destruction," "Tartaras," etc., and it will be recognized that most of these other terms are found only in the Book of Revelation. (In this last book of the Bible we get much vindictiveness, inconsistent with the main thrust of the New Testament, for the Book was written in a time of persecution under the Emperor Domitian [c. 95 A.D.] and consequently represents a natural reaction to the fear that Christianity might soon be crushed by the pagan forces of Rome.)

Christ himself, let it be observed, though he willingly uses the symbols of damnation current in his day, also describes those who fail to accept the opportunity of the Kingdom as being in a place where there is "weeping and gnashing of teeth." Thus when he likened the Kingdom to a householder who has "risen up and shut the door," those excluded will "weep and gnash [their] teeth."[9] Or, as Matthew relates the Parable of the Great Feast, God is compared to a king who gives a wedding banquet for his son. An offending guest is ordered to be "cast ... into ... outer darkness, [where] men will weep and gnash their teeth."[10] These passages and others like them imply that the person who chooses not to follow the straight path to the light of the Kingdom will indeed be left in the darkness of his own misery. The impact of the whole Gospel suggests that this understanding of Hell is much more in keeping with the idea of the Lord of Love than the Hell of fiery torment. While we cannot conceive of a loving God who condemns to eternal fire even the worst, yet we can easily conceive of a person, who, turning his back on God, chooses the miserable condition of one in darkness, isolated from all good fellowship.

We know many sad people who live around us now, men and women who love to "stew in their own juice," as the saying goes. These people have a love for self-centeredness and misery and don't want to be relieved

Hell

of what has become for them the pleasure of constant stewing. It is Hell, but some people prefer—or think they prefer—that kind of an existence to the one God intended for them.

Dr. Caird of McGill University used to tell the story of the bus which made a daily trip back and forth from Hell to Heaven. It was a free ride, and anyone wanting to leave Hell and journey to Heaven was allowed to do so. But, as the story goes, there were few takers, and even those who did make the trip to Heaven found they just couldn't stand it and soon found themselves back in Hell.

Let us not go too far, however, in thinking of Hell as purely a matter of one's own choosing. There is the good possibility of Hell's being a matter of God's decision, his judgment on someone who *must* be separated from the rest of God's people. Modern criminal justice regards imprisonment for habitual offenders not as punishment per se (which does little if any good), but as segregation, separation from others whom they would victimize. In human society here, at least, it is not true that re-education and love and reform programs *always* bring about a change in character. Rather experience shows that some individuals, like Satan himself, are determined to do wrong, no matter what. We have to protect society by the long-term imprisonment of these offenders. We wonder whether this determination to do wrong cannot go beyond this earth, and we wonder whether the need to segregate for the protection of others must also go beyond this earth. Milton in *Paradise Lost* makes the point that those in Heaven are *not* beyond corruption—only God is perfect—and, therefore, we ask, is it not possible to corrupt those of the Christian fellowship in the world beyond?

For what it's worth, the need for segregation seems to be substantiated by at least some parapsychological experiences. The author of *Journeys out of the Body* (a book mentioned in chapter 3) speaks of his traveling by "the borders of hell," where he comes in contact with some utterly despicable beings who are bent on inflicting their evil on others. From the grip of these characters, Robert Monroe relates, he had much trouble escaping.[11] More than this, there do seem to be demonic beings who from time to time are successful in possessing otherwise good people. Dr. Ritchie, in his *Return from Tomorrow* (an amplification of his experience related in chapter 3), describes how hellish spirit characters wait for a chance to enter a living earthly body.[12] *Occult Phenomena*, a book by a Roman Catholic writer which bears an imprimatur, has a disturbing section on possession and describes a case in which there can be absolutely no doubt about possession.[13] Biblical evidence indeed supports this contention, and my physician step-son is sure of it. Exorcisms, and only exorcisms, have cured some mentally ill humans. Are these demonic beings (those who would possess if they could) normally in Hell? I am inclined to believe that they are imprisoned there; I also believe that these beings are more than just the self-centered characters whom we usually think of as dwelling in Hell: they are bent on poisoning God's good work at every opportunity. There are people in Hell who would, if they could, make a Hell of Heaven. If in this life we pray "Lead us not into temptation," and we are assured that this prayer is answered, does it not follow that God will also keep us from temptation in the next life as well? We need to be protected from corrupting personalities wherever they are. Hell, then, must to some extent be a prison-house for spirits of all sorts who would pervert God's purpose for us.

Everyone seems to have his own favorite description of Hell, some versions worked out from real insight into the horror of alienation from God, others worked out as a result of vindictiveness and the desire for revenge.

A favorite human temptation is to wish one's arch-enemy in Hell. When one is absolutely convinced he is in the right and the opposition is in the wrong, there is, understandably, the tendency to believe God will take care of the punishment of the opposition in the next life. This vindictiveness is surely the main shortcoming of the Book of Revelation. Here the enemies of the Church are thought to be so wicked that something absolutely dreadful must be in store for them either at the end of the world or in the life to come—such as torture from sulphur-pit locusts,[14] a cavalry of fire-belching horses,[15] earthquakes,[16] and the flow of blood from the wine press of God's wrath as a river five feet deep and two hundred miles in length,[17] and, if those torments are not enough, there is threatened in the next world "the lake of fire and brimstone . . . [where those who oppose God] will be tormented day and night for ever and ever."[18] The terrible oversight of this book is its underestimation of the power of God's redeeming love, the failure to realize that God would one day convert these enemies of the Church, even the leaders of the pagan Roman Empire.

There are countless humorous stories about the frustrations of Hell, too, such as the one about the man who loved golf above all other things, especially on Sunday morning when he should have been in church. Over and over again he was told that he would end up in Hell, until he became quite sure that he would do just that—but he felt that this bit of green heaven here was well worth the price. Finally the time came for him to hit his last ball on earth. He collapsed of a heart attack on Easter Day, just as he was finishing up on the eighteenth hole.

Imagine this sport addict's surprise when he found himself on the other side of life, not amid the flames of the sulphur pit but still dressed in his golfing togs, approaching the most beautiful golf course he had ever seen! Ecstatic, the man asked if he could use the course. Indeed, he could. The best of drivers, irons, and putters were also available for his use. "Let's get going," he called to the caddy. When they reached the first fairway, the golfer placed the tee in the ground. The caddy handed him the driver. "All right now," he commanded, "let's have the ball."

"I'm sorry, Sir," replied the caddy. "There are no balls here."

"No balls," screamed the golfer. "No balls, and this beautiful course and everything to go with it, but no balls!"

"That's right, Sir. No balls. You see, that's the *hell* of it."

Yes, Hell is frustration; it is nonfulfillment; and such stories, lacking though they may be, tell us something of the plight of one there.

Trevor Huddleston likens Hell to what has happened in South Africa:

> Hell is not a bad description of South Africa, nor a very great exaggeration. For, as I understand it theologically, the real pain and agony (expressed symbolically but very definitely by Christ in the Gospels) of hell is frustration. Its atmosphere is dread. Its horror is its eternity. When you are in hell, you see the good but you can never reach it; you know that you are made for God but between yourself and Him "there is a great gulf fixed." It is not a bad description of the ultimate meaning of apartheid.[19]

Hell is not only separation from God but also, to a large extent, separation from one's fellow man. "I think this is Hell; it is so lonely here." These are the alleged words of a son to his father, via a psychic, following the son's suicide.[20] It would be judgmental to say that this boy was in Hell, but really his situation had the potential of Hell—loneliness. In Heaven we have fellowship. In Hell we have the opposite of this—loneliness. Heaven is a place where there are no separations. Hell is a place where separations are dominant. One often hears it jokingly said, "I want to go to Hell when I die, so I can be with my friends." But this is nonsense, for in a situation where self-centeredness dominates, friends will be lacking. Just as there is love in Heaven, there is hatred in Hell. The French existentialist Sartre, in his one-act play *No Exit*, describes Hell as a room in which three people who cannot stand each other are forced to live together for eternity.

On the other hand, it must be admitted that there can be a fellowship of sorts in Hell—a circle of those who hate God and mankind as a whole and share that hatred. Milton's picture of Hell suggests as much. There can be some kind of companionship among thieves, just as there can be family and social ties in the Mafia. Yet, as we have seen from the record of organized crime, whatever honor there is among anti-God people, it is never enough to prevent their killing one another whenever self-interest or expediency requires it.

Most of the mystics are fond of associating Hell with fire. This tendency persists despite everything we moderns would like to say in opposition. Typical is the way St. Hildegard of Bingen (1089–1179) describes the place:

> I saw a well, deep and broad, full of boiling pitch and sulphur, and around it were wasps and scorpions, who scared but did not injure the souls of those therein. . . .
>
> Near the pond of clear water I saw a great fire. In this some souls were burned and others were girdled with snakes, and others drew in and again exhaled the fire like a breath, while malignant spirits cast lighted stones at them.[21]

My Vermont mystic friend reports this description of Hell given to her by her grandson John:

> I've seen it over here—the "bottomless pit," I think they call it—and there isn't language to describe it. It almost strangles you to get anywhere near it. The stench of it is still in my nostrils now, although it was some time ago I saw it. I wouldn't want any of my dear ones headed for that place! God help us.

It is said that the Eskimos picture Hell as a region of unmitigated cold, for that is the worst that people who live near or within the Arctic Circle can imagine. So maybe if we understand all the descriptions of Hell in terms of fire as largely symbolic language for the worst that can happen to us, we approach the truth. Our Lord certainly minced no words about the dread involved. He clearly stressed the imperativeness of making a decision for the Kingdom before it is too late—"Enter by the narrow gate: for the gate is wide and the way is easy, that leads to destruction. . . . For the gate is narrow and the way is hard, that leads to life, and those who find it are few."[22]

Our final hellish consideration has to do with the hopelessness of the place. Dante placed over the entrance of Hell these words: "All hope abandon, ye who enter here."[23] And Milton says, "hope never comes / That comes to all." Such a characterization has been the standard Christian understanding of Hell—a choice from which there is no retreat. Is there, then, any hope for the hopeless? Many moderns say Yes, God never shuts the gate of opportunity, either in this life or in the life to come, and eventually the power of his love will prevail (a doctrine known as Universalism).*

But, we may well ask the Universalists, is there not a point in the course of a person's journey through eternity when he cannot turn back? Bishop Pike, in one of his recorded eschatological sermons,[24] reminds us of a sign posted a few miles above Niagara Falls—"No boating beyond this point." Though, it may well be that the exact spot where it is dangerous to boat is debatable—it depends on such factors as the type of boat used or the current of the Niagara River on that particular day—there *is* a point where there *is no* turning back; the current created by two hundred thousand tons of water a minute will carry you over the falls and down into a gigantic whirlpool, and you won't have a chance. Likewise there is a point in the course of a person's journey through eternity where there is no retreat.

In chapter 10 we made mention of the sin against the Holy Ghost, the unforgivable sin, and we will go into the subject again in the next chapter. When a person turns black into white, evil into right, when he loses all

---

* The classic proponent of Universalism is the patristic writer Origen (c. 185–254 A.D.), especially in his *Contra Celsum*, where he argues that eventually even the Devil will be saved and returned to Heaven. An example of a modern Universalist is Bishop John A. T. Robinson. He writes, "But no amount of human sin . . . can affect or deflect the loving purpose of God in Christ . . . since God has elected all for *eternal* fellowship with Him, that He loves every man beyond any power of his to sin himself out of the relationship in which he is created." (*In the End, God,* James Clarke & Co., London, 1950, p. 81.) He would agree with Origen that "Christ remains on the cross as long as one sinner remains in hell" (p.123).

contact with the moral universe, he has done a good job at shutting out all help.

If you go out swimming or boating in the Niagara River above the warning sign, it may be dangerous but you can always row back into shore, or, if you are a good swimmer, you can always swim back, and you'll be all right. But beyond that sign you won't be all right. It may be that God will forgive and forgive and forgive again; it may be that God will receive us into his Kingdom even at the eleventh hour; but we must also realize that we can wait too long, so long that we lose all desire to get right with God and be forgiven. It is the sin that cannot be forgiven because, if one shuts out God and does it over and over again, one can become so accustomed to calling good evil, or evil good, that it is impossible to know the difference or to go back. If one turns black into white, or white into black, and keeps on doing that, one can lose sight of the truth and become impervious to the pleadings of the Spirit. Such a person finds himself being carried down the river of life, down to destruction. The arrival at the end of that journey is Hell.

13

The Intermediate State

"Not Good Enough for Heaven—Not Bad Enough for Hell." That is the title of a pamphlet put out by an organization that publishes evangelical tracts.[1] Despite the implied optimism of the title, however, the conclusion of the pamphlet is anything but optimistic. It says, in effect, "Well, that's just too bad, buster; you're going to Hell." This has been the traditional Protestant position: Heaven or Hell—nothing between.

Yet when you stop to think about it, just how many of us are really angelic enough for Heaven or horrible enough for Hell? Is eternal judgment simply a pass-fail system? We can be fairly sure that if anyone is interested in reading this book in the first place, he can't be bad enough for Hell; the people destined for Hell don't want to know about eternal life. On the other hand, when we look at the perfect example given to us by Jesus, we realize at once just how far short of the ideal we have fallen. With the exception of a few saints, most of us will have to do a lot of polishing up before we are ready for Heaven.

Look at it this way: A child is born into the world. This particular child happens to have intelligent parents, and all indications are that he or she will have a good future in the university. But that child certainly won't be ready for the university for a long time to come, not until, in fact, he or she has had twelve years of elementary and secondary education.

It's like that with every one of us, too, when it comes to our spiritual development. Average Mr. and Mrs. Churchmember, through the grace of God, may well be good Christians, but are they good enough, or will they be good enough at the time of death, to behold the King on his throne? After all, the scripture says nothing unclean can enter Heaven.[2] How many of us are spotless?

That is why the historic Church, along with many modern Christians of *most* denominations, has come to believe in some kind of intermediate state, or purgatory. No matter what else we can say for this doctrine, it is a matter of logic. While writing this chapter, I happened to mention the subject to an English physician, a member of a Pentecostal Baptist fellowship. "Do you believe in an intermediate state?" I asked. "I don't know for sure," the doctor replied, "but I certainly hope there is one." A lot of people respond that way. The need for purification makes sense.

I hesitate to use the term *purgatory* because of the implications of that word. In the preceding chapter we admitted that Hell has had a bad press. Purgatory has had an even worse one. Mention the word and immediately there comes to the mind of the average Protestant, at best, the descriptions found in Dante's *Divine Comedy*, and at worst, the commercialization of the afterlife.

Dante was very much the man who believed in letting the punishment fit the crime. The proud are purged by being bent down beneath the weight of an enormous stone tied to their backs; the envious are made to sit like blind beggars with eyes sewn shut with fine wire; the slothful are compelled to run at top speed, continuously encircling Mount Purgatory; the covetous must lie face-downward where they can see nothing to covet; the gluttonous are forced to look upon richly-laden fruit trees, but the fruit they dare not touch; finally, the lustful are purged by purifying fire. All of this is medieval Purgatory at its best.

Purgatory at its worst brings to mind a celestial accounting system where each sin and each good deed is weighed to determine its exact value for better or for worse. It brings to mind the muttering of innumerable Masses for the repose of the souls, the hawking of indulgences, and the purchase of pardons.

The account of Johann Tetzel, the Dominican monk appointed by the Archbishop of Mainz to sell indulgences, illustrates the custom of trafficking in holy favors. He was accused of saying,

> When in the box the money rings,
> The soul from Purgatory springs.[3]

The Intermediate State

It was this whole matter of indulgences that aroused Martin Luther to post on the door of the castle church in Wittenberg his famous ninety-five theses, for he rightly protested Tetzel's "sales pitch," that anyone could actually buy his way into Heaven. With Tetzel's technique for cashing in on Purgatory, it is small wonder that the doctrine has had a bad press. That kind of purgatory deserves a bad press.*

But there is another side to the whole idea of a purgatory. Despite the abuses to which the doctrine has been subjected, many modern churchmen contend that it both makes good sense and that it is scriptural.

The purpose of Purgatory, as its name implies, is to purify, to purge the dross, to enable the newly-arrived soul to grow until he is ready to go higher. Where the Intermediate State leaves off and Heaven takes over we cannot say. If we were to be that precise in our definition of the limits and bounds of the Intermediate State, we would fall into the same sin as did the medievalists who knew precisely what each sin and virtue was worth, or we would be no better than the camp-meeting preacher I once heard describe in detail the architecture of Heaven. But we do know that life in Christ is a life of growth. We agree with Cardinal Newman who wrote, "Growth is the only evidence of life."[4] Also we know that just as life does not stop at death, neither does growth: it continues as the individual develops. Many modern prayers take this growth for granted, as, for example, this one found in the Eucharistic intercessions of the American 1979 Prayer Book:

> And we also bless thy holy Name for all thy servants departed this life in thy faith and fear..., beseeching thee to grant them continual growth in thy love and service; and to grant us grace so to follow the good examples of... all thy saints, that with them we may be partakers of thy heavenly kingdom.[5]

In the Anglican Communion, though the doctrine of Purgatory is seldom identified per se, it is taken for granted. For example, when the American 1943 Hymnal comes to list the hymns under various headings,

---

* The chief theological argument the Protestants had for rejecting the doctrine of Purgatory is that it implies that the atonement made on the Cross was incomplete. They would state that there could be no struggle with sin in the hereafter. Consequently, they believed that the sanctification begun on earth is miraculously completed at the moment of death for those destined for Heaven. As the Westminster Shorter Catechism words it, "The souls of believers are at their death made perfect in holiness."

under "Church" it has three subheadings—"The Church Militant" (i.e., the Church on earth), "The Church Expectant" (The Church immediately after death), and "The Church Triumphant" (The Church around the throne of God). Hymns such as "The Church's One Foundation" belong to the theme of the Church Militant, while "Let Saints on Earth in Concert Sing with Those Whose Work Is Done" belongs to the Church Expectant theme, and "Jerusalem the Golden" belongs to the theme of the Church Triumphant. The Haggerston Catechism (of the Church of England) describes Purgatory as the "Church waiting to get well," and the author of this work in his own inimitable way illustrates this for children by his drawing of a church building immersed in a big bottle of medicine.[6]

Does the doctrine of the Intermediate State have any basis in Scripture? Contrary to the old fashioned Protestant assertion, indeed it does, but not so obviously as would make it immediately apparent. The most frequently quoted Gospel reference is the words of our Lord to Simon Peter, in the farewell address found in the Fourth Gospel:

> Let not your hearts be troubled.... In my Father's house are many mansions [rooms]; if it were not so, I would have told you. I go to prepare a place for you. And if I go and prepare a place for you, I will come again, and receive you unto myself; that where I am ye may be also.
> John 14:1–3, KJV

It may well be argued that this passage is about Heaven itself, for obviously Christ was going to prepare a place in Heaven for his apostles. On the other hand, no matter what name you give it, in the afterlife there are many levels of development. On leaving this life one goes first to that mansion or room or level for which he is fitted, and this is essentially what is meant by the "Intermediate State." It is the idea of development through which a person goes as he or she progresses upward toward the throne of God.

The concept of growth is presented in a more obvious form by St. Paul in his Second Letter to the Church in Corinth:

> And we all, with unveiled face, beholding the glory of the Lord, are being changed into his likeness from one degree of glory to another.
> II Corinthians 3:18

Again, in a strict sense, this is a reference to Heaven as such—for theologically speaking no one sees the Lord's face in a state of purgation—but it

The Intermediate State

is a passage which makes clear the principal of development or growth, and this, we firmly believe, is a most necessary ingredient of the life after death no matter how it is categorized.

Forgiveness also has its place in the Intermediate State theology. This fact is found in St. Matthew's version of Jesus' warning concerning the sin against the Holy Spirit:

> And whoever says a word against the Son of man will be forgiven; but whoever speaks against the Holy Spirit will not be forgiven, either in this age or in the age to come.
> Matthew 12:32

This gives the clear implication that sins other than the one against the Holy Spirit *are* forgiven in the age to come. There is opportunity for increased understanding, and repentance, and healing.

The symbolism of purging with fire—a first-century Jewish belief that I will discuss presently—is found in St. Paul's First Letter to the Church in Corinth:

> For no other foundation can any one lay than that which is laid, which is Jesus Christ. Now if any one builds on the foundation with gold, silver, precious stones, wood, hay, stubble—each man's work will become manifest; for the Day will disclose it, because it will be revealed with fire, and the fire will test what sort of work each one has done. If the work which any man has built on the foundation survives, he will receive a reward. If any man's work is burned up, he will suffer loss, though he himself will be saved, but only as through fire.
> I Corinthians 3:11–15

Perhaps it would be wrong to base the affirmation of the doctrine of Purgatory on these scripture passages alone, but knowing the Jewish background thinking that was accepted during New Testament days and for some time earlier—a belief which Jesus in no way refutes—one can indeed take seriously these scripture passages as supportive evidence. In fact, it would be difficult to make any sense of the Fourth Gospel's "many rooms" [RSV] or "many mansions" [KJV] without this background.[7]

Again we return to the concept of Sheol, as it became altered during the late pre-Christian period. As has been previously pointed out, in this intertestamental period religious thinkers came to realize that God did not forget those in Sheol. The belief that the departed were segregated to await final judgment came into being. There were rooms in Sheol, different areas for the good, for those in a middle position, and for those considered bad. While the idea of progress or movement from one area to another was not spelled out, it certainly was implied.

As the Book of I Enoch tells the story, Enoch is given a guided tour of the underworld, where he sees "four hollow places, deep and wide and very smooth . . . and dark to look at." The spirits of the souls of the dead are to assemble in these places until "the day of their judgment."[8]

> Then I asked regarding all the hollow places: "Why is one separated from the other?" And he [Raphael the Archangel] answered me saying: "These three have been made that the spirits of the dead might be separated. And this division has been made for the spirits of the righteous, in which there is the bright spring of water. And this has been made for sinners when they die and are buried in the earth and judgment has not been executed upon them in their lifetime. Here their spirits shall be set apart in this great pain, till the great day of judgment, scourgings and torments of the accused for ever, so that there may be retribution for their spirits."
>
> I Enoch 22:8–11

In such manner, Enoch goes on to describe various other categories of those imprisoned in Sheol, some awaiting judgment with hope, others without hope. The implication of the rooms or "mansions," is clear: the afterlife is not a simple entity or monolith. Nor is it an assembly of all the departed in one area. There are gradations —maybe not literally rooms or mansions or places as such—but in terms of a nonspatial state of existence, areas of a kind. It is difficult to say how far upward or downward a person is, spiritually. It may well be that personal locations in this respect are recognizable only to our Lord. Yet we can be sure that very few leave this life and find themselves immediately in Heaven. As my Vermont mystic friend put it (quoting her departed grandson), "You don't enter Heaven just by going over. You stay put for a time, and then you go to the plane for which you are fitted in your life on earth. After that you can go on."

Some Anglican writers (as we mentioned in chapter 10) have attempted to use the term *Paradise* for this Intermediate State, and they base their assumption on the words our Lord addressed to the penitent thief, "Truly, I say to you, today you will be with me in Paradise."[9] The argument these writers give is that certainly the thief had to go through some kind of purgation before he could enter Heaven itself. A Church of England pamphlet puts it this way:

"To-day thou shalt be with me." Jesus, then, was going that day to Paradise. He and the penitent had been together on Golgotha, and would be together in the Garden of the Lord. Jesus at His death went into the state of the dead. "He descended," as the Creed has it, "into Hell"—into Hades, as the Greeks called it, into Sheol, as the old Hebrews would have said. And lo! it was no longer Hell or Sheol, no longer a dark cavernous prison, but a Garden, the Garden of happy souls, the Garden of the Lord. It was no longer a prison-house from which there was no escape, but the ante-chamber of Heaven, the waiting-place of souls expecting their resurrection.[10]

The writer of this pamphlet is quite correct in equating the word *garden* with Paradise, for *paradise* is a Persian word which originally meant a garden. But to equate Paradise with Hades is wrong, or to confuse the "Descent into Hades" (which is quite another story) with the entrance into Paradise is wrong. Also Paradise is not an "ante-chamber of Heaven"; it is Heaven itself. *Paradise* meant something like the Garden of Eden, a place always located either on this earth or, at the end of time, in the heavens above. It was never associated with a sub-earthly situation.[11]

With respect to the promise our Lord made to the penitent thief and the question of whether or not he was fit for Heaven, who knows just how repentant the thief was or what was the state of his worthiness, or who can be sure *exactly* what our Lord meant? All we can say is that our Lord conveyed the assurance that the man would be with him, *that day*, in the life beyond this life and thereby be enabled to enter the Heavenly Kingdom. The thief was thinking of a future Kingdom at the end of the world, but Jesus was saying, in effect, "You don't have to wait for the end of time for my Kingdom; *today* you are going to be with me on the other side of life."*

To return to the development of the idea of Purgatory, it is worth noting that for the Jews, shortly after the New Testament period, Gehenna

---

* There is no intention here of depreciating the importance of the "descendit ad inferna" ("he descended into Hell"). On the contrary it is very important to understand this descent in terms of how the victory of the Cross is effective for all men and women who have ever lived or will ever live on this earth, that His victory is both retroactive and eternal. Three scriptural passages in particular support the idea of the "descent into the lower parts of the earth"—I Peter 3:19, I Peter 4:6, and Ephesians 4:8–9. The idea is that Christ's redemptive activity had to be made available to all the good people both before the time of Christ and after that time. He had to preach to the "spirits in prison," those waiting in Hades. All this is, however, another story and must not be confused with what Jesus said to the penitent thief.

became a place of purification. As Pilcher puts it, "Gehenna became Purgatory." He quotes the School of Shammai showing how the words of Zechariah 13:9 became interpreted to apply to the cleansing and refining power of the fires of Gehenna: "And I will bring the third part through the fire, and will refine them as silver is refined, and will try them as gold is tried: they shall call on my name, and I will hear them." From the beginning of the second century A.D. it was common for the rabbis to speak of the purgatorial aspect of Gehenna.[12]

The traditional Catholic concept of Purgatory—and I am using the term *Catholic* broadly—is that at death, body and soul separate. As I pointed out in my discussion of the "Resurrection of the Body" in chapter 11, the soul as a disembodied spirit begins in a state of purgation. At the end of the world, the soul re-unites with the body (now glorified) and goes into Heaven. This exact time sequence is no longer strictly followed by most modern Christians, for we cannot impose our system of time and space upon the prerogatives of God. What we can say, though, is that there is growth in the state of purgation and it continues until finally the person is ready to enter Heaven as such and ultimately look upon the face of the Lord.

Now, another aspect of the Intermediate State—Prayers for the Departed. It is a controversial subject in modern Christendom, but one that is part and parcel of the whole doctrine of purgation and growth. Just how controversial it is is illustrated by an item which appeared in the "Dear Abbey" column of our American newspapers a number of years ago. A bereaved woman telephoned a minister, asking for a prayer she could say for her recently departed mother. The reply was: "What good will prayers do her now? If she is in Hell, she is beyond hope. If she is in Heaven, she won't need your prayers. Don't bother me about prayers for the dead."

This refusal to pray for the dead may have been the traditional Protestant position, but it is now very much on the wane. My favorite example comes from England, from a small book by the late chaplain to King George VI:

> Why should any one hesitate to pray for the dead? When I was young one of the outstanding men of the Free Churches was Dr. Parker . . . , minister of the City Temple, London. For years he inveighed against the habit of praying for the dead as popish, superstitious, and dishonoring to Christ. Then his wife died and the next Sunday he had the courage and sincerity to say he had been wrong. He said, "She has been in my

prayers all these years. I cannot think God wants me to take her out of them now."[13]

Once again I present my mystic friend from Vermont. Her grandson John had died while only a nominal believer. As a devout Christian, my friend was very much concerned about the state of the young man's soul. As a mystic, she continuously perceived his presence "in an earthly plane," where, of course, he didn't belong anymore. My friend prayed for him and kept up those prayers. Success came in due time. A year or so after his death, when John was again permitted to "come through" to his grandmother, he confessed, "It came pretty nearly being too late for saving for me—as it would have been without you, Big Mummy—prayers for me ever since I came over here are what saved me. The Father has listened to you for me." My friend also wrote (upon another occasion), "And then [John] asked me to say a little prayer for him every day and [promised] to do the same for me."

If you ask Why pray for the dead? you also have to ask Why pray for the living? Praying for those on the other side of life is just another form of intercessory prayer, interceding for others before the Throne of Grace. Does this kind of prayer do any good? The Christian answers, Very much. Prayer is power. We are commanded to pray for one another. While we haven't space here to go into the theology of prayer or to explain why it is a power that God can use, let it be said that Christians by experience have found it effective. Now, if prayer is effective for those in this world, it is also effective for those in the other world, for "all are alive unto God."

In my own prayer life I never miss a day without prayers for at least all members of my immediate family—and many others—both in this life and in the next one. Moreover, I have the habit of naming them before the Throne of Grace in random order, as their names come into my mind, irrespective of which world they happen to be in. There are David and Stephanie (our two children who died in the sixties) and Robert, William, Susan, and Sarah, together with grandchildren and great-grandchildren (all of whom are very much in this world). There is also my first wife Jane who died in 1981, and my second wife Valerie (much a part of my present life). And there are Mother and Dad (who have been gone from this plane for some time). And, in addition to my two brothers still with us, I never forget Henrietta, Catherine, George, and Frederick (siblings now in the next life). And it goes on like that, in varying order, night after night. I might also add that I even pray regularly for one child who suffered a stillbirth.

Perhaps a word more is needed about praying for David and Stephanie, our two children who died, each of them, just before their third birthdays. And the same goes for unknown children who died before birth. Children do not need to be purified in the same manner as adults do. They enter the other world in the innocence of life. Traditionally it has been felt that baptized children who leave this world for the next enter Heaven immediately, that there is no Intermediate State for them, no need for intercessory prayer. As an example of this reasoning, we have the Burial Service for Children from the 1928 Prayer Book. While there are a number of prayers for departed adults, strictly speaking there are none for departed children. The only thing that comes close to a prayer for departed children is a modified form of the Aaronic blessing—"The Lord bless *him* and keep *him*, the Lord make his face to shine upon *him* and be gracious unto *him*, the Lord lift up his countenance upon *him*, and give *him* peace, both now and evermore."[14] Or we have the prayer in the 1979 Prayer Book, which in part reads, "O God, whose beloved Son took children into his arms and blessed them: Give us grace to entrust *N.*, to your never-failing care and love."[15]

Yes, I am sure that our David and Stephanie are much, much closer to the Throne of God than I will be when my time comes, yet it is difficult to imagine that a child, however innocent he may be, is fully prepared for highest Heaven immediately upon death. Such children may not need purgation, but certainly there is much growth yet to take place, and toward that end our prayers can help. I am inclined to appreciate the way Cardinal Cushing of Boston put it at the time of the death of the baby born to President and Mrs. Kennedy (July 1963). The Cardinal said, "The child is entering the Nursery School of Heaven." While we should not think of children as being in Purgatory as such, I do want to state that it is perfectly right and proper to commend them to the Lord's keeping, praying that they may mature in their heavenly home, as He would have them. Perhaps we are right, too, in asking that our Lord remember us to them and assure them that they are ever in our hearts and minds, just as they were when on earth and in the physical body. Surely this prayer support and the realization on the part of the child that his parents continue to love and to pray will help the child grow and increase in the knowledge and love of the Lord.

The Intermediate State

In the development of the Hebrew religion, prayer for the dead (except the forbidden ancestor worship) makes its first appearance at the time of the Maccabeean revolt:

> On the next day . . . Judas and his men went to take up the bodies of the fallen and to bring them back to lie with their kinsmen in the sepulchres of their fathers. Then under the tunic of every one of the dead they found sacred tokens of the idols of Jamnia, which the law forbids the Jews to wear. And it became clear to all that this was why these men had fallen. So they all blessed the ways of the Lord, the righteous Judge, who reveals the things that are hidden; and they turned to prayer, beseeching that the sin *which* had been committed might be wholly blotted out. And the noble Judas exhorted the people to keep themselves free from sin, for they had seen with their own eyes what had happened because of the sin of those who had fallen. He also took up a collection, man by man, to the amount of two thousand drachmas of silver, and sent it to Jerusalem to provide for a sin offering. In doing this he acted very well and honorably, taking account of the resurrection. For if he were not expecting that those who had fallen would rise again, it would have been superfluous and foolish to pray for the dead. But if he was looking to the splendid reward that is laid up for those who fall asleep in godliness, it was a holy and pious thought. Therefore he made atonement for the dead, that they might be delivered from their sin.
> II Maccabees 12:30–45

There is also one passage in the New Testament which appears to support the practice of praying for the dead—II Timothy 1:16–18:

> May the Lord grant mercy to the household of Onesiphorus, for he often refreshed me; he was not ashamed of my chains, but when he arrived in Rome he searched for me eagerly and found me—may the Lord grant him to find mercy from the Lord on that Day—and you well know all the service he rendered at Ephesus.

It may be that Onesiphorus was alive at the time Paul wrote but, if on the other hand, as the Scottish Presbyterian scholar William Barclay suggests, Onesiphorus was dead, then this passage clearly supports prayer for the dead. The use of "that Day" is eschatological, i.e., having to do with Judgment Day. Barclay writes in connection with this, "It is clear that Paul was brought up in a way of belief which saw in prayers for the dead, not a hateful, but a lovely thing."[16] The Jews of the New Testament era did, indeed, pray for the dead, as do the Jews of our modern era, although admittedly the practice is not as widespread in Judaism as it is in Christianity.

One final thought with respect to Purgatory or the Intermediate State: Perhaps we should again ask What does happen to those people who *really* are not bad enough for Hell and maybe will *never* be good enough for Heaven? The traditional Christian concept is that eventually people with any potentials at all will be *made* good enough for Heaven, and eventually Purgatory, having served its purpose, will disappear. If it is not heresy, however, I would like to suggest that there may be a permanent place for those who are not terrible people but who would feel out of place in anything that resembles Heaven as Christians understand it. Perhaps the answer is Limbo. Limbo is a doctrine formulated by the medieval Church. It was conceived then as the proper place for all unbaptized infants, who, while not being able to participate in the Beatific Vision, were nevertheless in a state of perfect natural happiness. In Limbo also were all pre-Christian pagans who had done well by the light available. For example, in Dante's *Divine Comedy*, Virgil abides in Limbo; that's why he could not be Dante's guide in Paradise, where Beatrice had to replace him.

The doctrine of Limbo has been interpreted by the theologians with considerable latitude. It could be the "the coolest spot in Hell," or, as in Dante, the outer ring of Hell, or it could be a place that is neutral between Heaven and Hell. This latter interpretation I would endorse, and I see nothing wrong with the idea that Hell in its extreme may very well suit the likes of Hitler, Stalin, Ivan the Terrible, the Godfather of Mafia fame, and perhaps a host of lesser demons who are determined to remain horrible for eternity. Why then not a permanent Limbo for those who just cannot or will not face God?

A case comes to mind from my pastoral ministry in St. Albans, Vermont. Since it is an incident that happened many years ago, and the people involved have long been absent from this earth, it is safe to tell the story. Just new in the parish, I was making the rounds of those on the mailing list. Within walking distance of St. Luke's I came upon a woman who willingly admitted that she rarely attended church.

She also volunteered that her husband *never* would have anything to do with "your church." He was a veterinarian, she explained, and when it came to animals, "he was the kindest man who ever lived. However," she continued, "he just can't stand human beings."

The wife went on to illustrate by insisting how he never forgets a cow.

The Intermediate State

"Once he's seen a cow, that cow becomes part of his life. But a man or a woman, why, he just wouldn't pay any attention to them."

She looked me right in the eye and said, "If my husband met you here today and tomorrow he happened to see you downtown, he'd never recognize you. But with cows, that's different. The other day, for instance, he was over at the Bloomingdale Farm, in Alburg. As he glanced over the herd he called out, 'Hey, Mr. Bloomingdale, this isn't your cow. This cow came from the McPherson Farm in St. Albans Bay, didn't it?' Mr. Bloomingdale had to admit that it was so. 'I knew it,' my husband said, 'This cow's name is Buttercup, and she used to be in the stanchion right next to Cloverleaf at the McPherson barn.'"

"So," this woman concluded, "you see what sort of person my husband is. He may not like people and he may not believe in God, but he'll get into Heaven a lot sooner than most of the people who go to your church."

Well, now, we ask you, will he really get into Heaven a lot sooner than the people who go to church? What would such a character want in Heaven, anyway? And what would he do there? In Heaven he would have to love other human beings and he would have to love and worship God, activities this man apparently hated. I'm sure such a person would be much happier outside of Heaven where he could have the company of his bovine friends. If he did need an occasional change of pace from his animal kingdom, maybe the Almighty could see fit to let him now and then speak to others of his type, others who love animals more than humans. If I may be forgiven for being judgmental, there are a number of animal lovers I know who would much prefer this kind of Limbo to Heaven. No, this veterinarian would not belong in Hell as such, for, after all, he was kind to many of God's lesser creatures and he could never be cruel like the notorious tyrants of history.

It may be that I am like the writer of the Book of Revelation in this respect, not giving proper credit to God and the power of his redeeming love. Maybe somewhere in eternity this veterinarian and others like him would come to love God and his fellow human creatures. I don't know. But, granting the precept of free will and assuming this man is determined to be spared for eternity the need of associating with his fellow humans and worshipping God, then why should he not be left in a situation where he would be happy?

Maybe, then, not all the places outside of Heaven are situations where there is "weeping and gnashing of teeth." Perhaps there are a few areas where there is just less joy than what there could be and should be. The person who lacks faith may not be "bad" in our usual understanding of the word; yet, with that lack of faith, he cannot be in fellowship with Christ. Surely God in his mercy for such people will provide a place akin to Limbo, in the Intermediate State.

14

The End of the World

"He will come again in glory to judge the living and the dead," states the Nicene Creed, and the Apostles' Creed says almost the same thing. Or, as it is found in many new liturgies, we recite in unison:

> Christ has died,
> Christ is risen,
> Christ will come again.

Christianity never loses sight of the fact that there will be an end to this world and a second coming of Christ, a belief that is firmly rooted in the Gospel: "But in those days . . . the sun will be darkened, and the moon will not give its light, and the stars will be falling from heaven, and the powers of the heavens will be shaken. And then they will see the Son of man coming in clouds with great power and glory."[1] The Book of Revelation puts it in even stronger language, and in more judgmental terms: "Behold, he is coming with the clouds, and every eye will see him, every one who pierced him; and all tribes of the earth will wail on account of him."[2]

There are many other places in the New Testament, too, where the end of the world is threatened and the Second Coming promised. *Maranatha*, Aramaic for "O Lord, come," was a common early Christian prayer, so common in the language of the early Church that at least in one instance St. Paul feels no need to translate it for his Greek-speaking readers.[3] In fact, as we acknowledged at the beginning of chapter 6, *every* follower of Christ in the New Testament and the apostolic period following expected this Second Coming, together with the end of this creation, within his lifetime. And the problem of this expectation is still with us.

But when will all this happen? Today? Tomorrow? A few years from now? Hundreds or thousands or millions of years from now? There are always groups within Christianity who are quite certain of the answer, as the following account, entitled "Preview of Judgment Day," demonstrates:

> In a little village of Haleysburg, in Southern Indiana, an abandoned schoolhouse was used by a religious sect as their meeting place. The building was on a grade and the lower side was supported by three large rocks.
>
> In the spring of 1920 it was believed by the credulous that the world would end on a certain day, and this religious group planned a meeting for that day, intending to be engaged in prayer when Gabriel blew his trumpet. Some mischievous lads heard of the proposed meeting and planned some vexation. Prior to the meeting they bored holes in the floor to insert Roman candles, and adjusted the supporting rocks so that they could be easily displaced.
>
> When the great day arrived and the congregation was engaged in prayer a sudden blast of dynamite shook the earth, a trumpet sounded a long, mournful blast up in the woods, and Roman candles shot off in all directions. The rocks under the building were moved enough to cause it to topple to one side and the frightened, screaming people ran away. The affair ended in a small riot, with the culprits thrown into the county jail.[4]

Not all stories of this sort, however, are so humorous. Most of them are quite pathetic, yet in American life they occur every few years, with the absolute certainty on the part of the participants that they have determined the exact date. The first recorded instance in America goes back to March 21, 1844, when a group of people known as Millerites fixed this date as the assured end of time. They based their assumption on Daniel 8:14—"And he said unto me, Unto two thousand and three hundred days then shall the sanctuary be cleansed." The days were interpreted as meaning years, and this added up to March 21, 1844. As a result of this figuring, so the history books tell us, people from Vermont to Virginia sold or gave away their possessions and waited. Following the non-fulfillment of the prophecy, the Seventh Day Adventists organized as a new denomination, and since then, along with other groups, have been predicting new dates.[5]

The great mistake in all this is a failure to heed the admonition of Christ: no one knows the day nor the hour when the consummation of the world will take place except the Father.[6] Also, as we observed at the beginning of chapter 6, there is not the slightest indication that the early Christians ever stopped work because of their expectations of the end; nor did they in any way just sit and wait. Rather, they went on living in the world, working and behaving like responsible citizens.

There is in the New Testament, we readily admit, much confusion as to the Second Coming and the End of Time, for, as with the idea of Judgment, there are diverse ideas in flux. There are inconsistencies, too, from one Gospel account to another, as we can see by a comparison of some key passages in Matthew, Mark, and Luke, which is illustrated by the table in the appendix. Mark, as the majority of scholars believe, is the original writing. It will be observed at once that Luke generally plays down the eschatology of Mark, while Matthew intensifies it. For instance in Mark 13:14 there is a reference to the "desolating sacrilege" (perhaps a reference to the Emperor Caligula's order to put an image of himself in the Temple of Jerusalem, c. 40 A.D.).[7] This threat Luke interprets as in Titus's siege of Jerusalem (67 to 70 A.D.). Thus Luke sees the warning as a historical event rather than as a sign of the end of time. Matthew, on the other hand, ties the warning to the prophecy in Daniel, implying something more catastrophic—an *eschaton* predicted from Old Testament times. Matthew has other eschatological language not found elsewhere. The phrase "consummation of the age" occurs five times in that book, but nowhere else.[8] Likewise *parousia* occurs only in Matthew.* Luke is much less inclined to be concerned about an imminent consummation. He accepts the Old Testament point of view that God is the Lord of history, that history will ultimately unfold as He has ordained it, that before anything else existed, He was there, and that after all else disappears, God will remain.

As was pointed out in chapter 4, the exact time of the *eschaton* was not a problem for the Hebrews. The Prophet Joel predicted a plague of locusts and identified this plague with the Day of the Lord, as if the end of time

---

* *Parousia* (παρουσία), the word used in the Greek New Testament for the Second Coming of Christ, literally means "presence," "arrival," or "coming." Matthew 24:3, 27, 37, 49.

were coming.⁹ Yet when the plague of locusts was past and life continued, no one was disturbed that the "end" had not come. This same way of looking at particular events we see among the Palestinian Christians. The historical events in the first century were constantly making churchpeople experience what they thought was the fulfillment of Jesus' predictions, and yet the first and second generations passed, and the Church went on its way, simply because that is the way eschatology works. Eschatology is primarily an assertion about God, that his purpose will not be defeated in the world, for he will ultimately overcome. For the Hebrews, the eschatological moment is when God breaks into time. In essence, then, Hebrew eschatology is, as Bishop Robinson would phrase it, "In the End, God."¹⁰

On the other hand, what was not a problem for Palestinian Christians became a problem for Gentile Christians. We see this, for instance, in I Thessalonians, where St. Paul admonishes the people (mostly Gentiles) in Thessalonica, the capital city of Macedonia, not to get too involved in thinking about the end of the world.

Likewise, we see the problem of trying to date the Second Coming in what is technically known as the "Little Apocalypse" of Mark 13, a small part of which is quoted at the beginning of this chapter. Jesus is asked about the end of time. Here is the reply as Mark relates it:

> "Take heed that no one leads you astray. Many will come in my name, saying, 'I am he!' And they will lead many astray. And when you hear of wars and rumors of wars, do not be alarmed; this must take place, but the end is not yet. For nation will rise against nation, and kingdom against kingdom; there will be earthquakes in various places, there will be famines; but this is but the beginning of the sufferings.
>
> "But take heed to yourselves; for they will deliver you up to councils; and you will be beaten in synagogues; and you will stand before governors and kings for my sake, to bear testimony before them. And the gospel must first be preached to all nations. . . .
>
> "But in those days, after that tribulation, the sun will be darkened, and the moon will not give its light, and the stars will be falling from heaven, and the powers of the heavens will be shaken. And they will see the Son of Man coming in clouds with great power and glory."
>
> Mark 13:9–28 (selected verses)

The manner of expression in the above we acknowledge to be that of Jesus, but the details of the "signs of the end" are generally thought to be editorial intrusions by the early Church,[11] for these intrusions are standard Jewish apocalyptic language of the time, and, in the sequence of events, parallel Revelation chapter 6, where we have the breaking of the seven seals and the riding forth of the four horsemen. The order of events in both cases is (1) wars of conquest, (2) international strife, (3) famine, (4) pestilence, (5) persecution, and (6) earthquakes and cosmic signs. These are all based on Old Testament prophecies and apocalyptic sources.[12]

The idea that the earth will be shaken is found, among other places, in the Prophet Haggai 2:5b–6:

> My Spirit abides among you; fear not. For thus says the Lord of hosts: Once again, in a little while, I will shake the heavens and the earth and the sea and the dry land.

This is reflected in Hebrews 2:26:

> His voice then shook the earth; but now he has promised, "Yet once more I will shake not only the earth but also the heavens."

It was because of this long association of earthquakes with the end of time that the young men of Haleysburg, Indiana, felt that they had to shake things up by dynamiting the foundation of the improvised church building where those expecting the end of the world were meeting.

The Haleysburg pranksters also provided a long, mournful trumpet blast. This association with the *eschaton*, likewise, goes back to the Old Testament. As the people of Israel journeyed toward the Promised Land, there were frequent assemblies, and these were called together by a long blast on a trumpet.[13] Also, after the land was settled and something important was to be proclaimed, the trumpet would call the assembly together. The Prophet Joel exhorts the people to repent. Consequently, he orders:

> Blow the trumpet in Zion;
>   sanctify a fast;
> call a solemn assembly;
>   gather the people.
>   Joel 2:15

As time went on, the trumpet blast inevitably became associated with the "Day of the Lord." as we also see in Joel:

> Blow the trumpet in Zion
>   sound the alarm on my holy mountain!
> Let all the inhabitants of the land tremble,
>   for the day of the Lord is coming, it is near. . . .
>
> Joel 2:1

Inevitably, too, the sound of the trumpet was connected with an apocalyptic event,[14] as in the so-called "Little Apocalypse" of Isaiah:

> And in that day a great trumpet will be blown, and those who were lost in the land of Assyria and those who were driven out of the land of Egypt will come and worship the Lord on the holy mountain at Jerusalem.
>
> Isaiah 27:13

The trumpet blast soon becomes firmly fixed in eschatological thinking, so that Matthew quotes Jesus as saying that when the Son of Man comes at the end of time, "he will send out his angels with a loud trumpet call."[15] And St. Paul, in his description of the "rapture,"* writes, "For the Lord himself will descend from heaven with a cry of command, with the archangel's call, and with the sound of the trumpet of God."[16] Likewise, chapters 8 to 11 of Revelation give us seven trumpet blasts.

The Haleysburg pranksters also provided Roman candles to simulate the falling of stars. This, too, was standard apocalyptic language.[17]

How Christ will come, who will see him come, what he will do after his coming—answers to all these questions are recorded in the Gospel in symbolic language. "Every eye will see him" simply means there will be no secret about Christ's coming.[18] It will be just as obvious as the lightning, which men see flash from the east to the west.[19] It's not a light "hid under a bushel." A comparison is made to the gathering of vultures (or eagles) over a dead carcass; scavenger birds from apparently everywhere flock to such a feast.[20] Regardless of how it is accomplished, there will be no doubt about Christ's coming in the mind of everyone.

The reference to the coming "in the clouds"[21] is also from apocalyptic literature. Again, we do not need to interpret this literally. But we do need to understand that Christ's appearance at the end of time will be in majesty and splendor. As one of our hymns words it,

---

* For those not familiar with the term, the *rapture* means an anticipated experience involving the faithful person's rising up in the air and meeting Christ at the time of his Second Coming. Many Fundamentalist Christians make much of this expectation.

> Not, as of old, a little child,
>   to bear, and fight, and die,
> But crowned with glory like the sun
>   That lights the morning sky.[22]

Concerning Christ's rule on earth following his Second Coming (what is known as the Millennium, a feature at the end of time that groups like the Seventh Day Adventists insist on)—again, we maintain, this must not be taken literally. Though the millennium doctrine is found throughout apocalyptic literature,* it is found in the canonical Bible in one place only—Revelation 20:4–6, as if the author of this book felt he just had to mention it somehow. And, incidentally, it was this millennium doctrine that kept the Book of Revelation outside the collection of the canonical New Testament for a long period of time.† The best way to understand Christ's reign on earth is to understand it as beginning with his first coming. Christ is reigning now, and at the end of time when he comes in glory, he will continue to reign, and for ever, but this time in the heavenly realm.‡

All these outward displays associated with the end of time—the cosmological signs, the earthquakes, the trumpet blast, and the falling stars, etc.—C. H. Dodd would call symbols.[23] These were standard symbols current during the first century, symbols which Christ and the New Tes-

---

* The duration of the Messiah's kingdom on earth was a favorite subject of speculation among the Jews; by some it was believed to last forty years, by others seventy years, or a hundred years, or four hundred (IV Esdras 7:28–32), or, as in the case of Revelation, a thousand years. The idea that the Messianic age will last for the full millennium is based on the belief that the world will last for 7,000 years. Psalm 90:4 states, "A thousand years in thy sight are but as yesterday." The Psalm is combined with the creation story in Genesis 1. Because God rested on the seventh day, there will be a kind of Sabbath Day's rest for the whole of creation. Millenarianism is also known by the terms *chiliasm* (from the New Latin *chiliasmus* and ultimately from the Greek *chiliasmos*—χιλιασμός) and by *Millerism* (after William Miller who was responsible for the date of March 21, 1943, for the Second Coming of Christ).

† The learned Roman presbyter Gaius (c. late second century) attributed Revelation to the heretic Cerinthus simply because he could not believe that an apostle would subscribe to millenarian teaching. See Massey H. Shepherd, Jr., *The Paschal Liturgy and the Apocalypse* (John Knox Press, Richmond, Virginia, 1960), p. 81.

‡ Proper treatment of the Book of Revelation would require a book in itself, but it should be pointed out here that millenarians generally hold to the theory—not accepted by the mainstream of Christianity—that there is a judgment when Christ comes at the beginning of the millennium (presumably to be identified with the one mentioned in the Gospel), and there is another judgment after the thousand years' reign.

tament writers simply picked up and used without attempting to analyze them. Symbols are not to be taken literally. When the Greek would philosophize, the Hebrew would paint a picture. These symbols, then, are only pictures to demonstrate that one day something catastrophic will happen to our world and that everything will be consummated in Christ. It is wrong to place tremendous importance on symbols as such, and it is wrong to think of all these signs as essentials to the real truth of the Second Coming and the End of the World.

Yet we can go too far in this line of reasoning, in our symbolic interpretation of the *eschaton*. The final consummation of the world and the return of Christ is in itself far more than symbolic. We don't know how the world will end or how Christ will return, but as Christians we must surely believe that one day these things will happen.

It is a simple cosmological fact that Earth will not exist forever. As to the termination of life on this planet, there are a number of possibilities:

First, there is the problem of tidal friction, caused by the gravitational attraction between the earth and the moon, as well as between the earth and the sun, thus slowing the rotation of the earth. Ultimately, this action will result in not only tides hundreds of feet high, inundating all the land masses in the path of the moon, but also producing large tidal waves within the earth's rocky crust and its underlying support, setting off devastating earthquakes and volcanic eruptions, destroying all land life on the planet.[24] At the same time, the length of the earth's day would continue to increase until finally the earth would present the same face toward the sun at all times; one half of our planet would be in unrelieved darkness, while the other half would be bathed in scorching heat, making the dark side a vast sheet of ice thousands of feet thick and the sunny side an ovenlike desert.[25]

Another possible end to life on our planet would occur from the sun's evolution into what scientists call a red giant or super giant and eventually a white dwarf. This is the evolutionary path that all stars take, according to current cosmological theory. As time goes on, more and more helium ash will be deposited in the sun's core, forcing it into hotter and more intense reaction. This will cause the sun to expand enormously. Though the surface will cool, turning first to orange and then to red, the increased size will mean tremendously increased radiation, thousands of times what it is today. From the red giant stage there will be a rapid movement toward its end, which would mean that all life on earth will be fried to a crisp.[26]

The End of the World

When all this will happen is debatable—maybe billions of years from now, maybe much sooner. But it will happen, for the sun is subject to the same immutable natural laws as are the other stars of the universe.

Perhaps, on the other hand, long before anything cosmological happens, we will have ended the world by our own doing, through self-extermination. There is more than one way this can be done: A major problem is pollution from our highly industrialized society, which belches into the atmosphere an ever-increasing concentration of contaminants. This is more than a question of autointoxication, more than a question of sewage and chemicals in our rivers, lakes, and oceans. It is more than a contamination of our air. It is primarily a question of altering the balance between the rate at which our earth absorbs solar radiation and the rate that our earth gives off heat and infrared rays. Carbon dioxide and other infrared-absorbing molecules in our atmosphere are steadily increasing, bringing about what is called the "greenhouse effect," a rising of the earth's temperature. In time this could be sufficient to destroy life on our planet.[27]

Related to the problem of the rising temperature is the balance between atmospheric oxygen and atmospheric carbon-dioxide. This is controlled by plant life. Any great change in the abundance or distribution of plant life would bring with it a change in the amount of oxygen available for animals to breathe. Plant metabolism is ever renewing the supply of free oxygen in the atmosphere; plants consume 500 billion tons of carbon dioxide every year by transforming it into oxygen, water, and organic matter. If this did not happen, it would take just 3,000 years for all our free oxygen to disappear.[28]

Still another possibility of self-destruction is what might happen to our protective ozone layer, which is found about thirty-two miles above the surface of the earth. Man's industrial activity is constantly threatening this. Without the ozone layer's work of absorbing ultraviolet radiation, all life would be destroyed; water would be separated into its ingredients of hydrogen and oxygen, with the hydrogen escaping the earth's gravitational pull and the oxygen oxidizing all matter. All the earth's water would eventually disappear. As we now know, because of our release into the atmosphere of chlorofluorocarbons, a huge hole has appeared over the Antarctic region and a lesser one over the Arctic.[29]

Perhaps the most frightening and the most immediate of the self-extermination threats is a holocaust made possible by our nuclear know-how.

This was horribly, though hilariously, illustrated by the 1964 screenplay *Dr. Strangelove, or How I Learned to Stop Worrying and Love the Bomb*.[30] As the story has it, a maniacal Air Force general in the Strategic Air Command sends a wing of bombers to make a nuclear attack on the Soviet Union. He arranges it so that the bombers could not be recalled. What the general did not know, though, was that the Russians had a retaliatory "doomsday device" as a deterrent to any foreign power which might be tempted into such a raid as was then taking place, and once this "doomsday device" was triggered, it could not be stopped—nuclear bomb after nuclear bomb would go off. The announcement of this deterrent was to have been made the very next day, on the Russian Premier's birthday. But now it is too late for any such announcement, and the story ends with one nuclear device exploding after another—all around the world—and the obvious end of all human life on earth just a matter of a few days away.

All of these possibilities are real threats—Damoclean swords that hang over our world.

Despite these awesome realities, however, we, as Christians, never need fear any purely materialistic threat. This story illustrates why:

A certain priest was one day meditating in his church. At that time (in the early sixties) there was much talk of building underground survival shelters. The priest, like many of us in those days, was very uneasy about the chance that nuclear war would become a reality and end our world—at least most of it.

It was late in the afternoon. As the priest continued to ponder these things, he fell asleep and dreamed. In his dream, God said to him: "Remember my words of old spoken through my Prophet Isaiah—'I am the Lord, and there is no other. I form light and create darkness.... I made the earth and created man upon it.... My counsel shall stand, and I will accomplish my purpose....'"[31]

Waking up, the priest suddenly recalled that the last book of the Bible also had something to say about God's being in control of all creation. He rushed over to the lectern, and there it was before him: "And he who sat upon the throne said, 'I am the Alpha and the Omega, the beginning and the end.'"[32]

The cleric then realized that if the world were to come to an end, it would not be the decision of any trigger-happy madman, for God created the world for his special purpose, and only when that purpose is accomplished will He end the present creation.

The End of the World

My own favorite story, and a true one, about the end of the world took place in my home state of Connecticut, May 19, 1780, during the War of American Independence. Though that morning broke with a clear sky, it was not long before an unexplained darkness fell, the cause of which nobody has known even to this day. As the morning went on, it soon became so dark that chickens went to roost and people had to carry lanterns to see. Many were convinced it was the prelude to the Second Coming of Christ and the end of the world. Panic arose. People stopped work and went home, while others stood gazing up into the black sky, expecting the spectacular appearance of Christ and his angels at any minute. In Hartford, the State Capital, the General Assembly was in session. While the House of Representatives adjourned, the Governor's Council kept working. There Colonel Abraham Davenport said in effect, "It may well be that this *is* the end of the world and the time for the Second Coming of Christ. I don't know. But if it is that time, and Christ is coming, then let him find us doing His work. I move we bring in candles and go on with the business before us."[33]

There has long been a common belief among Christians (based on several verses in scripture) that the world will *not* end until the Gospel is spread over the entire globe and all people everywhere have the opportunity to know Christ.[34] This belief is logical enough, when we consider why God created the world in the first place. There are still vast numbers of people who have never heard of Jesus Christ. Only about one-quarter of the world's population is even nominally Christian. Until this has changed, let us continue our work as Christians living on this earth. We don't know when or how Christ will come again, but we can be sure he will come, and for all people. Then the work in this world will be finished. Until then, let him find us very busy working in the present world, doing his Will.

Appendix

A Comparison of Eschatological Passages of Mark, Luke, and Matthew

I

Mark 8:38. "For whoever is ashamed of me and of my words in this adulterous and sinful generation, of him will the Son of man also be ashamed, when he comes in the glory of his Father with the holy angels."

Luke 9:26. "For whoever is ashamed of me and of my words, of him will the Son of man be ashamed when he comes in his glory and the glory of the Father and of the holy angels."

Matthew 16:27. "For the Son of man is to come with his angels in the glory of his Father, and then he will repay every man for what he has done."

II

Mark 9:1. And he said to them, "Truly, I say to you there are some standing here who will not taste death before they see the kingdom of God come with power."

Luke 9:27. "But I tell you truly, there are some standing here who will not taste death before they see the kingdom of God."

Matthew 16:28. "Truly, I say to you, there are some standing here who will not taste death before they see the Son of man coming in his kingdom."

III

Mark 13:4. "Tell us, when will this be, and what will be the sign when these things are all to be accomplished?"

Luke 21:7. And they asked him, "Teacher, when will this be, and what will be the sign when this is about to take place."

Matthew 24:3. As he sat on the Mount of Olives, the disciples came to him privately, saying, "Tell us, when will this be, and what will be the sign of your coming and of the close of the age?"

Appendix

IV

Mark 13:14. "But when you see the desolating sacrilege set up where it ought not to be (let the reader understand), then let those who are in Judea flee to the mountains."

Luke 21:20. "But when you see Jerusalem surrounded by armies, then know that its desolation has come near. 21. Then let those who are in Judea flee to the mountains, and let those who are inside the city depart, and let not those who are out in the country enter it."

Matthew 24:15. "So when you see the desolating sacrilege spoken of by the prophet Daniel, standing in the holy place (let the reader understand), 16. then let those who are in Judea flee to the mountains."

V

Mark 13:26. "And then they will see the Son of man coming in clouds with great power and glory. 27. And then he will send out the angels, and gather his elect from the four winds, from the ends of the earth to the ends of heaven."

Luke 21:27. "And then they will see the Son of man coming in a cloud with power and great glory."

Matthew 24:30. "Then will appear the sign of the Son of man in heaven, and then all the tribes of the earth will mourn, and they will see the Son of of man coming on the clouds of heaven with power and great glory; 31. and he will send out his angels with a loud trumpet call, and they will gather his elect from the four winds from one end of heaven to the other."

VI

Mark 14:62. And Jesus said, "I am; and you will see the Son of man sitting at the right hand of Power, and coming with the clouds of heaven."

Luke 22:67. "If you are the Christ, tell us." But he said to them, "If I tell you, you will not believe; 68. and if I ask you, you will not answer. 69. But from now on the Son of man shall be seated at the right hand of the power of God."

Matthew 26:64. Jesus said to him, "You have said so. But I tell you, hereafter you will see the Son of man seated at the right hand of Power, and coming on the clouds of heaven."

Notes

CHAPTER 1
DEATH AS PART OF LIFE

1. The original may come from Benjamin Franklin, whose exact words are, "No matter what else happens, in this world nothing is certain but death and taxes."

2. William Hazlitt, "On the Feeling of Immortality in Youth," *Selected Essays of William Hazlitt* (Nonesuch Press, London, 1948).

3. For the sake of accuracy, it should be pointed out that some of the Epicureans of later years far excelled the master's idea of the pursuit of pleasure. Epicurus's definition of pleasure was simply "Freedom from pain in the body and turmoil in the soul."

4. Epicurus, *Letter to Menoeceus*, vol. 3.131.

5. Theodor Gomperz, *Greek Thinkers* (Charles Scribner's Sons, New York, 1901), vol. 1, p. 428.

6. Arthur Schopenhauer, *The World as Will and Idea*, trans. Haldane and Kemp, (Paul, Trench, Trübner & Co.), vol. 1, p. 253.

7. Schopenhauer, *World as Will and Idea*, vol. 3, pp. 112 and following.

8. Bertrand Russell, *Mysticism and Logic* (Longmans, Green & Company, London, 1918), pp. 47–48.

9. Jean-Paul Sartre, *Nausea*, trans. Lloyd Alexander (New Directions, Norfolk, 1959), p. 180.

10. Sartre, *Existentialism and Humanism*, trans. Philip Mairet (Methuen, London, 1948).

11. Sartre, *Being and Nothingness*, trans. Hazel E. Barnes (The Philosophical Library, New York, 1956), p. 627.

12. Albert Camus, *The Myth of Sisyphus and other Essays*, trans. Justin O'Brien (Alfred A. Knopf, 1958), p. 56.

13. I Corinthians 6:19.

14. C. G. Jung, *The Structure and Dynamics of the Psyche*, trans. R. F. C. Hull (Routledge and Kegan Paul, London, 1960), p. 402.

15. Jung, *Structure and Dynamics of the Psyche*, p. 407.

16. Luke 24:46.

CHAPTER 2
SOURCES OF INFORMATION

1. Luke 12:20, 21.
2. Matthew 19:29.
3. Luke 12: 4, 5, as an example .
4. This will be treated in detail in chapter 8.
5. The subject of chapter 9.
6. Jess Stern, "Yesterday, Today, Tomorrow," *This Week*, March 27, 1966, p. 5.
7. Venerable Bede, *A History of the English Church and People,* trans. Leo Sherley-Price (Penguin Books, 1955), bk. 2, chap. 6, pp. 108–109.
8. Bede, *History of the English,* bk. 4, chap. 3, pp. 204–205 .
9. See also chapter 9 for a discussion of this.
10. An article by Andrew M. Greeley and William C. McCready, *The New York Times,* January 26, 1975, sec. 6, pp. 12–25.
11. George Gallup, Jr., *Adventures in Immortality* (Souvenir Press, London, 1983), p. 17.
12. *The Catholic Encyclopedia,* 1910, vol. 7, p. 351, quoted from *Pitra.*
13. Evelyn Underhill, *Mysticism,* 4th ed. (Methuen and Company, London, 1912), pp. 296, 299.
14. Acts 26:3. Also cf. Acts 9:13 and 22:6.
15. Lucy Menzies, *Mirrors of the Holy* (A. R. Mowbray, London, and Morehouse, Milwaukee, 1928), p. 8, quoted from *Epistle* xlviii.
16. Helen Fiske Evans, *The Garden of the Little Flower and Other Mystical Experiences* (Sutherland Press, Baltimore, 1947). Distributed by Morehouse, Gorham, New York. Unfortunately this book had a very limited printing and is now available only in a few large libraries, including the Library of Congress.
17. Evans, *Garden of the Little Flower,* p. vii.
18. Evans, *Garden of the Little Flower,* p. ix.
19. Evans, *Garden of the Little Flower,* p. 4.
20. Hebrews 12:1.
21. Underhill, *Mysticism,* p. 532.
22. Isaiah 6.
23. Origen, *Contra Celsum,* bk. 2, chap. 2.

CHAPTER 3
THE UNIVERSALITY OF BELIEF IN LIFE AFTER DEATH

1. For example, James G. Frazer, *The Belief in Immortality and the Worship of the Dead* (Macmillan and Company, London, 1913), vol. 1, p. 468.

Notes

2. Colin Renfrew, *Before Civilization* (Jonathan Cape, London, 1973), p. 120.

3. Jamake Highwater, "Shadows of Forgotten Ancestors," *The Christian Science Monitor*, July 27, 1989.

4. John Baillie, *And the Life Everlasting* (Oxford University Press, London, 1934), pp. 62, 63.

5. J. G. Frazer points out that among some tribes in southeastern Australia, all of a person's property is deposited with the body. *Belief*, vol. 1, p. 145.

6. James Hastings, *Encyclopaedia of Religion and Ethics* (Charles Scribner's Sons, New York, 1912), vol. 4, p. 430.

7. Sir Leonard Woolley, *Ur of the Chaldees* (W. W. Norton & Company, New York, 1965), pp. 58–64.

8. Audrey Topping, "An Emperor's Clay Army Unearthed in China," *The Sunday Sun*, Baltimore, Maryland, May 23, 1976, sec. D, p. 1.

9. Psychologists are wont to place the whole cause of belief in an afterlife on "wish fulfillment," but J. G. Frazer has a convincing discussion on the impossibility of man's gaining any idea of such a life from intuition or "natural theology" (*Belief*, vol. 1, p. 26).

10. Noel F. Busch, "A Who's Who of English Ghosts," *Life*, vol. 23, no. 12 (September 22, 1947), p. 126.

11. Margaret A. James, "The Monk's Warning," *Church Times*, vol. 140, no. 4,904 (February 8, 1957), p. 6.

12. *The Living Church*, vol. 133, no. 14 (September 30, 1956), p. 18.

13. *The Living Church*, vol. 134, no. 18 (May 5, 1957), p. 8.

14. Gallup, *Adventures*, p. 6.

15. S. Ralph Harlow, *A Life after Death* (Doubleday and Company, Garden City, New York, 1961), p. 164.

16. *Guideposts*, June 1963, reprinted January 1966, pp. 20–23. An enlargement of this experience entitled *Return from Tomorrow*, was published by Guideposts, Carmel, New York, 1978.

17. Harlow, *Life after Death*, pp. 131–133.

18. Raymond A. Moody, Jr., M.D., *Life after Life* (Stackpole Books, Harrisburg, Pennsylvania, 1976). This was also published the same year in paperback by Bantam, New York. A sequel entitled, *Life after Life and Reflections on Life after Life*, was published by Guideposts, Carmel, New York, 1977.

19. Elisabeth Kübler-Ross, M.D. is the author of *On Death and Dying* (Macmillan, New York, 1969); *Questions and Answers on Death and Dying* (Macmillan, 1974); and *Death—The Final Stage of Growth* (Prentice-Hall, Englewood Cliffs, New Jersey, 1975). One very important statement by Dr. Kübler-Ross occurs on page 167 in the second of these three books: "Before I started working with dying patients, I did not believe in a life after death. I now believe in a life after death, beyond a shadow of a doubt."

20. Moody, *Life after Life*, p. 7.
21. Moody, *Life after Life*, pp. 19, 23, 24.
22. Raymond A. Moody, Jr., M.D., *The Light Beyond* (Bantam Books, New York, 1988).
23. Moody, *Light Beyond*, p. 5.
24. Moody, *Light Beyond*, pp. 141–142.
25. Moody, *Light Beyond*, p. 134.
26. Kenneth Ring, *Life at Death* (Quill, New York, 1982).
27. Maurice Rawlings, M.D., *Beyond Death's Door* (Thomas Nelson, Nashville, 1978).
28. Marvin Ford, *On the Other Side* (Logos International, Plainfield, New Jersey, 1978).
29. Robert A. Monroe, *Journeys out of the Body* (Anchor Books, Garden City, New York, 1971).
30. Charles Tart, *Out-of-Body Experiences*, A Psychology Today Cassette (Ziff-Davis Publishing Co., New York, 1978).
31. C. G. Jung, *Memories, Dreams, and Reflections* (Vintage Books, div. of Random House, New York, 1963), pp. 305, 312–313.
32. Matthew 2:18–21.
33. Frederic W. H. Myers, *Human Personality and its Survival of Bodily Death* (Longmans, Green, and Company, New York, 1903) vol. 1, pp. 682–683.
34. Luke 16:31.

CHAPTER 4
OLD TESTAMENT ESCHATOLOGY

1. See R. H. Charles's *Eschatology—The Doctrine of a Future Life in Israel, Judaism and Christianity* (Schocken Books, New York, 1963), page 15 and following. Archdeacon Charles is generally regarded as the grandfather of all modern Biblical eschatological study. Modern scholars will differ with his details of textual criticism and some of his dating, but certainly not with his discovery of the basic truths underlying Old Testament belief in life after death.
2. Charles, *Eschatology*, p. 22.
3. I Samuel 19:13, 16.
4. Charles, *Eschatology*, p. 23.
5. Judges 17:1, 4, 5.
6. Charles, in his *Eschatology*, pages 29–30, gives us the following Biblical references for these customs: *(a)* For the use of sackcloth—Genesis 37:34; I Samuel 3:31; I Kings 20:31; Isaiah 3:24, 15:3, 22:12; Jeremiah 6:26, 48:37; *(b)* The removal of shoes—II Samuel 15:30; Ezekiel 24:17; *(c)* The cutting off of the hair—Isaiah 22:12; Jeremiah 7:29; Amos 8:10; Micah 1:16; Ezekiel 7:18, 27:31.

Notes

The removal of beards—Jeremiah 41:5. The cutting of both hair and beards—Isaiah 15:2; Jeremiah 48:37. The making of baldness between the eyes—Deuteronomy 14:1,2; *(d)* The making of incisions in the flesh—Deuteronomy 14:1; Leviticus 19:28; *(e)* The covering of the head (as a substitute for removal of the hair)—II Samuel 15:30; Esther 6:12; Jeremiah 14:3. The covering of the beard—Ezekiel 24:17. Though generally these rites are mentioned for purposes of condemnation, there are places where no impropriety is implied—Amos 8:10; Michah 1:16; Isaiah 15:2, 22:12; Jeremiah 41:5.

7. Deuteronomy 25:5–10.
8. Charles, *Eschatology*, p. 25.
9. Luke 20:27–33, Matthew 22:23–33, Mark 12:18–27.
10. Exodus 20:5, 34:7; Numbers 14:18; Deuteronomy 5:9.
11. II Kings 9:10.
12. Genesis 25:8, 25:17, 35:29, 49:33; Numbers 20:24, 20:26, 27:13, etc.
13. Charles, *Eschatology*, p. 33.
14. R. H. Charles, *Religious Development between the Old and the New Testaments* (Henry Holt and Company, New York, n.d.), pp. 10–11.
15. Exodus 20:5, 34:14; Deuteronomy 4:24, 5:9, 6:15; Joshua 24:19.
16. Leviticus 19:31, 20:6, 20:27; Deuteronomy 18:11; Isaiah 8:19, 19:3.
17. Deuteronomy 18:14.
18. I Chronicles 10:13.
19. John Baillie, *And the Life Everlasting*, p. 64.
20. Aristotle, *de Anima*, 1.2; 411a7.
21. Gomperz, *Greek Thinkers* (Charles Scribner's Sons, New York, 1901), vol. 1, p. 448. A fragment from Protagoras's book, *On the Gods*.
22. John Burnet, *Early Greek Philosophy*, 4th ed. (Adam and Charles Black, London, 1930), p. 84.
23. Socrates, *Apology*, p. 18 and following. Compare Gomperz, *Greek Thinkers*, vol. 2, p. 85 and following.
24. *Apology*, p. 30d.
25. A. E. Taylor, *Socrates* (D. Appleton and Company, New York, 1933), p. 123.
26. *Phaedo*, p. 81a.
27. I am indebted to the Rev. George B. Caird, D.Phil., formerly of McGill University, Montreal, for much of this line of reasoning.
28. Amos 1:3 to 2:3.
29. Jeremiah 19:1.
30. All of this is written in that part of the Book of the Prophet Isaiah known as "Deutero-Isaiah" (chapters 40–66). Again, this is a portion of the book written by someone in the "School of the Prophet," and for want of a better name, we call him "The Poet-Prophet of the Exile."

31. Carlton J. H. Hayes and James H. Hanscom, *Ancient Civilizations* (Macmillan Company, New York, 1968), p. 174.

32. Isaiah 45:12, 45:18, 48:12–13.

33. *Interpreter's Dictionary of the Bible*, vol. E-J, (Abingdon Press, New York, 1962), p. 204. This passage in Ezekiel is the origin of the "four living creatures" of Revelation 4.

34. Robert Martin-Achard, *From Death to Life: A Study of the Development of the Doctrine of the Resurrection in the Old Testament*, trans. John Penney Smith (Oliver and Boyd, Edinburgh, 1960), p. 99.

35. Ch. Guignebert, *The Jewish World in the Time of Jesus*, trans. S. H. Hooke (Routledge and Kegan Paul, Ltd., London, 1951), p. 118.

36. The word *apocalypse* together with *apocalyptic*, etc., is explained later in this chapter.

37. Stanley B. Frost, trans., *Old Testament Apocalyptic* (Epworth Press, London, 1952), pp. 151–152.

38. Compare with Ezekiel 39:17–20, Zephaniah 1:7.

39. Frost, *Apocalyptic*, p. 152.

40. For much of the material of the Seleucian period and its effect on the eschatological development of Israel and for some of the subsequent development I am indebted to Dr. Burton Scott Easton.

41. Charles, *Eschatology*, p. 125.

42. Compare with Frost, *Apocalyptic*, p. 189.

43. Arthur Jeffery, "The Book of Daniel," *The Interpreter's Bible* (Abingdon Press, New York, 1956), vol. 6, p. 543.

44. Charles Venn Pilcher, *The Hereafter in Jewish and Christian Thought*, Morehouse Lectures, 1938 (Macmillan Company, New York, 1970), pp. 150–151.

45. II Maccabees 12:39–45.

46. R. H. Charles, *The Apocrypha and the Pseudepigrapha of the Old Testament*, (Oxford, 1913), vol. 2.

47. Since the Hebrew Enoch is a recent discovery, it is not included in Charles's collection. Archdeacon Charles died in 1931.

48. Frost, *Apocalyptic*, p. 166.

49. H. H. Rowley in his *Jewish Apocalyptic and the Dead Sea Scrolls* (University of London, The Athlone Press, 1957, p. 8 and following) offers what I regard as convincing evidence that II Enoch is generally of the Maccabean period, despite Charles's theory of the diversity of dates stretching over the whole intertestamental period. Not all Old Testament scholars, however, agree with Rowley: some of them place parts of II Enoch well into the first century A.D. Ulrich Simon in his *Heaven in the Christian Tradition* (Harper, New York, 1958) summarily dismisses this work with the statement, "A. Vaillant . . . has shown convincingly . . . that it

is a medieval product." With the help of a French-speaking parishioner I have carefully gone through A. Vaillant's work, *Le Livre des Secrets d' Henoch* (Institut d'Etudes Slaves, Paris, 1952), but am unable to come to the same conclusion as Simon and accept rather the findings of Rowley.

50. R. H. Charles, *The Book of Enoch*, with an introduction by W. 0. E. Oesterley, Translations of Early Documents—Series I (S.P.C.K., London), p. x.

51. Oesterly's introduction in Charles, *Enoch*.

52. Sigmund Mowinckel, *He That Cometh*, trans. G. W. Anderson (Abingdon Press, New York, 1964).

53. Charles feels that this doctrine of a catastrophic end of our present world is one of the three great doctrines of apocalyptism, the other two being a belief in a blessed future life and the expectation of a new Heaven and a new earth. (R. H. Charles, *Religious Development*, pp. 98–99.)

54. This is dated by H. H. Rowley, *Jewish Apocalyptic*, p. 11, as c. 150 B.C.

55. This work is not to be confused with the Book of Baruch in the Apocrypha. The Apocrypha of Baruch (often called Baruch II) is contemporaneous with the chief writings of the New Testament and is described by Charles as the "last noble utterance of Judaism before it plunged into the dark . . . years that followed the destruction of Jerusalem." (*The Apocalypse of Baruch*, Adam and Charles Black, London, 1896, p. vii).

56. Pilcher, *Hereafter*, p. 92 (from Berakoth 28b, 23).

57. Pilcher, *Hereafter*, p. 149.

58. Charles, *Religious Development*, p. 96.

59. Charles, *Religious Development*, p. 97.

60. Mowinckel, *He That Cometh*, pp. 264, 271, 273, 275 and following.

CHAPTER 5
THIS IS LIFE ETERNAL

1. John 17:3, KJV.

2. John 11:22–26.

3. Compare with the treatment of the word *eternal* in Alan Richardson's *A Theological Word Book of the Bible* (SCM Press, London, 1951), p. 266.

4. Seventy-seven percent of the American population, according to the latest survey, now believe in Heaven. *Newsweek*, April 3, 1989, vol. 113, no. 14, international ed., p. 41.

5. John Baillie, *And the Life Everlasting* (Oxford University Press, London, 1934), p. 120.

6. H. J. Carpenter, "The Resurrection of the Body," *The Gospel of the Resurrection* [A course of sermons preached in the Chapel of Pusey House, Oxford] (A. R. Mowbray & Co., London, 1962), p. 21.

7. J. G. Frazer, *The Belief in Immortality and the Worship of the Dead*, (Macmillan and Company, London, 1913), vol. 3, p. 48.

8. Frazer, *Belief*, vol. 1, p. 286 and following.

9. R. H. Charles points out that these passages "attest belated survivals of Ancestor Worship." The poet Homer, Charles claims, is mistaken in thinking that the restoration of the consciousness of the shades is brought about by the blood of the slaughtered animals. Rather in primitive times the blood is an offering to the shades to comfort and feed them. By Homer's time the meaning of these sacrifices had been largely forgotten (*Eschatology*, p. 144).

10. Homer, *The Odyssey*, line 484 and following.

11. *Odyssey*, IV, line 562 and following.

12. Psalm 94:17, 115:17.

13. Ezekiel 26:29; 31:14, 16; 32:18, 24, 25, 29, etc.

14. Daniel 12:2; Job 7:21, 17:16.

15. Our word *gospel* is from Old English, meaning "good tale."

16. The subject of the Second Coming will be considered in the last chapter of this book.

17. Matthew 19:28, Luke 22:30.

18. Matthew 8:11.

19. Revelation 11:15.

20. C. H. Dodd, *Parables of the Kingdom* (Charles Scribner's Sons, New York, 1961), p. 23. His reference is "*Kaddish* in the Jewish *Authorized Daily Prayer-Book*, translated by S. Singer, authorized by the chief rabbi, and published by Eyre and Spottiswoode, 1908, p. 86."

21. Mark 4:30–32. Parallel passages: Matthew 13:31–32, Luke 13:18–19.

22. Matthew 13:33, Luke 13:20–21.

23. Luke 10:9.

24. Luke 11:20.

25. Luke 17:21. Dr. Pierson Parker, former Professor of New Testament at General Seminary, New York, points out that "within" is a preferable translation of eutoz (*entos*) to "in the midst" (*Christ our Hope*, S.P.K., London, 1958, p. 161).

26. Mark 12:34.

27. Romans 14:17.

28. Matthew 19:16–30, Mark 10:17–31, Luke 18:18–30.

29. Luke 18:24. Parallel passages: Matthew 19:23, Mark 10:23.

30. Matthew 19:26, Mark 10:27, Luke 18:27.

31. Luke 23:43.

32. Luke 23:46.

33. Luke 24:21.

34. John 18:36.

35. Emil Brunner, *Eternal Hope*, trans. Harold Knight (Westminster Press, Philadelphia, 1954), p. 142.
36. Luke 24:34, I Corinthians 15:5.
37. John 20:11–18.
38. Matthew 18:20.
39. Matthew 28:20, KJV.
40. Brunner, *Eternal Hope*, p. 143.
41. John A. T. Robinson, *The Body—A Study in Pauline Theology*, Studies in Biblical Theology (SCM Press, London, 1957), no. 5, p. 49.
42. I Corinthians 6:15.
43. Brunner, *Eternal Hope*, p. 145.
44. John 16:33.
45. John 11:25.
46. Romans 6:3–11.
47. Romans 6:23.
48. Baillie, *Life Everlasting*, p. 97.
49. St. Thomas à Kempis, *Imitation of Christ*, Book III, p. 59.
50. John Greenleaf Whittier, "Our Master," lines 123–4.

CHAPTER 6
LIFE HERE

1. Plato, *Theaetetus*, 174 A; see also Diogenes Laertius, *Lives and Opinions of Eminent Philosophers*, Book I, p. 8.
2. Walter Russell Bowie, *On Being Alive* (Charles Scribner's Sons, New York, 1931), p. 219.
3. Karl Marx, *Kritik der Hegelschen Rechtsphilosophie* (A Critique of the Hegelian Philosophy of Right), 1844, Introduction.
4. Quoted by William Henry Chamberlin, *Soviet Russia—A Living Record and a History*, revd. ed. (Little, Brown, and Company, Boston, 1931), p. 306.
5. I Thessalonians 5:35.
6. Mark 13:32, Matthew 24:36.
7. I Peter 4:7.
8. I Corinthians 7:20,21.
9. I Peter 2:15.
10. I Corinthians 3:17; 1 Titus 1:10; Jude 8; I Timothy 1:5, 5:22; II Timothy 2:21–22, 3:9; etc.
11. II Corinthians 4:1, 7:2, 8:21; Philippians 4:8; I Thessalonians 4:11; Hebrews 13:18; etc.
12. Luke 15:3–7, Matthew 18:12–13.
13. Luke 15:8–10.

14. Luke 15:11–32.
15. Matthew 18:1–14, 19:13–15; Mark 9:33–37, 10:13–16; Luke 9:46–48, 18:15–17.
16. Luke 7:36–50.
17. Matthew 9:10–13, Mark 2:15–17, Luke 5:27–32.
18. Matthew 10:29–31, Luke 12:6–7.
19. Philemon 16.
20. Matthew 25:31–46.
21. Aristotle, *Politics*, I, 4, p. 1253d.
22. Ray C. Petry, *Christian Eschatology and Social Thought* (Abingdon Press, New York, 1956), p. 16.
23. See C. P. S. Clarke, *Short History of the Christian Church* (Longmans, Green and Co., London, 1941), p. 291. During the summer of 1975 when I first visited the ancient battlefield at Senlac, I heard our guide say that this action was to finance Henry's romance with Anne Boleyn. Actually, his main purpose was to finance his government, though it is true that he wasted a great deal of the money on his favorites. Also, it must be acknowledged, Henry regarded the monasteries as centers of Papal intrigue.
24. See *The Book of Common Prayer*, 1977, p. 59, etc.
25. Petry, *Christian Eschatology*, p. 100.
26. Petry, *Christian Eschatology*. Quoted from Homer, XLIII, 7.
27. Petry, *Christian Eschatology*, p. 103.
28. Petry, *Christian Eschatology*, p. 16 and following.
29. C. W. Kennedy, *The Poems of Cynewulf Translated into English Prose*, (Routledge & Kegan Paul, Ltd., London, 1910), pp. 193–194. Quoted by Petry in *Christian Eschatology*, pp. 119–120.
30. Petry, *Christian Eschatology*, p. 150.
31. R. H. Tawney, *Religion and the Rise of Capitalism* (Harcourt, Brace and Company, New York, 1926), p. 4.
32. Tawney, *Religion*, p. 5.
33. Percy Dermer, "Socialism and Christianity," in Stewart D. Headlam, et al., *Socialism and Religion*, Fabian Socialist Series (A. C. Fifield, London, 1909), no. 1, 2d ed., p. 54.
34. William Temple, *The Hope of the World* (Macmillan Company, New York, 1943), p. 71.
35. David Sheppard and Derek Worlock, *Better Together* (Hodder & Stoughton, London, 1988).
36. Jonathan Lewis and Phillip Whitehead, *Stalin—A Time for Judgement* (Thames Methuen, London, 1990), p. 1.
37. I am indebted to Dr. Henry Walsh, Professor of Church History, McGill University, for this thesis.

38. In his *Critique of the Gotha Programme* (1875), Karl Marx would have society write on its banners: "From each according to his ability, to each according to his need!"

39. See Trevor J. Saxby, *Pilgrims of a Common Life* (Herald Press, Scottdale, Pennsylvania, 1987).

40. Leviticus 18:21, II Kings 23:10, Jeremiah 32:35.

41. James Klugmann, "The Marxist Hope," *The Christian Hope*, ed. G. B. Caird, (S.P.C.K., London, 1970), p. 65.

42. I Thessalonians 4:13.

43. John 10:10.

44. John 1:14—"And the Word became flesh and dwelt among us."

45. Raymond A. Moody, Jr., The Light Beyond, (Bantam Books, New York, 1988), p. 131.

46. Moody, *Light Beyond*, p. 27.

47. Moody, *Light Beyond*, p. 29.

48. Moody, *Light Beyond*, p. 33.

CHAPTER 7
I AM THE GOOD SHEPHERD

1. Amos 1:1. Tekoa is a rugged country in the highlands of Judah.
2. Isaiah 40:11.
3. Matthew 18:12–13, Luke 15:3–7.
4. Luke 15:8–10.
5. Matthew 22:23–33, Mark 12:18–27, Luke 20:27–40.
6. Exodus 3:1–6.
7. Romans 14:8.
8. I Corinthians 15:12–14—free translation.
9. I Corinthians 15:19.
10. Catherine Marshall, *A Man Called Peter* (McGraw-Hill Book Company, New York, 1951), p. 273.

CHAPTER 8
THE TRANSFIGURATION

1. I Kings 21:1–24.
2. I Kings 16:31 and following.
3. Matthew 16:1–4 and parallel passages in Mark 8 and Luke 11.
4. Matthew 14:1–2.
5. John 6:15.

6. Matthew 16:13–23, Mark 8:27–33, Luke 9:18–22.
7. Matthew 16:16.
8. Luke 9:21–22.
9. Isaiah 53:8.
10. I am following the chronology in the chapter on this subject by Alfred Edersheim, *The Life and Times of Jesus the Messiah* (Longmans, Green and Company, New York, 1905), chap. 2, p. 92 and following.
11. Edersheim, *Jesus the Messiah*, chap. 2, p. 94.
12. Luke 9:28.
13. Luke 9:29.
14. Matthew 17:2.
15. Mark 9:3. Phillips translation.
16. Edersheim, *Jesus the Messiah*, chap 2, p. 93.
17. Matthew 17:3, Mark 9:4, Luke 9:30–31.
18. Matthew 17:3, Mark 9:5–6, Luke 9:32–33.
19. Edersheim, *Jesus the Messiah*, chap. 2, p. 97.
20. Matthew 17:5.
21. Mark 9:7.
22. Matthew 17:5–8, Mark 9:7–8, Luke 9:34–36.
23. Matthew 17:9, Mark 9:9–10.

CHAPTER 9
THE EVIDENCE FOR THE RESURRECTION OF JESUS

1. I am indebted to the Rev. George Bernard Caird, D.Phil. (from whom I have previously quoted) for the essentials of these three arguments, from a lecture given at McGill University, March, 1954, when I was doing graduate work there. A brief summary of his three arguments is also presented in his book *The Truth of the Gospel* (Oxford University Press, London, 1950), pp. 85–87.
2. Luke 24:2–3
3. Matthew 27:57–61, Mark 15:42–47, Luke 23:50–56, John 19:38–42.
4. Most scholars are inclined to fix the date of the crucifixion at 30 A.D., but an article by Robert C. Cowen (*Christian Science Monitor* science editor), titled "British Scientists Find an Astronomical Clue to Help Date Crucifixion of Jesus," claims "we can assign the crucifixion the Julian calendar date of April 3, 33" (*Christian Science Monitor*, January 3, 1984).
5. Matthew 27:62–66. This account of the securing of the guard is also found in two apocryphal sources: The Gospel of Peter and in some manuscripts of the Gospel according to the Hebrews (Burton H. Throckmorton, Jr., ed., *Gospel Parallels*, Thomas Nelson and Sons, New York, 1957, p. 186). We would also call

attention to the fact that, although these sources are labeled "apocryphal," they contain much nonapocryphal material. Consider footnote number 38 for what I believe is the only logical source of this guard.

6. Matthew 27:61, Mark 15:47, Luke 23:55–56.

7. The Right Reverend David Jenkins, Bishop of Durham, was interviewed by British Television on Saturday, March 25, 1989. News of his disbelief in the physical resurrection of Christ was featured in all the main English newspapers on Easter Day, March 26th. "I am pretty certain," he said, "the disciples did not think of it as a physical resurrection."

8. Acts 2:32.

9. Acts 10:41.

10. Acts 1:21–22.

11. II Corinthians 11:23–27.

12. Tacitus, *Annals*, 15:44.

13. See Matthew 28:8 or Luke 24:41,52, for example.

14. Matthew 26:69–75, Mark 14:66–72, Luke 22:54–62.

15. Acts 2:14 and following.

16. Acts 4:5–22.

17. John 20:24–30. The martyrdom of Thomas in India is in accord with the tradition found in *The Acts of Thomas* (a third- or fourth-century work).

18. The fact that James was not a disciple during the ministry of Jesus is based on Matthew 12:46–50, Mark 3:31–35, Luke 8:19–21, and John 7:5; yet he was a witness to the Resurrection, as is certified by I Corinthians 15:7, and he became an important figure in the life of the early Church, as proved by such passages as Galatians 1:19, Galatians 2:6–10, and Acts 15:12–21. Eusebius, *History of the Church*, 2:23 and Josephus, *Antiquities of the Jews*, 20:9, 197–203 relate the death of James.

19. Acts 8:1.

20. Acts 8:3, KJV.

21. Galatians 1:13.

22. Acts 23:6.

23. Philippians 3:5.

24. Acts 9:1–22, 22:4–16, 26:9–18; Galatians 1:13–17.

25. Burton Scott Easton, *Why the Resurrection?*, Problem Paper no. 15 (Holy Cross Press, West Park, N. Y., n.d. [purchased by the author about 1943]), pp. 13–15.

26. Michael Ramsey, *The Resurrection of Christ*, (Fontana Books, Glasgow, 1961), p. 9.

27. Ramsey, *Resurrection*, p. 13.

28. *Letters of Pliny the Younger*, number 96. Pliny the Younger (Caius Plinius Caecilius Secundus, c. 62–113 A.D.) was an orator and statesman. He is famous

for his letters, which are an excellent mirror of Roman life of that time.

29. Luke 24:13–35.

30. Luke 24:36–43. Dr. George B. Caird, in his commentary on Luke (*The Gospel of Luke*, Penguin Books, Baltimore, Maryland, 1963), makes the point that both John and Luke are careful to emphasize the corporeal nature of the body of Jesus. Luke, for one thing, wants to be true to his Aramaic sources, "a tradition which spoke of Jesus eating and drinking with his disciples after he had risen (Acts 10:36–43)" (p.260). Dr. Caird also points out that the very use of the word *resurrection* meant for the Jew a resurrected *body*, nothing else (pp. 255–256).

31. John 20:27–39.

32. John 21:1–14.

33. John 20:6–7

34. Leslie D. Weatherhead, *The Manner of the Resurrection—In the Light of Modern Science and Psychical Research* (Abingdon Press, Nashville, 1959), p. 44.

35. Weatherhead, *Manner of the Resurrection*.

36. Rudolf Karl Bultman, a German Lutheran scholar, in 1941 published a very controversial monograph entitled *Neues Testament und Mythologie*. It is available in an English translation by Reginald H. Fuller, *Kerygma and Myth* (SPCK, London, 1953). Bultman's idea of the myth is also expounded in a U.S. paperback, *Primitive Christianity in its Contemporary Setting*, (trans. R. H. Fuller, Living Age Books, Meridian Books, New York, 1957), p. 196. According to Bultman, Christian "myths" about the Lordship and pre-existence of Jesus come from the Gnostics and are the cause rather than the result of the idea of the Resurrection. Bultman, however, never quite answers the question of how the early Christians permitted themselves to be fed to the lions in defense of a myth.

37. *The Living Church*, vol. 134, no. 16, April 21, 1957, p. 18.

38. I Corinthians 15:20.

39. Acts 2:36.

40. William Temple, *Palm Sunday to Easter* (Morehouse-Gorham Company, New York, 1942), pp. 40–42.

41. Matthew 28:20, KJV.

CHAPTER 10
THE JUDGMENT

1. Acts 10:40–42.

2. II Timothy 4:1 and I Peter 4:5. The use of the word *quick* in the King James version of the Bible and in the Creed prior to the modern version is based on the first meaning of the word found in the Oxford English Dictionary—"characterized by the presence of life."

3. Acts 17:31.

4. Romans 2:16.
5. Romans 2:2.
6. Romans 14:10.
7. Romans 14:12.
8. Luke 22:30, Matthew 19:28.
9. Matthew 25:31–46.
10. Matthew 5:20.
11. Matthew 7:1–2a, Luke 6:37.
12. Matthew 7:13–14, Luke 13:23–24.
13. Matthew 7:24–27, Luke 6:47–49.
14. Luke 12:4–5, with parallel in Matthew 10:28.
15. Matthew 11:22, Luke 10:13–14.
16. Matthew 11:23–24, Luke 10:15.
17. Matthew 12:41–42, Luke 11:31–32.
18. Matthew 12:42, Luke 11:31.
19. Matthew 9:1–8, Mark 2:1–12, Luke 5:17–26.
20. Matthew 12:31–32, Mark 3:28–29, Luke 12:10. I have more comment on this text in chapter 12.
21. Luke 23:43.
22. Matthew 23, with parallel in Luke 11:42.
23. Mark 11:15–17, with parallels in Matthew 21:12–13 and Luke 19:45–46. Mark makes clear the words of the Prophet in Isaiah 56:7—"My house shall be called a house of prayer for all peoples;" and the Prophet Jeremiah's words in his book in 7:11—"Has this house, which is called by my name, become a den of robbers. . . ?" There is involved here the purpose for which God called Israel into being, as is put forth in Exodus 19:6—"and you shall be to me a kingdom of priests and a holy nation." To be a kingdom of priests meant to mediate (communicate) the knowledge of God to all nations. By allowing this commercial traffic to go unabated in the Court of the Gentiles meant that the Gentiles were at that time being excluded from the opportunity to know the one true God.
24. Matthew 21:18–21, Mark 11:12–14, 20–21.
25. Mark 13:26–27 with parallels in Matthew 24:30–31 and Luke 21:27–28. This same claim Jesus makes as he stands on trial before the Sanhedrin (Mark 14:62, Matthew 26:64, Luke 22:69).
26. Raymond A. Moody, Jr., *Life after Life*, (Stackpole Books, Harrisburg, Pennsylvania, 1976), p. 22.
27. J. Patterson-Smyth, *The Gospel of the Hereafter* (Fleming H. Revell Company, New York, 1930), pp. 34–37.
28. Pilcher, *Hereafter*, (Macmillan Company, New York, 1970), pp. 81, 82, 91, 92. The Slavonic Enoch (which we considered in chapter 4) removes the

righteous from Hades entirely; they enter Heaven immediately upon death. II Baruch 51:10 states the same idea.

29. Augustine, *De anima et eius origine*, 2:4.8. Compare with *New Catholic Encyclopedia*, vol. 8, pp. 26–40.

30. Revelation 20:11–15.

31. I John 2:2.

32. II Corinthians 5:21.

33. See chapter 5, page 75.

34. John 3:17–19.

35. This is to some extent a paraphrase of Burton Scott Easton's lecture on the Fourth Gospel, General Theological Seminary, January 8, 1945.

36. Patterson-Smythe, *The Gospel*, p. 163c.

37. The Book of Common Prayer, 1928 ed., p. 98; 1979 ed., p. 160.

CHAPTER 11
HEAVEN

1. The account of the sending out of the Mission of the Seventy is found in Luke 10:1–24.

2. Matthew 5:10, 12.

3. Matthew 6:33, with parallel passages in Mark 10:29–30 and Luke 18:29–30.

4. Matthew 6:19–21, with parallel passage in Luke 12:33–34.

5. Matthew 13:45–46.

6. James 1:17.

7. Theodore H. Epp, *Heaven—that Better Country*, Back to the Bible broadcast, Lincoln, Nebraska, 1958, p. 22.

8. I John 4:8, 4:16.

9. I John 1:3.

10. I John 3:11, 14.

11. I John 4:20–21.

12. Moody, *The Light Beyond*, (Bantam Books, New York, 1988), p. 33.

13. I Corinthians 13:13.

14. Tertullian (160–230 A.D.), *Apologeticus*, p. 39.

15. Luke 16:19–31. The beggar is said to be carried "to Abraham's bosom." This is an idiomatic expression which is tantamount to saying, "In the place of honor at Abraham's right." At this celestial banquet table the guests are portrayed lying on couches, in the Roman fashion of the time.

16. Mark 14:25, with parallel passages in Matthew 26:29 and Luke 22:18.

17. Moody, *Life after Life*, (Stackpole Books, Harrisburg, Pennsylvania, 1976), p. 42.

18. Luke 2:10, KJV.
19. Luke 6:23.
20. Luke 15:10.
21. John 15:10.
22. John 16:20,22.
23. Romans 15:13.
24. One book written on the subject is Elton Trueblood's *The Humor of Christ*, (Harper & Row, New York, 1964).
25. Mary B. Abett, in "Letters to the Editor," *The Living Church* (August 18, 1974), vol. 169, no. 7, p. 3.
26. John Donne,—"That a Wise Man is Known by Much Laughing," in *Paradoxes and Problemes*. The Latin quotation—"Laugh, if you be wise, girl laugh"—is a fragment attributed to Ovid, but of uncertain authenticity; it is not found in the text of his major works and may have come from a lost work.
27. David A. Redding, "God Made Me To Laugh," *Christianity Today*, vol. 6, no. 20 (July 6, 1962), p. 3.
28. Burnett H. Streeter, *Immortality* (Macmillan and Company, London, 1930), p. 160.
29. Streeter, *Immortality*, p. 161.
30. John 5:17
31. See S. G. F. Brandon, *Man and His Destiny in the Great Religions* (Manchester University Press, 1962), p. 247 and following, where he quotes Surah 18:29–30 and 35:31–32.
32. Thomas Moore, *Intercepted Letters*, no. 6, 1.32.
33. A short account of this fascinating life is found in *Strange Stories, Amazing Facts* (Reader's Digest Association, Pleasantville, New York, 1976), pp. 414–415.
34. Streeter, *Immortality*, p. 157.
35. Philippians 3:20–21—free translation.
36. I Corinthians 15:36–38,42,44.
37. We find the beginning of this thinking in Clement (first century Bishop of Rome) in his *Epistle to the Corinthians*, and in II Clement chapter 9 we find it stated "In like manner as you were called in the flesh, you shall come also in the flesh." Compare with Charles Venn Pilcher, *The Hereafter in Jewish and Christian Thought*, p. 172 and following.
38. Moody, *Life after Life*, p. 23.
39. Moody, *Life after Life*, p.42.
40. Compare Plato, *Phaedo*, 64 and following and *Phaedrus*, 148 and following, where the author makes it clear that the soul is quite an independent entity and can be placed in any body whatsoever.
41. S. Ralph Harlow, *A Life after Death*, p. 162, gives us a good example of a mother who was able to see her child, who died at three, grown up in Heaven. I

also have in my files a tape recording of a woman who lost her son at the age of two; during an operation she was granted a mystical experience, seeing her child again, but this time the boy, much to her surprise, appeared an eight-year old, for six years had gone by since his death. When she met the boy in this experience she could not believe that he was her son until finally he convinced her that he was.

42. Moody, *Light Beyond*, pp. 134–135.

43. Editors of Time-Life Books, *Psychic Voyages*, in Mysteries of the Unknown series (Time-Life Books, Alexandria, Virginia, 1987), pp.14–15, 52.

44. Other places in Hebrews where this word is used include 3:11, 3:18, 4:1, 4:3, 4:5, 4:8.

45. Dr. George B. Caird, "Lectures in New Testament" 3-A, (McGill University, Montreal, October 20, 1953).

46. E. L. Mascall, *Grace and Glory*, p. 7. (At the time Dr. Coggan wrote this introduction he was Archbishop of York.)

47. Matthew 6:33.

48. Matthew 5:6. "*For* righteousness" is the RSV translation.

49. John 16:8,10.

50. Revelation 21:27.

51. Revelation 22:3.

52. Revelation 22:15.

53. The Book of Common Prayer (Church Hymnal Corporation, New York, 1979), p. 323.

54. John 8:32.

55. Streeter, *Immortality*, p. 158.

56. Peter J. Kreeft, *Everything You Ever Wanted to Know about Heaven but Never Dreamed of Asking* (Harper & Row, San Francisco, 1982), pp. 30–31.

57. Moody, *Light Beyond*, p. 35.

58. W. C. Piggott, hymn no. 222, *The Hymnal, 1940*.

59. Ritchie, *Return from Tomorrow*, p. 72.

60. II Corinthians 12:3–4.

61. I Corinthians 2:9.

62. Revelation 4:3–2.

63. Revelation 4:6.

64. Revelation 4:4, 5, 8, 10; 5:12 (KJV).

65. Revelation 21:1.

66. Revelation 21.1.

67. Revelation 21:10 and following.

68. Revelation 22.

69. In The Hymnal, 1940, John Mason Neale's translation forms four cantos which make up hymns 595, 596, 597, and 598. We have selected the stanzas used from hymns no. 597 and 598. As The Hymnal, 1940 Companion, puts it,

this is one of those exceptions in which the translation is far more famous than the original and, we might add, much better poetry (p.350).

70. Matthew 5:8.
71. I John 3:2.
72. Frank Biggart, C. R., *And Then the Judgment* (Dacre Press, Westminster, 1946), p. 30.
73. Kenneth E. Kirk, *The Vision of God—The Christian Doctrine of the Summum Bonum* (The Bampton Lectures for 1928), 2nd ed. (Longmans, Green and Company, London, 1932), p. 1. The quotation of Irenaeus is from *Adversus Haeresus*, iv, 20.7.
74. Kirk, *Vision of God*.
75. Mascall, *Grace and Glory*, pp.63–66.
76. Streeter, *Immortality*, pp. 161–162.
77. The inspiration to use this illustration comes from the Reverend Moultrie Guerry, D.D., my much-admired professor of Bible and chaplain during my first two years at the University of the South.
78. This is the last stanza of a hymn entitled "The Eternal Father," the first line of which is "My God, how wonderful thou art," hymn no. 284 in The Hymnal, 1940, and no. 441 in The English Hymnal, 1933. The "gaze and gaze" stanza, though included in the English Hymnal, for obvious reasons was omitted from the American edition.
79. Moody, *Light Beyond*, p. 10; Ritchie, *Return from Tomorrow*, p. 48; etc.
80. Mascall, *Grace and Glory*, p. 33 and following.
81. Exodus 33:19–20.
82. Isaiah 6.
83. Ezekiel 1:26–28.
84. John 14:9.
85. I Corinthians 13:12.
86. II Corinthians 2:12 ff.
87. II Corinthians 4:6.
88. Matthew 18:10.
89. Proverbs 29:18, KJV.
90. Stanza 2 of a hymn by John Cennick, no. 587, in The Hymnal, 1940.
91. Romans 13:12.

CHAPTER 12
HELL

1. Henry Bamford Parkes, *Jonathan Edwards—The Fiery Puritan* (Minton, Balch and Company, New York, 1930), pp. 101–102.
2. Robert Burns, "The Holy Fair," stanza 22.
3. Milton, *Paradise Lost*, Book 1, lines 61–67.
4. I confess ignorance as to the source of this quotation from John Henry Cardinal Newman. I picked up the quotation from a lecture I heard.
5. I Enoch 22:2–23. This passage will receive further comment in the next chapter. Enoch, it should be noted, is inconsistent as to where Sheol is placed. In the passage referred to, Sheol is not strictly in the underworld but in the far west, a location suggested by the glow of the setting sun. But as Pilcher (*Hereafter*, Macmillan Company, New York, 1970, p. 81) points out, the word *Sheol*, etymologically speaking, means an abyss. The doctrine of Sheol originally goes back to the Babylonian idea of a subterranean hollow which receives all the dead.
6. See II Kings 23:10; II Chronicles 28:3, 33:6; Jeremiah 7:31, 32:37.
7. Note the parallel to Mark 9:44–48.
8. See *The Interpreter's Dictionary of the Bible*, vol. E–J, p. 361, or Pilcher, *Hereafter*, pp. 81–83.
9. Luke 13:25–28.
10. Matthew 22:13.
11. Monroe, *op. cit.*, pp. 119–121.
12. George G. Ritchie, M.D., *Return from Tomorrow* (Guideposts, Carmel, New York, 1978), p. 59 and following.
13. Alois Wiesinger, O.C.S.O., *Occult Phenomena in the Light of Theology*, trans. Brian Battershaw (Burns & Oates, London, 1957), p. 243 and following.
14. Revelation 9:3–11.
15. Revelation 9:15–19.
16. Revelation 11:13.
17. Revelation 14:20.
18. Revelation 20:10.
19. Trevor Huddleston, C.R., *Naught for Your Comfort* (Collins, St. James's Place, London, 1956), p. 24.
20. See James A. Pike, *The Other Side* (Doubleday & Company, Garden City, New York, 1968), p. 114. The quotation is from a source other than Bishop Pike's book.
21. H. O. Taylor, *The Mediaeval Mind*, vol. 1, 2nd ed. (Harvard University Press, Cambridge, Massachusetts, 1914), p. 468. Quoted from *Pitra*.
22. Matthew 7:13–14, with parallel in Luke 13:23–24.

Notes

23. Dante Alighieri, trans. Henry Francis Cary, *Divine Comedy*, "Inferno," canto 3, line 9.

24. James A. Pike, "Hell," a recorded radio talk, The Parish of the Air, Atlanta, Georgia. (Date unknown, probably about 1950.)

CHAPTER 13
THE INTERMEDIATE

1. Willard M. Aldrich, American Tract Society, New York, 1965. The title for the tract comes from J. B. Priestly's novel, *Delight*.

2. Revelation 21:27; Hebrews 12:14, 23.

3. These lines occur in "Die Wittenbergisch Nachtigall" by Hans Sachs—"Sobald das Gelt in Kasten Klingt, / Die Seele aus dem Fegfeuer springt." For a good explanation of all that happened in this controversy, see the book by Roland H. Bainton (professor at Yale), *Here I Stand—A Life of Martin Luther*, available in paperback (Abingdon, Nashville, 1978), pp.51–78.

4. John Henry Cardinal Newman, *Apologia pro Vita Sua* (George Routledge & Sons, London), p. 6

5. The Book of Common Prayer (Church Hymnal Corporation, New York, 1979), p. 330.

6. H. A. Wilson, *Haggerston Catechism*, part 2: "The Creed" (A. R. Mowbray & Company, London, 1958), pp. 112–113.

7. The actual Greek used here is μονή (singular) or μοναί (plural), meaning a residence or abode.

8. I Enoch 22:2,3.

9. Luke 23:43.

10. H. B. Swete, *The Intermediate State*, no. 151 in Little Books on Religion series (S.P.C.K., London, n.d.), p. 15.

11. See Pilcher, *Hereafter* (Macmillan Company, New York, 1970), pp. 89–90; James Hastings, *Encyclopaedia of Religion and Ethics* (Charles Scribner's Sons, New York, 1910), vol. 2, p. 704 and following.

12. Pilcher, *Hereafter*, p. 84. He makes reference to Rosh Hashana 16b, 34 Baraitha.

13. Peter Green, *Old Age and the Life to Come* (A. R. Mowbray & Co., London, 1950), p. 59.

14. The Book of Common Prayer, 1928 ed., p. 341.

15. The Book of Common Prayer, 1979 ed., pp. 470, 494.

16. William Barclay, *The Letters to Timothy, Titus and Philemon* (Westminster Press, Philadelphia, 1960), pp. 179–181.

CHAPTER 14
THE END OF THE WORLD

1. Mark 13:24–26.
2. Revelation 1:17.
3. I Corinthians 16:22. The Greek Μαρὰν ἀθή is transliterated by St. Paul directly from the Aramaic מרן אתא, and this in turn is transliterated by KJV as *maranatha.* The RSV *translates* this (rather than transliterates it) as "Our Lord, come!" The Greek translation of the Aramaic is found in Revelation 22:20— ἔρχου Κύριε Ἰησοῦ, "Come, Lord Jesus."
4. Mrs. J. D. Barnett, *The Journal-Courier Magazine* (Louisville, Kentucky, *Courier Journal*), vol. 191, no. 148, Sunday, May 28, 1950, p. 32.
5. The Adventists get around this by a most literal interpretation: "We are not to know the day or the hour, but we can know the week or the month."
6. Matthew 24:36, Mark 13:32, Acts 1:7.
7. I Peter 4:12. Peter sees this event in terms of a great persecution setting in.
8. Or "completion of the age" συντέλεια τοῦ αἰῶνος —Matthew 13:39, 40, 49; 24:3; 28:20.
9. Joel 1:4 ff.
10. J. A. T. Robinson, *In the End, God* (James Clarke & Co., Ltd., London, 1958).
11. R. H. Charles, *Eschatology* (Schocken Books, New York, 1963) pp. 377–385.
12. This sequence has been pointed out by many expositors. See for example Massey H. Shepherd, Jr., *The Paschal Liturgy and the Apocalypose* (John Knox Press, Richmond, Virginia, 1960), p. 89.
13. As in Exodus 19:13.
14. The Oracle of Zechariah in 9:14 also involves the trumpet.
15. Matthew 24:31.
16. I Thessalonians 4:16. Also Cf. I Corinthians 15:52.
17. Isaiah 13:10; Ezekiel 32:7; Joel 2:10, 3:15; Matthew 24:29; Mark 13:25; Luke 21:25; Revelation 6:13, 8:12.
18. Revelation 1:7.
19. Matthew 24:27.
20. Matthew 24:28.
21. Matthew 24:30, 26:64; Mark 13:26, 14:62; I Thessalonians 4:17; Revelation 1:7. The reference to the clouds reflects Daniel 7:13—"with the clouds of heaven there came one like a son of man. . . ."—which in turn reflects Jeremiah 4:13—"Behold, he comes up like clouds, his chariots like the whirlwind."
22. Hymn no. 11 in The Hymnal, 1940. Translated by John Brownlie from a Greek source.

23. C. H. Dodd, *The Coming of Christ* (Cambridge University Press, 1954), pp. 2–4.

24. Lloyd Moltz, *The Universe—Its beginning and End* (Charles Scribner's Sons, New York, 1975), p. 282.

25. Moltz, *Universe.*

26. Moltz, *Universe,* pp.283–285; David Bergamini, et al., *The Universe,* Life Nature Library series (Time-Life Books, New York, 1971), pp. 94–99.

27. Moltz, *Universe,* p. 267.

28. Moltz, *Universe,* p. 268.

29. Moltz, *Universe;* "The Heat Is On," *Time,* (intl. ed.) vol. 130, no. 16, October 19, 1987, p.46 and following.

30. The screenplay was by Stanley Kubrick, based on the story *Red Alert* by Peter George.

31. Isaiah 45:6b, 7, 12; 46:10.

32. Revelation 21:6.

33. This story was first introduced to me by my New Testament professor Burton Scott Easton. The account is found, among other places, in the *Connecticut Courant* (now called the *Hartford Courant*), no. 800, May 23, 1780.

34. This is based on the command to spread the Gospel as found in Matthew 28:19, Luke 24:45–48, and in the longer ending of Mark 16:15 (found in some ancient manuscripts). Also see Mark 13:10.

Index

A

Acts, Book of 83, 85
Amos, Book of 52, 53, 103
Ancestor worship 23, 44-45, 49-50
And the Life Everlasting 50
Angels 11, 13, 14, 40, 166, 198, 202
   Archangel Gabriel 14
   Archangel Michael 14, 66
Annunciation 14
Apocalypse 88, 193-203
   events of in Bible 197
   meaning of term 65
Apocrypha 9, 9-10n, 65, 68, 71
   meaning of term 65
Apocrypha, Bridge of the Testaments, The 72n
Apology 51
Apostles' Creed 140, 193
Aquinas, Saint Thomas 144
Aristotle 92
Atonement 136
Augustine, Saint 90, 133, 142

B

Babylonian Captivity 55-59
Baillie, John 50, 76, 86
Barclay, William 189
Beatific Vision 162-166
Beatitudes 139, 146, 156, 163-164, 165
Bede, Venerable 12
Bernard of Cluny 161-162
Better Together 95
Beyond Death's Door 38
Bible Atlas 112n
Body, The 86
Book of Common Prayer 151n, 181, 188
Brunner, Emile 85
Buddhism 150
Burns, Robert 169

C

Caird, George B. 119, 155, 173
Caligula, Emperor 195
Camus, Albert 4
Catholicism
   concept of Purgatory 186
Charles, R. H. 44, 65, 69, 74
Christ. *See* Jesus
Christian Eschatology and Social Thought 92
Christian(ity) 5, 6, 7
   attitude about death 4-7, 108-109
   birth of the church 123
   characteristics of Heaven 142-166
   concepts of Heaven 141-142
   concepts of Hell 168-170, 172-177
   concepts of Eternal Life 75-76, 79-87, 163
   concepts of the Intermediate State (Purgatory) 180-192
   concepts of resurrection 151-154
   concepts of Second Coming 193

Christian(ity) *(continued)*
  concerns for social welfare 90, 92-100
  expectations of the Apocalypse 194-196, 202-203
  fellowship with Christ 142-144
  following Christ 137
  free will 170
  fundamentalism 135
  growth in early years 124
  highest goal (*See* Beatific Vision)
  importance of Transfiguration 114-115
  mystics 15-19, 142
  nature of Christian life 142
  sacredness of human life 99-100, 104
  view of the Judgment 128-136
Christianity Today 147
I Chronicles, Book of 43
Chrysostom, Saint 93
City of God, The 90, 142n
Coggan, Donald 155
Communion of Saints 145, 149
Communism 89-90, 96-99
Connecticut General Assembly 203
Contra Celsum 177n
Corinthians, Letters to 107, 142, 151, 182, 183
Cushing, Richard J. 188
Cynewulf 94

D

Daniel, Book of 8, 63-64, 65-67, 194
Dante 141, 155, 177, 180, 190
Davenport, Abraham 203
David (Hebrew king)
  story of wife 45

Day of the Lord 52-57, 89, 195, 197-198. *See also* Judgment Day
Death
  modern attitudes toward 1-7
  See also Eschatology; Near-death experiences; Visions of the departed;
De Contemptu Mundi 161
Denton, Robert C. 72n
Dermer, Percy 95
Deuteronomy, Book of 46, 46n, 68
Diaspora 55
Divine Comedy, The 141n, 180, 190
Divine Institutes 133, 133n
Dodd, C. H. 199
Dominicans 163
Domitian (Roman emperor) 172
Donne, John 147
Dr. Strangelove 202

E

Easton, Burton Scott 122, 155, 167
Ecclesiastes, Book of 48
Ecclesiasticus, Book of 9
Edwards, Jonathan 168
End of the world 193-203 *See also* Apocalypse
Enoch, Books of 68, 69, 70, 71, 160, 171, 184
Ephesians, Letter to 185n
Epicurus 2, 6
Erskine, John 87
Eschatology *(Inasmuch as eschatology is the principal subject of this book, only special references are included under this topic.)*
  impact in Christian thought 89-91
  meaning of term 43
  realized eschatology defined 76, 81
  treatment in Old Testament 43-74

Index

See also Eternal Life; Heaven; Hell; Judgment; Resurrection
Esdras, Book of 43, 199n
Essenes 112n
Eternal Life 10, 75-87, 143, 163
Eucharist 144, 145, 157
Evans, Helen Fiske 16-17
Evil 73
Existentialism 4
Exodus, Book of 45
Ezekiel, Book of 58-60, 80

F

Faber, Frederick William 164
Ford, Marvin 39
Fourth Gospel. *See* John's Gospel
Franciscans 163
Free will 170

G

Gabriel (the archangel) 14
Garden of the Little Flower and Other Mystical Experiences 17
Gehenna 171-172, 186. *See also* Hell
Genesis, Book of 44, 68, 152
George VI, King 186
Ghosts 11, 21, 25-31. *See also* Spirits
God 10, 11, 19, 20
   Christians' vision of 104
   in control of creation 202
   described by Jesus 172
   concept of God among Hebrews 47-50, 52-64, 67-73
   "God of the living" 106
   God's omnipotence and omnipresence 58-74, 170
   humor of 147-148
   in judgment of mankind 128-138
   knowing God 164-165
   as love 144

   nature of 19, 58, 138
   as a personal God 103, 106-107, 109
   providing Heaven and Hell as a choice 169
   seated in Heaven 140-141
Godfrey, Arthur 11
Gospel of the Hereafter, The 133
Grace and Glory 142n, 155
Greek philosophers 50-51, 140, 149
Greeks, Ancient
   impact of Alexander the Great 63
   impact of Antiochus 63-66
   attitude toward death 3-4
   attitude toward human life 92
   contrast with Judaism 152
   concept of life after death 50-51, 77-78, 152
Guideposts 33, 35

H

Hades 47, 171-172. *See also* Hell
Haggai, Book of 197
Hallucinations 14, 37
   possibility among Christ's followers 120-122
Harlow, S. Ralph 21, 32, 35
Hawthorne, Nathaniel 164
Hazlitt, William 2
Heaven 69, 106n, 133-134, 139-167, 169, 188, 190, 191
   Christian concepts of 141-166
   Christ's teachings on 139-140
   concepts of 140-167
   speculation on location 140-141
   ten characteristics of 142-167
Hebrews. *See* Judaism
Hebrews, Letter to the 128, 155, 197
Hell 8-10, 168-178
   concept in Christian theology 170, 172-178

Hell *(continued)*
  concept in Judaism 170-171
  in New Testament 170
  place to separate offenders 173-174, 175
  See also Hades; Purgatory; Sheol
Heraclitus 50
Hildegard of Bingen 15-16, 19, 168
Hinduism 144, 150
Hinnon, Valley of 171
Holy Spirit 18, 19, 20, 80, 81, 82, 85, 86, 131, 147, 177-178, 183
Homer 50, 77-78
Huddleston, Trevor 175
Human Personality and Its Survival of Bodily Death 40-41

I

In the End, God 177n
Intermediate State 179-192. *See also* Purgatory
Irenaeus 163
Isaiah, Book of 47, 53-54, 55-56, 57-58, 61-63, 145, 171, 198
  Little Apocalypse 61-62, 198

J

Jacob (Hebrew patriarch)
  story of wife's gods 44
Jehovah's Witnesses 170
Jeremiah, Book of 43, 54-55, 56-57
Jesus 1, 5, 10, 76, 79, 151
  on children 165
  on continuing creation 148
  crucifixion and resurrection 83, 85n, 86, 107, 114-115, 117-118, 127
  at the End of Time 198-200
  on Eternal Life 10, 75-76, 79-85
  fellowship with 85-86, 87, 143-144
  foretelling death and resurrection 111
  as judge 129, 131, 136-138
  mention of Hell 172, 177
  humor of 147-148
  on the Kingdom of Heaven 81-84
  on nature of resurrected body 117
  parables 80, 91, 105-106, 132, 139-140, 145, 146, 171-172
  and penitent thief 185
  as personal savior 80-87, 151
  at prayer 112
  on sacredness of individual 91-92, 99
  Second Coming 132
  Sermon on the Mount 146, 130-131
  as shepherd 101, 103, 108-109
  teaching on judgment 10, 91, 130-132
  teaching on spirits 139
  at tomb of Lazarus 75
  at the Transfiguration 110-114
  See also Second Coming of Christ
Jews (see Judaism)
Job, Book of 9, 48, 72, 78
Joel, Book of 197
John (the apostle) 112, 123n
John, Letters of 144, 162-163
John of Patmos 10, 11, 20
John's Gospel 20, 75, 81, 85, 86, 101, 104, 111, 137, 165-166, 182
Josephus (Roman historian) 65n
Journeys out of the Body 39, 173
Jubilees, Book of 70-71
Judaism 15, 90, 152, 183, 184
  impact of Alexander the Great 63
  ancestor worship among primitive Hewbrews 44-45
  impact of Antiochus 63-67

concept of corporate person 135
concept of Eternal Life 78-79, 85
concepts of God 47-50, 52-53, 59-61, 64, 67-74
Hebrew eschatology 44-50, 52, 63-67, 196-197
concept of Hell 170-171
injunctions against sacrifices 46
concepts of life after death 44-50, 52, 60-74
monotheism 46
mysticism 19
prayer for the dead 189-190
concept of Sheol 46, 78-79, 170-171, 183-184
theology of free will 170
Judgment 43, 75, 128-138, 184
of all creation 136
judging one another 129, 130
ongoing judgment 136-138
in Sermon on the Mount 130-131
See also Judgment, Final; Last Day
Judgment Day 94, 189, 194, 199n. See also Apocalypse
Judgment, Final 91, 134-138
attitudes toward 135-136
nature of 132-138
time of 132-138
See also Judgment; Judgment Day; Last Day
Jung, Carl 6, 39-40

K

Kayyam, Omar 128
Kingdom of God. See Kingdom of Heaven
Kingdom of Heaven 8, 79-87, 90-91, 96, 130, 136, 139-140, 145, 185
I Kings, Book of 53n

Kirk, Kenneth E. 163
Kraeling, Emil G. 112n
Kreeft, Peter J. 157
Kübler-Ross, Elisabeth 36

L

Lactantius 133, 133n
Larsen, Caroline 153
Last Day 82, 89, 90. See also Apocalypse; Day of the Lord; Judgment Day; Eschatology
Lazarus 42, 75
Lenin, V. I. 89
Life after death. See Eschatology
Life after Life 132
Life at Death 38
Light Beyond, The 99, 144
Limbo 190. See also Purgatory
Living Church, The 126, 147
Luke's Gospel 14, 90, 91, 118, 128, 139, 146, 171-172, 195
Luther, Martin 181

M

MacBeth 3
Maccabees, Book of 65, 189
Manner of the Resurrection, The 125
Mark's Gospel 118, 193, 195, 196
Marshall, Peter 108
Marx, Karl 89
Marxism. See Communism
Mary (mother of Jesus) 14
Mascall, E. L. 155, 165
Mason, T. W. 80
Matthew's Gospel 81, 93-94, 117, 146, 172, 183
Messiah 57, 62, 80, 113, 199n. See also Jesus
Michael (the archangel) 14, 66

Milton, John 169, 173, 176, 177
Monroe, Robert A. 39
Moody, Raymond J. 36, 37, 38, 99, 132, 144, 146, 152, 153, 157, 165
Moore, Thomas 90, 93, 149
Morrison, Frank 125n
Moses 49, 110, 165
Moslems
   concept of Heaven 149
Mowinckel, Sigmund 69, 74
Myers, F. W. H. 40
Mystery religions 51
Mystic(ism) 14-20, 115, 141-142, 153, 159-160, 161
   contrasted with spiritualism 19
Mystical experiences 11-19, 39-42, 149, 187
   See also Out-of-body experiences
Myth of Sisyphus 4

N

Neale, John Mason 139
Near-death experiences 31-39, 99-100, 132-133, 144, 152-153, 159-160
New York Times 14
Newman, John Henry 170, 179
Nicene Creed 140, 193
No Exit 176

O

Occult Phenomena 173
Odyssey 77-78
Oesterley, W. O. E. 69
On the Other Side 39
Origen 20, 177n
Out-of-body experiences 11, 39-42, 153-154, 173

   See also Mystical experiences
Out-of-Body Experiences 39

P

Paradise 142, 184-185. *See also* Heaven
Paradise Lost 169, 173
Parapsychology 11, 19, 31-42, 153, 159-160, 173. *See also* Mystical experiences; Out-of-body experiences
Paschal Liturgy 199n
Patterson-Smythe, J. 133, 137
Paul (the apostle) 1, 4, 5, 10, 11, 16, 85n, 86, 87, 89-90, 91, 98-99, 120, 121-122, 129, 182, 189, 196
   on joy 147
   on love 144
   on three virtues 144
   on resurrection of the dead 107
   on seeing God 166
   on Heaven 142, 151, 160-161, 167
   on the Judgment 129, 136
Percy, W. A. 107-108
Pessimism 3, 4, 6
Peter (the apostle) 89, 111-113, 117, 128-129
Peter, Letters of 185n
Petrey, Ray C. 92, 93
Phaedo 51
Pharisees 130, 131
Philippians, Letter to 154
Pike, James A. 177
Pilcher, Charles Venn 186
Plato 90, 92, 152
Prayer 67, 75, 112
Prayer for the dead 186-190
Primitive man
   concepts of life after death 21-27

Prodicus 3
Prominent American Ghosts 26
Protagoras 50-51
Proverbs, Book of 166
Psalms, Book of 9, 47, 48, 62, 79, 103, 199n
Ptolemy 140
Purgatorio 155
Purgatory 133-134, 148, 151, 179-192
  as Paradise 184-185
  meaning of term 181
  levels of 182-184

R

Ramsey, Michael (archbishop) 123
Rapture 198n. *See also* Second Coming of Christ
Rawlings, Maurice 38, 153
Redating the New Testament 114n
Reincarnation 154
Religion and the Rise of Capitalism 94
Republic, The 90, 93
Resurrection of Christ 20, 83, 85n, 86, 107, 114-115, 136
  affirmation of Jesus' teaching 126-127
  assurance of Christ's deity 127
  evidence of 117-127
Resurrection of the body 67, 68, 70-72, 86, 136, 151-154, 164
  nature of resurrected body 124-126, 151-154
Resurrection of the dead 59-62, 105-107, 114-115, 151
Return from Tomorrow 173
Revelation, Book of 129-130, 133, 134, 141, 143, 161, 172, 174, 193-194, 197, 198, 199, 199n

Righteousness 156-157
Ring, Kenneth 38
Ritchie, George C. 33, 34, 35, 36, 37, 160, 173
Robinson, John A. T. 86, 114n, 168
Romans
  concept of life after death 78
Romans, Letter to 87, 136n
Russell, Bertrand 3

S

Sadducees 46, 105-106
Saints. *See* Communion of Saints
Salvation. *See* Heaven; Judgment; Purgatory
Samuel, Books of 9, 43
Sartre, Jean-Paul 4, 176
Saul (Hebrew king) 8, 9
Schopenhauer, Arthur 3
Second Coming of Christ 80-82, 132, 193-196, 198-200, 203. *See also* Apocalypse; Final Judgment
Semele 165
Seventh Day Adventists 21, 28, 44, 134, 194-195, 199
Shakespeare 3
Sheol 46, 49, 61, 62, 67, 78-79, 140, 170-171, 183-184. *See also* Hell
Shepherd, Massey H. 193
Sheppard, David 95
Sin 86, 137
Social reform
  attitudes toward 88-90
  among Christians 90-100
Socrates 51-52, 88
Son of Man in Daniel, Enoch, and the Gospels, The 80n
Soul, The 10, 13, 16, 49, 52, 61
Spirit(s) 13, 19, 22, 60, 61, 70, 139, 149-150, 173, 184

Spirit(s) *(continued)*
  possession by demonic beings 173-174
Spiritual experiences. See Mystical experiences
Spiritualism 19
Streeter, Burnett 148, 150, 157, 163
Stuck, Hudson 21, 28-29, 149
Suicide 3, 4, 175

T

Tart, Charles 39
Tawney, R. H. 94
Temple, William 95, 127
Tertullian 133, 144
Tetzel, Johann 180-181
Thales 50, 88
Thessalonians, Letter to 196
Thomas (the apostle) 121, 127
Thomas à Kempis 86-87
Timothy, Letter to 75, 189
Transfiguration 10, 110-116
  Jesus' explanation of 114
  significance of 115-116
Tutu, Desmond 95

U

Udali, Daudi W. 21, 25-27
Underhill, Eveyln 16
Universalism 177, 177n
Utopia 90, 93

V

Valley of Hinnon 168
Vision of God. *See* Beatific Vision
Visions. *See* Mystical experiences; Visions of the departed
Visions of the departed 11-14, 18, 24-31, 149, 187. *See also* Mystical experiences

W

Weatherhead, Leslie D. 125
Wedell, Theodore 156, 170
Whittier, John Greenleaf 87
Who Moved the Stone? 125n
Wisdom of Solomon, Book of 9, 71-72
Woolley, Leonard 22, 23
World as Will and Idea, The 3
Worlock, Derek 95
Worship
  as characteristic of Heaven 158-159

Y

Yahweh 48, 49, 49n. *See also* God
Yahwehism 49

Z

Zeus 165
Zoroastrianism 74